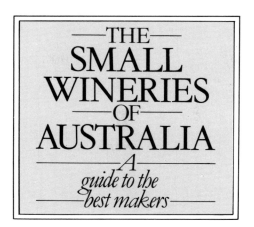

THE SMALL WINERIES OF AUSTRALIA

A guide to the best makers

Other books by Robin Bradley

Three Days of Wine 1977
The Australian Wine Pocket Book 1979
Australian Wine Vintages 1979, 1981

THE SMALL WINERIES OF AUSTRALIA

A guide to the best makers

ROBIN BRADLEY

First published 1982 by
THE MACMILLAN COMPANY OF AUSTRALIA PTY LTD
107 Moray Street, South Melbourne 3205
6 Clarke Street, Crows Nest 2065

Associated companies in
London and Basingstoke, England
Auckland Dallas Delhi Hong Kong
Johannesburg Lagos Manzini Nairobi
New York Singapore Tokyo Washington Zaria

National Library of Australia
cataloguing in publication data
Bradley, Robin, 1937-   .
   The small wineries of Australia.

   ISBN 0 333 33848 0.

   1. Wineries — Australia. I. Title.
663'.2'0994.

Cartography: Robyn Smith
Set in Garamond by Savage & Co., Brisbane
Printed in Hong Kong

Contents

Foreword by Harry Waugh   vii

Introduction   ix

The Wineries   1

Area Maps   183

Index   204

Foreword

I have not unfortunately had the same, can one say 'intimate' experience, of Australian wines as I have those of California, but from an outsider's point of view the two wine producing regions appear remarkably similar with their futures pointing in the same direction.

Although old established, for long years neither area had broken through on to the world scene in so far as quality is concerned. Indeed some fifteen years ago in the United States the magic word 'imported' had to appear on the label and very few people considered buying their domestic product which one must admit with but a few exceptions, was nothing much to write home about! Now, with the almost miraculous advent of the smaller growers (unkindly termed boutique wineries) the whole scene has been transformed. The standard of quality has been raised dramatically and the good example has rubbed off on the larger old established firms which are now exporting to markets where in the past they had made little or no impact.

The situation appears to be almost identical in Australia where small producers have been redeveloping the former vinous areas with increasing success and they too are blazing a trail. Modern methods of oenology have made all the difference and in a number of cases the new world has begun to teach the old. For example a mere twenty years ago there were no stainless steel fermenting vats to be seen in the Médoc, but now, like mushrooms, whole sets of them are springing up at the famous châteaux.

During the course of extensive lecture tours throughout the United States the subject of Australian wine seldom cropped up, but within the past two years, in spite of the highly successful domestic wine, a lively interest has been emerging. In Vancouver as well there was talk of the exciting wines beginning to arrive from Australia. Just as the boutique wineries of the Napa Valley have placed the wines of California on the map, so it seems the small producers of Australia are helping to make their own wine receive the recognition it deserves.

Pithily informative, but humourous and easy to read, Robin Bradley's book relates to these very wines and opens a window on the exciting things burgeoning on the Australian scene. It will prove invaluable not only to Australian readers but also to enthusiasts in the United States, Canada and last but not least, here in the United Kingdom. Wine lovers are greedy for knowledge and this book will make an admirable addition to this author's excellent 'Australian Wine Vintages' now in its second edition.

Harry Waugh,
London, 1982

Introduction

If not actually a labour of love, writing this book has been for me at least a labour of deep affection. Like many others I have somewhat of a prejudice towards small producers, without whom most of Australia's best wines would not exist. It is hard to remember that even a decade ago small makers were regarded by the big companies as being mere flea-bites on the industry's hide. My, how the fleas have multiplied.

This book should really be entitled 'The Small, High Quality Wineries of Australia', as I have deliberately excluded those makers — particularly in some of the traditional areas — the quality of whose product leaves much to be desired. Similarly I have not included irrigation areas.

It seemed too inflexible arbitrarily to create a cut-off point based on vineyard size or crush tonnage and apply such with unthinking rigour. Instead I relied heavily on the publicly held image of each particular candidate for inclusion as a 'small' maker. Here too there are exceptions, the most marked being Lindeman's 'Ben Ean' vineyard and winery in Pokolbin, whose 600 tonne crush of high quality wines which are all kept quite separate from the rest of the giant's products certainly qualifies the winery for inclusion. There will be arguments of the 'why have you got Chateau Smith when you have omitted Clos de Brown?' sort, no matter what parameters were used anyway. So be it.

The format is standard throughout the book. In the background information about each winery I have tried as much as possible to give an evocation of the spirit of the venture rather than a litany of historical details. Re-reading it, I think I was patchily successful. Then come the winemaker details — bare bones and little else there I am afraid, although it is interesting to note how often the Riverina College crops up in the background of small makers.

The 'Range of Wines' section is self explanatory, although sometimes a little boring when the list includes 'tourist trap' wines. However, in each case I have selected the two or three most important wines to be dealt with under the Style section.

Which brings us to the hard part. 'Style', probably a misnomer, is ambitiously intended to give some indication of what can fairly be expected to lie behind the relevant label, regardless of vintage variations. Obviously this is entirely subjective, and because of such I have gone to very considerable trouble to avoid any unwitting unfairness. A perennial problem rears up when one tries to describe some three hundred odd wines without tedious repetition. What words does one use? There are different schools of thought, the one I find most offensive being the currently growing trend towards describing tastes and smells in terms of organic chemistry. Such a coolly analytical approach is of extreme importance to the winemaker, particularly in identifying specific faults with a view to correction, but dangerous if we consumers start mouthing organic compound names, persuading ourselves that the unimaginably complex taste structure of even the simplest wine can be reduced to a handful of oenological buzzwords. Leave such to the winemakers — their art is infinitely less subtle than that of the winedrinker.

I suppose most words used to describe the non-verbal are liable to criticism or satire: a piece of music can be loud or soft, but it is begging the readers' indulgence to call it contemplative or mystical. If this is the case, then I beg the readers' indulgence in suffering my litany of subjectively lyrical and often distressingly adjectival wine terms.

Those unfamiliar with my prejudices may be surprised at the almost total lack of reference to wine shows, trophies and medals. Briefly throwing a leg over my hobby-horse, this is because I believe that a wine's impression grows from a one-to-one confrontation between bottle and drinker, rather than by the frozen moment of a wine show line-up. Using the analogy of a beauty contest, I suppose that means that I think the judge should sleep with each contestant. Yes.

Brief details of ownership, production, new plantings and market follow, together with representations of the labels, winery visiting details and maps. The maps were specially drawn for the book, working from ordnance surveys upwards — deleting some of the irrelevant clutter, and adding any aspects germane to the oenophile. I must not let slip by this opportunity to express my gratitude to my cartographer Robyn Smith, who has produced for this book what I believe are palpably the best Australian wine maps ever conceived. Well done, Robyn.

Finally, as a piece of subjective trivia, I offer gratuitously the following list of the dozen wines, encountered in researching this book, which impressed me most. This selection is entirely personal and you are invited — even exhorted — to make your own list.

For what it's worth, and in alphabetical order:

Allandale Chardonnay (Dawson) 1980
Katnook Chardonnay 1980
Lakes Folly Cabernet Sauvignon 1980
Leeuwin Estate Chardonnay 1980
Moorilla Estate Rhine Riesling 1981
Moss Wood Cabernet Sauvignon 1979
Moss Wood Chardonnay 1980
Mount Mary Cabernets 1979
Petaluma Chardonnay 1977
Pipers Brook Cabernet Sauvignon 1981
Seville Estate Trockenbeerenauslese 1980
Wantirna Estate Pinot Noir 1978

The Wineries

ALKOOMI

Less is heard of the Frankland development as a vignoble than of the neighbouring area of Mount Barker (both of these frequently being lumped together by wine writers, in spite of their marked differences in soil and climate). And most Australian wine consumption is by the Eastern States anyway, where we are all still trying to adapt ourselves to the quality phenomenon of Margaret River. Well, it doesn't stop there.

Merv and Judy Lange are friendly but shy, almost self-effacing people, who it is difficult to realize make one of the best Rhine Rieslings in Australia.

They had, and indeed still have, a sheep grazing property almost 11 kilometres west of Frankland in 1971 when they succumbed to the then prevalent temptation to start a vineyard. They went to some considerable trouble to select the best soil on the property and began to plant vines. A total of 11.5 hectares was eventually established comprising 3.5 hectares of Cabernet Sauvignon, 3 of Rhine Riesling, 2 Shiraz, 1 each of Malbec and Sauvignon Blanc, and 0.5 each of Merlot and Semillon.

While this planting programme was under way, the Langes built a small but modern and well-equipped winery, set into the side of a hill and constructed of local granite. 1976 arrived, and with it the first vintage — a small quantity of Rhine Riesling and Cabernet Sauvignon. This and the next two vintages were made under contract, but the Alkoomi winery was finished in time for the 1979 vintage.

Alkoomi wines are setting a very high standard for the area. It will be most interesting to see if other Frankland makers can achieve a similar quality.

Winemaker

Merv Lange has had no formal training in oenology, but is one of those many current winemakers who have 'risen to the occasion'. He studies winemaking textbooks, and retains consultants.

Range of Wines

Alkoomi Cabernet/Malbec/Shiraz
Alkoomi Cabernet Sauvignon
Alkoomi Malbec
Alkoomi Rhine Riesling
Alkoomi Shiraz
Alkoomi Vintage Port

Style

Alkoomi Cabernet Sauvignon

Superb, dense, tight and convincing Cabernet with intense varietal flavour and an almost coffee nose. Fining is not what it could be though, and the wines I have seen lack brilliance, to say the least, and can be muddy, to say the most. Very impressive cool climate Cabernet Sauvignon.
Best years: 1979, 1980

Alkoomi Malbec

These are big and soft, but still quite tight and again showing emphatically distinct fruit character. I know of no other Malbec in Australia which so strongly shows the individual profile of this voluptuous but elegant variety. For all that, one feels that sooner or later the Alkoomi Malbec should take its rightful place in marriage with the Cabernet Sauvignon (without Shiraz making the arrangement a *ménage à trois*).
Best years: 1977, 1979

Alkoomi Rhine Riesling

I think this wine is quite lovely, and indeed I drink far too much of it. Fragrant and soft, the wine is nevertheless in excellent balance, and the palate has a weight and power to it which almost suggests honey. The only wine of comparable style I know of is the Vasse Felix Riesling, and it should live very well (although not in my cellar unless I can keep my hands off it).
Best years: 1980, 1981

Owned by Merv and Judy Lange.

Production

Currently about 4000 cases, but this should rise to 7000 cases as the vines come to full bear. About 75 per cent of this is red.

(Not yet yielding.) Nil, but some of the established vines are not yet yielding fully.

Market

Mostly cellar door and mailing list, with a few bottles in specialist merchants.

Winery Visiting Details

Monday to Saturday 9 am to 5 pm, Sunday by appointment only. The address is R.M.B. 234, Frankland, 6396 Telephone (098) 55 2229.

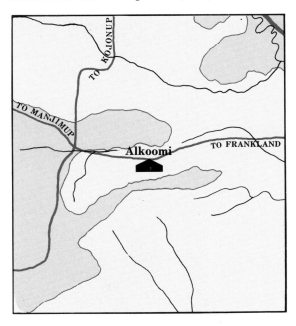

ALLANDALE Pokolbin, NSW

This venture is almost* unique in Australia. The Allandale concept was to build an efficient and adequately modern winery to process small amounts of grapes purchased from a handful of independent local growers. Only very high quality fruit is used and, most importantly, there is a continuity of vintages from each grower, attribution to whom is given on the relevant labels.

In California such a practice is almost standard for many of the best wineries, although they usually own their own vines as well. (Heitz 'Martha's Vineyard' Cabernet Sauvignon is perhaps the most brilliant example; many believe this to be America's best wine, but Joe Heitz annually buys all the grapes from this prime vineyard, and it would be unthinkable for any to be sold to another maker.)

Ed Joualt created the Allandale project, establishing the winery in 1977. He felt it was most

*(See 'Redbank')

unfortunate that the individual character of a small vineyard's grapes should be swamped by a lake of other fruit when the grower sold to a large producer. He also observed that such individual characteristics are substantially responsible for the extreme quality of all great European wines, as distinct from the Australian 'superstar winemaker' cult. More power to his elbow.

Allandale handles parcels of grapes ranging from two to sixteen tonnes (150 to 1200 cases). Obviously the resultant wines are of severely limited availability. In about two years Allandale will become one of its own suppliers (conceptually, I am sure that is how Ed Joualt would regard it) as a few hectares of Pinot Noir, Semillon and Chardonnay were planted on the winery land in 1980.

As consumers we should be deeply appreciative of the philosophy and practice inherent in Allandale; it is as a direct result of this kind of purism that the world's greatest wines are made.

Winemaker

Ed Joualt arrived in Australia in 1964 as a chartered accountant. Falling in love with Hunter Valley wines, he opted out of accountancy in favour of wine, and for him now a trial balance means checking a dry red for the harmonious integration of its components. He gained experience of winemaking with Saxonvale, Rothbury Estate, Robson and McPherson wineries, and was one of the first students for the degree course in wine science at Riverina College.

Range of Wines

Allandale Cabernet Sauvignon (Leonard)
Allandale Chardonnay (Dawson)
Allandale Chardonnay (Leonard)
Allandale Chardonnay (Peterson)
Allandale Chardonnay (Sutherland)
Allandale Semillon (Kindred)
Allandale Semillon (Latara)
Allandale Semillon (Leonard)
Allandale Semillon (Peterson)
Allandale Semillon/Chardonnay (Leonard)
Allandale Semillon/Chardonnay (Sutherland)
Allandale Shiraz (Leonard)
Allandale Shiraz (Peterson)
Allandale Traminer (Kindred)
Allandale Traminer (Leonard)

Style

Allandale Chardonnay (Dawson)

The Allandale concept of small parcels with relevant attribution makes it difficult to identify specific styles without somewhat arbitrarily selecting a particular grower's produce. So this is just what I have done. The Dawson is, quite simply, a superb Chardonnay; very Californian but very elegant. The nose is fine and intense, with all the apricots, figs and peaches that any devotee of this wonderful variety could desire. *Best year: 1980*

Allandale Semillon (Leonard)

Ed Joualt's conception of Semillon ('Hunter River Riesling') is markedly different from the traditional area style. Finesse and considerable delicacy are not normally attributes of this uniquely Australian style and neither is sweetness of fruit. Without turning my back on the many glorious whites of the district over the last three decades, I wholeheartedly welcome his approach and his sensitivity with the variety.
Best years: 1979, 1980

Ownership

The enterprise is owned by Villa Villetini Pty Ltd, a company whose shareholders are E. R. J. Joualt, W. Atallah, S. Rocca and D. Roberts-Thomson.

Production

Total production is currently 7500 cases, but is expected to increase to double this figure over the next few years.

New Plantings

The Allandale block has been planted with 1.5 hectares each of Pinot Noir and Semillon and 2 hectares of Chardonnay.

Market

Apart from a small quantity which is made available to specialist merchants, Allandale wines are sold by mailing list and cellar door.

Winery Visiting Details

9 am to 5 pm Monday to Saturday, noon to 5 pm Sundays. The address is Allandale Road, Pokolbin, 2321 Telephone (049) 90 4526.

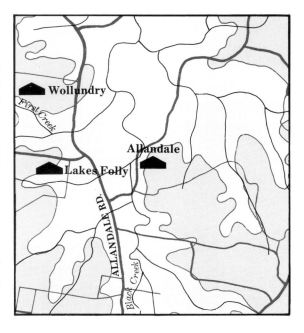

AMBERTON WINES

The concept of Amberton Wines was born in the mid-1970s when a group of Sydney-based wine and food lovers decided to diversify their interests into the wine industry. They were familiar with the Mudgee district and saw its potential for producing both red and white table wines of high quality. The result was the purchase of some 121 hectares of gently undulating land in the Parish of Eurunderee about 12 kilometres north of Mudgee township and the establishment of a 20 hectare vineyard planted to premium varieties. Industry trends had already become obvious and 60 per cent of the vineyard was planted to white varieties — Chardonnay, Sauvignon Blanc, Traminer, Rhine Riesling and Semillon. The balance is evenly divided between Cabernet Sauvignon and Shiraz.

The idea was to produce small batches of high quality wines and market them principally through cellar door and mail order facilities. That concept was given a firmer foundation in early 1980 with the construction of a modern winery and the appointment of a full-time winemaker, John Rozentals. The dream was at least partially realized in 1981 when Amberton took out both trophies and seven of eight gold medals awarded in the dry/medium dry white classes at the 1981 Mudgee Wine Show.

The winery has been in the forefront of technology in Mudgee, the first with must-chilling facilities and the first with diatomaceous earth filtration facilities. There is also a 'vine library', three vines each of some sixty different varieties, and this is being expanded in association with the local Department of Agriculture. As these vines come into full production, experimental batches will be made to assess their relevance to viticulture and winemaking in the Mudgee district.

Winemaker

John Rozentals gained his Bachelor of Applied Science (Wine Science) degree at Riverina College of Advanced Education in 1979, studying under Brian Croser and Andrew Birks. He graduated winning the College Medal — a very creditable feat. John believes that the next major step forward for Australian wine will be in the viticultural rather than the oenological area. He is certainly not alone in this belief.

Range of Wines

Amberton Chardonnay
Amberton Cabernet-Sauvignon Bin 1
Amberton Cabernet-Sauvignon Bin 2
Amberton Dry Red
Amberton Rhine Riesling
Amberton Sauvignon Blanc
Amberton Semillon
Amberton Semillon/Chardonnay
Amberton Shiraz
Amberton Traminer/Rhine Riesling

Style

Amberton Chardonnay (Lowe's Peak)

Lowe's Peak is the name given to the Amberton vineyard proper, as distinct from separately owned patches of premium vines, the fruit from which will sometimes be purchased by Amberton, made separately and identified as such on the label (*à la* Napa Valley). This Chardonnay is a graceful, dense-fruited wine, skilfully made to achieve a nicely honed balance unusual for the area.
Best years: 1980, 1981

Amberton Cabernet Sauvignon, Bin 1

A remarkable wine, the successful result of some courageous experimentation, Bin 1 Cabernet is cold fermented over a long period and released without any wood aging. This unique 'Cabernet Nouveau' is light on the palate but sweetly complex and with very little of the hard vinosity which bedevils most attempts at slender Cabernets. A delightful wine.
Best year: 1980

Amberton Cabernet Sauvignon (Lowe's Peak) Bin 2

Much more substantial than the Bin 1, this is the Rip Van Winkle of the Amberton range, needing a decade to develop. The young wine is full of promise and redolent of what is fast becoming the Amberton trademark; beautiful fruit.
Best years: 1980, 1981

Ownership

The major partners in the Amberton venture are four Sydney radiologists: Drs Ted Jackson, Bill Vautin, Colin Franklin and Peter Kitchener.

Smaller shareholdings are owned by Cynthia Jackson, John Rozentals and Beverley Brill.

Production

Increasing annually, but 1981 figures were 3450 cases, being Chardonnay 100 cases, Semillon/Chardonnay 500 cases, Semillon 500 cases, Traminer/Rhine Riesling 500 cases, Sauvignon Blanc 350 cases, Cabernet Sauvignon 500 cases, Shiraz 500 cases and Vintage Port 500 cases.

New Plantings

(Not yet yielding.) 2 hectares of Chardonnay planted and sufficient rootlings for a further 3.5 hectares of this variety and 2 hectares of Sauvignon Blanc.

Market

Ninety per cent of Amberton wines are consumed in New South Wales (and Australian Capital Territory), with 5 per cent each going to Queensland and Victoria.

Winery Visiting Details

Monday to Saturday: 10 am to 4.30 pm, Sundays 12 noon to 4.30 pm. The postal address is PO Box 305, Mudgee, 2850 Telephone (063) 73 3910.

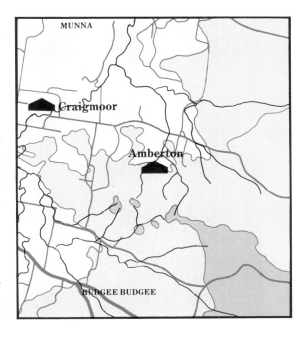

ANAKIE

Anakie is a two-part story. Tom Maltby estab-lished the vineyard some twelve years ago in a quest for that romantic Holy Grail which, to the great benefit of you and me as consumers, has infected so many dedicated 'dilettantes' who eventually make some of our finest wines. Tom, who could be called Geelong's answer to Stuart Anderson, made some superb Cabernets, but had planted some odd varieties (Dolcetto, Biancone) as well as the predictable Shiraz and Rhine Riesling. Unlike Stuart, Tom Maltby wearied of the annual crisis called vintage and leased out his vineyard.

Which starts the second part of the story. Ian Hickinbotham has been a quixotic figure in Australian wine for thirty years. Like a king in exile, Ian has held court as an oenology popularist for a decade, and now — together with his son Stephen — has purchased a new kingdom. The Hickinbothams are strongly influenced by Bordeaux vinification techniques and have totally changed the concept of the Anakie project. An obvious starting point

was to graft and replant, to replace the whim-sical varieties with Chardonnay, Cabernet Franc and Merlot. The combination of Ian's pre-occupation with scientifically assured vinous health and Stephen's Bordelaise predilections promises some extremely rewarding results in the very near future, as long as practicality is not trammeled by pedantry.

The Anakie vineyard is some 400 metres above sea level, a fact which, together with its southerly latitude, brings it loosely into the 'cool climate' range, with a consequent en-hancement of fruit quality in terms of grace and power. Currently, Anakie-made wines include some made from grapes grown in other cool areas (Adelaide Hills, Mornington Peninsula and even Tasmania). It is to be hoped that this will be maintained, with a continuity of vin-tages from these specific growers: a system which operates most successfully in California.

Whether from altruism or consumer self-interest, we all wish the Hickinbothams well.

Winemaker

Stephen Hickinbotham has an impressive list of both qualifications and experience. Academi-cally, he has a Bachelor of Agricultural Science and a *Diplome National d'Oenologue* with honours from Bordeaux. He has worked in Australia with Hollydene, Saltram, Mildara, Arrowfield, Lindemans and Seppelts, and in France with Mumms, Bollinger, Chateau Clark and the *Station de Recherches Viticoles et Oenologiques* in Alsace.

The appeal of cool climate wines is seasonal variation. Victoria's 1981 summer was abnormally long enabling us to leave our Riesling grapes on the vines to attain the extraordinary sweetness of 15° Beaumé. (About 11° is normal).

After vinifying by Alsatian methods new to Australia, we offer a seldom to be repeated living wine full of lusciousness and lingering flavour.

Stephen Hickinbotham

Diplôme national d'oenologue (Hons.)

HICKINBOTHAM WINEMAKERS PTY. LTD.
ANAKIE, VICTORIA 3221, AUSTRALIA.

HICKINBOTHAM WINEMAKERS

ANAKIE
RIESLING
Very late picked (Auslese)
1981
VINEYARD: MT ANAKIE

PRODUCE OF AUSTRALIA   **750 ml**

Range of Wines

Anakie Cabernet Sauvignon
Anakie Riesling
Anakie Semillon
Anakie Shiraz
Clarendon Cabernet Sauvignon
Elgee Park Cabernet Sauvignon
Meadowbank Riesling

Style

Note: There is little point in describing the established style of the Maltby wines, as the change in both theory and practice has been extreme since the Hickinbothams assumed command. I am left then with just the one vintage to date to give an indication of the new style of Anakie wines — an inadequate basis for any reliable parameters to be established.

Ownership

The vineyard and winery are still owned by Tom Maltby, with the Hickinbotham family having taken a long lease in February, 1981, with option to purchase.

Production

As about half of the vineyard is being progressively grafted, a current production figure would be meaningless. Expected full production after all 8 hectares are yielding is about 2500 cases, most of which will be the Cabernet Sauvignon/Cabernet Franc/Merlot blend.

New Plantings

(Not yet yielding.) Nil, but much grafting and replanting as mentioned.

Market

As yet unestablished, apart from cellar door and 'word of mouth' mailing list. Anakie wines will remain hard to buy.

Winery Visiting Details

Currently weekends only — Saturday 10 am to 5 pm, Sundays 1 pm to 5 pm. The address is Staughton Vale Road, Anakie, 3221 Telephone (052) 84 1256.

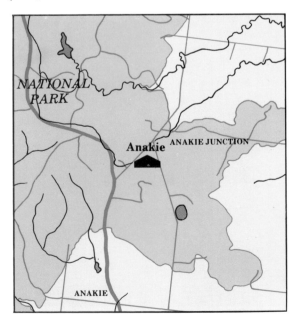

ASHBROOK ESTATE

Ashbrook Estate, owned by the Devitt family, is a 160 hectare property situated at Willyabrup, a small hamlet about 15 kilometres north of Margaret River. The property is located some three kilometres from the Indian Ocean in gently undulating country covered in large eucalypt forest and dissected by streams.

Since the property was purchased in 1975, eight hectares of vines have been planted and a mud brick and jarrah winery constructed. The winery is in the colonial style with a high-pitched roof and wide verandahs. The Devitt family is also developing a beef cattle herd and a cropping programme on the remainder of the property.

The major varieties planted in the vineyards are Cabernet Sauvignon, Semillon, Chardonnay, Verdelho and Sauvignon Blanc. Rhine Riesling is purchased from the nearby Hillcrest Vineyard of Brian Batley. Further plantings are not envisaged at this stage.

To date only small quantities of wine have been produced, however the eventual production should reach 25 000 litres. The major interest will be in producing dry white and dry red table wines in most cases as varietals. It is anticipated that all dry reds will receive 12 to 18 months of new French oak while some whites will also receive French oak maturation. However, the aim of the winemakers, brothers Tony and Brian Devitt is to make wines to highlight the varietal flavours and character so pronounced in the fruit of this region.

Initially the company will aim to market its wine through the cellar door, by mail order, locally through restaurants and retailers and in Perth in private clubs and restaurants. At this stage cellar door sales will be conducted on weekends only, and on public holidays. An information board is placed at the entrance to the property to inform customers of the wines currently available and the business hours.

Winemaker

Tony Devitt graduated with Honours in Agricultural Science from the University of Western Australia in 1968 and with Honours in Oenology from Roseworthy Agricultural College in 1975. Currently Senior Viticulturist and Oenologist, Western Australian Department of Agriculture.

Brian Devitt graduated with a Science Degree majoring in Organic Chemistry in 1970 and a Diploma of Education in 1975, both from the University of Western Australia. Initially employed as an industrial chemist with Monsanto and then as a mathematics and science teacher.

Range of Wines

Ashbrook Estate Cabernet Sauvignon
Ashbrook Estate Chardonnay (not till 1983)
Ashbrook Estate Rhine Riesling
Ashbrook Estate Semillon
Ashbrook Estate Verdelho

Style

As none of the wines had been released at the time of writing, I am indebted to Tony Devitt for the following winemaker's notes:

Ashbrook Estate Cabernet Sauvignon

First produced in 1980 — no release has been made of this wine as yet. It is intended that the wine will receive 12 to 18 months aging in oak and a further 2 to 3 years bottle aging before release. Typical of the Cabernets of this region the wine has a deep red/purple colour and a strong Cabernet flavour integrated with French oak. The wine has been made as a lighter bodied style with a very dry finish.

Ashbrook Estate Rhine Riesling

An almost dry, light bodied wine exhibiting a fresh fruity flavour and firm acid. The fruit naturally contains about 22° Brix of sugar, 8 grams per litre acid and a pH of 3.1 making for excellent balance.

Ashbrook Estate Semillon

A dry light bodied wine demonstrating varietal flavour with a soft palate and clean acid finish. It is anticipated that this variety may receive wood treatment in the future.

Ashbrook Estate Verdelho

A dry, light bodied wine with an obvious crisp acid finish. This wine is made in a lighter more acid style than the traditional Western Australian verdelho which is generally full-flavoured and very soft wine.

Ownership

Ashbrook Estate is owned by the Devitt family.

Production

When the vineyard is in full production it is expected that the annual output will be about 3000 cases.

New Plantings

(Not yet yielding.) Nil, but none of the vines is yet producing fully, the Chardonnay, for example, not being of a quantity worthy of separate fermentation until 1983.

Market

Obviously still to evolve, but cellar door and mailing list is expected to play a major role.

Winery Visiting Details

As mentioned before, the Ashbrook Estate Winery is open at weekends and public holidays only. At the time of writing, precise hours of opening have not been determined. The postal address is C/- Post Office, Cowaramup, 6284 Telephone (097) 55 6238.

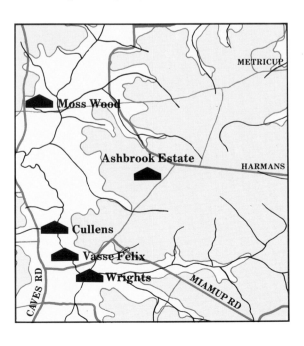

BAILEYS Glenrowan, Vic.

In common with a great many other Melbourne based tipplers of my vintage, one of my most pleasant memories is of drinking bottles beyond number of the famous 1953 Baileys Hermitage, the wine for which the horrific but unchangeable 'Old Matured Hermitage' label was created, at some four shillings the bottle. It was undoubtedly one of the greatest wines of this country's history, and is still in magnificent condition.

Devotees of Baileys (and they are legion) were shocked when they learned in 1972 that the vineyard had been taken over by Davis Consolidated Industries as a commercial giant's whimsical diversification. We need not have worried. No change of style or concept was undertaken; no sparkling port introduced; no whiz-kid marketing procedures adopted. On the contrary, the Davis company installed as winemaker and manager a man whose entire determination was to maintain the unique style and position won by Baileys.

The vineyard, of about 40 hectares, is planted on a freak belt of red granitic soil about 5 kilometres long and only a few hundred metres wide. It is very deep, and drains efficiently to a generous water table; facts which engender mammoth root development in the vines, and consequent high levels of flavour components in the fruit.

Proof that the old-timers who established the wines (in 1870) knew what they were about was readily demonstrated when Harry Tinson had a deep channel dug through the vineyard for a pipeline. The last row of vines coincided exactly with the sudden change in soil type.

Many and oft-quoted are the startled remarks bursting from the lips of overseas experts upon first encountering Bailey reds. Perhaps more significant is Hugh Johnson's carefully thought out statement: 'If they ever made a wine like any vintage of Baileys Hermitage in the Rhone Valley, they would promptly declare it the vintage of the century'.

Winemaker

Harry Tinson took an honors degree in physical engineering at Sydney University in 1951. A year later he had his Masters. He rose through the serried ranks of Davis Consolidated to become a corporate planner. It was as such that he recommended to his company that they buy the Bailey vineyard. They agreed, moved him across to manage the place on a 'temporary' basis, and left him there. The scientist/corporate planner had to become a winemaker, so he did. His advent meant only fairly minor changes to the style of the major wines, the most significant being lavish wood treatment for the reds, generally lower pH's, and attempts to create a range of saleable whites for economic reasons.

Range of Wines

Baileys Cabernet Sauvignon
Baileys Cabernet Hermitage
Baileys Chardonnay/Traminer
Baileys Chasselas
Baileys Colombard
Baileys Hermitage
Baileys Liqueur Muscat
Baileys Rhine Riesling
Baileys Tokay
Baileys Vintage Port

Style

Baileys Cabernet Sauvignon

Cabernet is the noblest of red grapes, and Taminick is a magnificent vignoble unique in the world. I am not convinced, however, that in this case the whole is as great as the sum of the parts. Baileys Cabernets rape rather than seduce the palate with their dogmatic and uncompromising intensity, leaving little room for grace or elegance. Very long aging prospects.
Best years: 1979, 1980, 1981

Baileys Hermitage

This is not only the great wine of the north-east Victorian range of reds, it is to my mind the best 100% Shiraz in the world. (No apologies to those lovers of Rhone Valley's *L'Hermitage* who labour under the misapprehension that all such is 100% Shiraz.) When young, the wine can smell remarkably like a handful of the earth on which the vines grow, but age brings grace. If Baileys Cabernet is like King Kong, the Hermitage is like a weight-lifting Doctor of Philosophy who writes poetry. In other words, powerful, complex and beautiful.
Best years: 1965, 1967, 1975, 1977, 1980

Baileys Liqueur Muscat

Which is the world's best Muscat; Morris's or Baileys? And if the Morris wine, how much of its aged base material was purchased from Baileys? Don't seek the answers here, but let it suffice to say that Baileys Muscat is rich and luscious and full and voluptuous and intense and languorous.

Ownership

Entirely owned by Davis Consolidated Industries Ltd.

Production

Baileys are coy about their production, giving totals only. These are: '70 to 80 thousand gallons. Dry red is the biggest volume, followed by Muscat, then Tokay, then the dry whites.'

New Plantings

Two hectares of Rhine Riesling, and a little over one hectare each of Traminer and Chardonnay.

Market

This information was withheld, one imagines in the interests of industrial security. The Davis Company has still a little to learn about the wine industry.

Winery Visiting Details

9 am to 5 pm Monday to Friday, 10 am to 5 pm Saturdays and holidays. The address is simply Glenrowan, Victoria, 3675 Telephone (057) 66 2392.

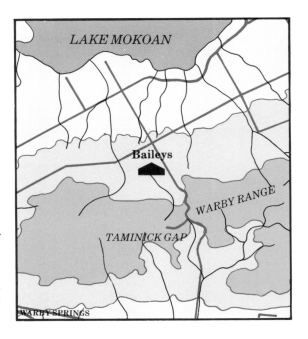

BALGOWNIE

Balgownie is the creation of Stuart Anderson, who conceived the project while in the process of growing bored with being a pharmacist in High Street, Bendigo.

Stuart, a many-sided man, was at the time an enduring Wine & Food Society member whose other interests included terrorizing the Victorian countryside in his Type 37 Bugatti and, although not simultaneously, playing the bassoon. (The latter he still pursues, and maintains a fully professional standard in his technique and musicality.)

He had always been impressed with the quality and taste-complexity of the local area fruit, particularly berry-fruit, and knew that the region had once been a vignoble. With hindsight one could say that for such a man as Stuart Anderson, those two facts could progress to only one conclusion. Finding a friendly bank manager, he arranged the purchase of 75 hectares of land at Maiden Gully a few kilometres west of Bendigo, and established about 10 hectares of vines.

Determined at all costs not to be a mere hobbyist, he voraciously devoured viticultural tomes and gained practical vintage experience at Lakes Folly while his vines were growing, during which time his by now hard-pressed bank manager reluctantly facilitated the building of a small but well-equipped modern winery.

His first small release of wine, the 1973 vintage, struck Melbourne like a planet. Almost on the instant Balgownie wine was accorded a respect and desirability which took it to the very forefront of Australian reds, a position which subsequent vintages have firmly entrenched.

Currently 12 hectares are in production, 3.5 of Shiraz and 7 of Cabernet Sauvignon, with smaller plantings of Chardonnay and Pinot Noir.

Winemaker

Stuart Anderson has made all the Balgownie wine. His background as a pharmacist helped him to achieve extreme oenological competence in a remarkably short time, as did his working for several vintages with Dr Max Lake at Lakes Folly. Of recent years Stuart has made an annual trip to France where he has done several vintages with Louis Vialard in the Haut Médoc.

Range of Wines

Balgownie Cabernet Sauvignon
Balgownie Chardonnay
Balgownie Hermitage
Balgownie Pinot Noir

Style

Balgownie Cabernet Sauvignon

Certainly among the great Cabernets of Australia, however short the short-list. Densely coloured but never inky, the wine is born with an intense and voluptuous aroma whose complex structure includes, for me, much more than a hint of desiccated coconut. Maturity tightens the generous fruit and develops distinct Pauillac overtones.
Best years: 1976, 1979, 1980

Balgownie Chardonnay

French rather than Californian in style, with profound but understated fruit character, this sadly rare wine is well worth acquiring by fair means or foul. It is an exemplary Chardonnay, and an object lesson to all but the very few top Chardonnay makers in Australia.
Best years: 1979, 1980

Balgownie Hermitage

Shiraz in Australia traditionally makes a heavily vinous, hard-finishing wine. Balgownie is quite atypical as the wine has an elegance and subtlety rarely seen since the old Maurice O'Shea Mount Pleasant reds of the 40s and early 50s.
Best years: 1973, 1979, 1980

Balgownie Pinot Noir

Very, very little of this is made, and indeed few people are fortunate enough to taste the wine at all, much less acquire a bottle. Deep brick-red in hue, its nose is redolent of the aristocratic Burgundian variety to a degree which would be quite exceptional in Bourgogne.
Best years: 1979, 1980

Ownership

Balgownie is a family-owned Proprietary Limited Company.

Production

Average current production is 4000 to 5000 cases, a little more than half of which is Cabernet, with Chardonnay and Pinot Noir accounting for only a couple of per cent of the crop.

New Plantings

(Not yet yielding.) Less than half a hectare each of Rhine Riesling and Chardonnay are established. No further expansion is envisaged.

Market

Effectively all of the production is placed by mailing list, including wine merchant and licensed restaurant orders.

Winery Visiting Details

The winery may be visited from 10 am to 5 pm Monday to Saturday. The address is Hermitage Lane, Maiden Gully, 3551 Telephone (054) 49 6222.

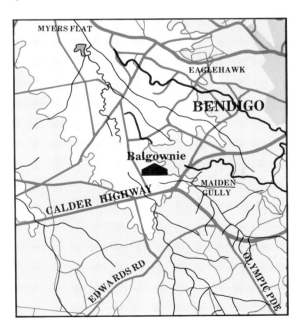

BANNOCKBURN VINEYARDS

Bannockburn, Vic.

Bannockburn, rather like Virgin Hills, strives to be not just low-profile but invisible, at least at the moment. Whether this is a reflection of its owner's, Stuart Hooper's, shyness of publicity or a well-orchestrated prelude to making a fanfare impact at a chosen time, we can only surmise.

Information is scarce. To date 11 hectares have been planted on the Hooper property, 3 in 1973 and a further 8 some distance away on sloping ground in 1975. Yield has been ridiculously low (how about 90 kilograms per hectare from seven-year-old vines in the 1980 vintage!) and shortage of water killed many vines. Drip irrigation equipment was installed in 1981, but is ruthlessly controlled to limit yields to 2.5 tonnes per hectare. Stuart Hooper's intention is to make great wine, and with this sort of purism success would appear ultimately achievable.

Currently planted varieties are Shiraz, Malbec, Cabernet Sauvignon, Pinot Noir, Rhine Riesling, Chardonnay and Sauvignon Blanc, and it is intended that the eventual size of the plantings will be 16 hectares.

The winery is superbly equipped and as modern as could be desired, with an impressive array of new wood, the whole being housed in an attractive wine-red building.

Incredibly, no wine has been released at the time of writing, although a quantity should become available during this year. I understand that the standard Bannockburn practice will be to hold white wines for 18 months and reds for 3 years before releasing them.

The Geelong vignoble is supremely promising with its cool climate engendering great intensity of flavour in the fruit and the Bannockburn operation seems destined to achieve notable success, combining as it does Geelong fruit quality, purism and no dearth of capital.

Winemaker

Gary Farr, the Bannockburn winemaker, seems to share his employer's predilection for avoiding the limelight. All I can tell you about him is that he is a graduate of Roseworthy Agricultural College and that he is in a Utopian situation, being able to play with extreme quality fruit in an extreme quality winery.

Range of Wines

Bannockburn Cabernet Sauvignon
Bannockburn Chardonnay
Bannockburn Pinot Noir
Bannockburn Rhine Riesling

Style

As I have been unable to obtain wines for tasting, the following is reprinted from 'Wines & Wineries of Victoria' by kind permission of the author, James Halliday:

Rhine Riesling 1981 (barrel-fermented; tasted from cask)

Brilliant green-gold colour. Intense vanillin-lime bouquet with Californian overtones. At three months of age had already developed depth of flavour and balance.

Chardonnay 1981 (tasted from cask)

Bright yellow-green. Intense grapefruit aroma to bouquet; similar fine flavour on the palate. Exceptional promise for a very young wine.

Rhine Riesling 1980

Very good colour. Similar vallinin-lime aromatics to the '81, but with more development. Very full flavour for a wine devoid of residual sugar. Slightly hard finish which should soften with bottle age.

Chardonnay 1980

Pale green-gold colour. Medium to full bouquet with complex fruit and oak aromatics. A deep and long palate in which the fruit flavour peaks early but is sustained right through. Barrel fermented: 7 months in cask.

Pinot Noir 1980

Medium to deep purple colour, very good for variety. Smoky, complex bouquet with varietal character yet to develop. A strongly flavoured wine, with glorious strawberry overtones on the palate. Should develop beautifully in bottle.

Cabernet Sauvignon 1979

Superb colour both in hue and depth. A smooth and rich bouquet, but not heavy, and showing good varietal character. Minty overtones add a flavour dimension to a smooth, long and perfectly balanced palate. A classic wine at the start of its life.

Ownership

The Bannockburn Vineyards operation is entirely owned by Stuart Hooper.

Production

Currently production is still very low: a mere 1200 cases annually. Maximum production when the vineyard is fully planted and yielding is likely to be in the vicinity of 5000 cases.

New Plantings

(Not yet yielding.) None of the plantings is yet yielding fully. As mentioned, the vineyard will ultimately be of 16 hectares.

Market

Not yet decided, but will include mailing list and specialist outlet distribution.

Winery Visiting Details

None. To be put on the mailing list, write to Bannockburn Vineyards, Midland Highway, Bannockburn, 3331 Telephone (052) 81 1363.

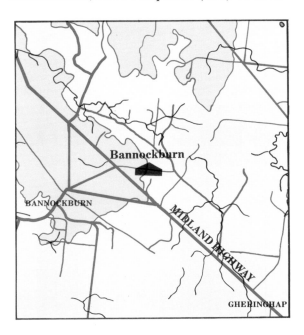

BESTS 'CONCONGELLA' Great Western, Vic.

The history behind the establishment of Bests vineyard is complex, fascinating and much too eventful to be recounted here. Leave that for those of historical bent, and suffice to say that the wines were first planted in 1866 by Henry Best. His knowledge of viticulture was quite negligible, but his capacity for work was mammoth, and the project flourished. On his death his son Charles carried on the business until he sold it in 1920 to Frederick Thomson, who already owned the 'St. Andrews' vineyard at Lake Boga.

Both vineyards are still in the Thomson family's hands. Today the old winery has a new face, but still the original viscera, with the hand-cut red gum beams in the cellars still (just) holding up the winery floor. The name, by the way, remains 'Bests', even after more than sixty years of Thomson proprietorship.

Bests, perhaps more than any other traditional producer of quality wines in Australia, refuse to develop late 20th century marketing procedures but maintain a 'what worked last year will work this year' attitude in their sales efforts. Remarkable, if puzzling. In winemaking, however, the company has always kept as much up to date as seemed prudent, while at the same time being unwilling to permit any dramatic technological revolution to overturn its admirable traditional styles, but has relied more on evolutionary changes.

Nevertheless such changes have developed, and their old style of, for instance, Rhine Riesling which, while still fine and delicate, depended on lengthy wood maturation for stabilization, has given way to the modern style at a cost (nostalgia might suggest) of profundity, complexity and longevity. It would be churlish not to admit that the benefits are reliably healthy, balanced and saleable wines of high quality.

Winemaker

Viv Thomson has responsibility for Bests winemaking, but no formal training beyond twenty years of experience and a deep understanding of the Bests style. He is ably supported by Trevor Mast, a graduate of Geisenheim who also had experience at Stellenbosch in South Africa and Seppelts 'across the road' at Great Western, before joining Bests in 1976.

Range of Wines

Bests Concongella Chardonnay
Bests Concongella Gewurztraminer
Bests Concongella Golden Chasselas
Bests Concongella Hermitage
Bests Concongella Malbeck (Dolcetto)
Bests Concongella Ondenc
Bests Concongella Pinot Meunier
Bests Concongella Rhine Riesling

Style

Bests Concongella Chardonnay

It is not possible to speak of a 'style' for this wine. At the time of writing three vintages only have been produced, the 1981 which is still resting in wood and stirring the occasional limb; the 1980, with which the winemaker was dissatisfied and was consequently blended with a fruit salad of other white varieties, and the 1979, which is one of the finest Chardonnays ever made in this country. The future looks promising.
Best year: 1979

Bests Concongella Hermitage

In its best years, this is a wine of remarkable beauty; soft, it is true, but with substantial depths underlying the beguiling gentleness of the fruit. Poorer, wetter years produce wines of lesser stature but almost similar charm.
Best years: 1967, 1971, 1976, 1980

Bests Concongella Rhine Riesling

One of the prettiest wines in Victoria, although at the moment undergoing a change of style. Notwithstanding the latter, the Rhine Riesling fruit from Concongella has always been characterized by much more than a hint of the smell and taste of ripe peaches, an idiosyncrasy which in fortunate years is quite enchanting.
Best years: 1977, 1979, 1981

Ownership

A private company entirely owned by the Thomson family.

Production

About 6500 cases being Hermitage 1500, Pinot Meunier 600, 'Malbeck' 600, Rhine Riesling 700, Chardonnay 700, Ondenc 1000, Chasselas 1200, Gewurztraminer 200.

New Plantings

Rhine Riesling 2.25 hectares, Pinot Noir 1 hectare, Cabernet Sauvignon 1.2 hectares.

Market

85 per cent Victoria, 10 per cent New South Wales, 5 per cent other states.

Winery Visiting Details

9 am to 5 pm weekdays. Saturday and public holidays 9 am to 4 pm. The address is just Great Western, 3377 Telephone (053) 56 2250.

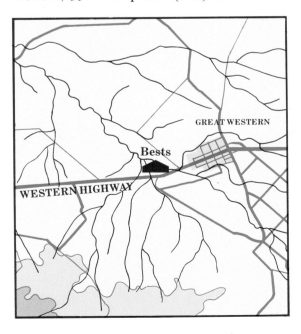

BLEASDALE

Climatically Australia has some extraordinary vignobles, but none more so than Langhorne Creek. Vineyards are planted along the banks of the Bremer River, on land which would be quite arid were it not for the intermittent flooding of the river. Floodgates force the water out over the banks, and *voilà* — the vines can drink. A wit once described the Langhorne Creek water system as 'natural floodfall'.

Frank Potts first planted some vines in 1860 on his 126 hectare property: 12 hectares of Shiraz and Verdelho on both banks of the river. (An intriguing quirk to the history of Bleasdale, as Frank Potts named the vineyard, is that his second wife had the maiden name 'Anne Flood'.) Potts' use of red gum is legendary: he used it to make wine presses, pumps, casks, ferry boats and even a piano. An extraordinary man.

His grandson John is at the Bleasdale helm now. The vineyard has grown greatly since the original plantings, and fruit is also purchased from other local growers. Grapes planted include Shiraz, Cabernet Sauvignon, Malbec, Grenache, Palomino, Doradillo, Verdelho, Crouchen, Muscat of Alexandria (Gordo Blanco) and Cinsault (Oeillade), together with new plantings of Rhine Riesling, Merlot, Colombard and, of course, Chardonnay. I am inclined to question the wisdom of such shotgun plantings, but I suppose Bleasdale know what they are doing. Certainly a very substantial part of their market has been taken by their very popular Charmat method sparkling wines whose total annual production now exceeds 20 000 cases.

But it is the smaller production of higher quality wines which interests us here — particularly with a view to the winery's intentions regarding the direction of its future development. The hotch-potch of Bleasdale plantings must, if nothing else, at least make for flexibility.

Winemaker

Ian Garnham is, at the time of writing, still an undergraduate at the Riverina College at Wagga, doing the Bachelor of Science course in Oenology and Viticulture as a part-time student. He gained practical experience working with the Settlement Wine Company in McLaren Vale and Orlando in the Barossa Valley before joining Bleasdale as winemaker in 1980.

Range of Wines

By my count there are 35 different wines on the Bleasdale product litany — far too many to list here. The major wines are:

Bleasdale Cabernet Sauvignon
Bleasdale Malbec
Bleasdale Pioneer Port
Bleasdale Shiraz/Cabernet Sauvignon
Bleasdale White Burgundy

Style

Bleasdale Cabernet Sauvignon

A reliably consistent, but never great, Cabernet Sauvignon of good deep colour and clarity, and particularly sensitively handled wood treatment (American oak puncheons). Fruit flavour is a little understated and the finish lacks distinction, but the wine is generally quite fine and makes attractive staple drinking.
Best years: 1976, 1978, 1979

Bleasdale Malbec

This really is an excellent 100% Malbec, and one which is useful to show just what this grape — which is usually blended — is like. The Bleasdale version has the velvet softness associable with the variety, but is tight and in far better balance than most attempts at straight Malbec. An interesting, well-made and admirable wine for which the winery is to be congratulated.
Best years: 1968, 1976, 1978, 1979

Bleasdale Pioneer Port

A good tawny, which is a blend of old ports made from Shiraz and Grenache aged for some years in old hogsheads. The nose is attractively spirituous, and the palate pleasantly lighter than many Australian Tawnies. Incidentally, the label of Pioneer Port shows the magnificent old red gum beam wine press which still exists at Bleasdale.

Ownership

A family owned Proprietary Limited Company.

Production

Not counting the lower grade fortifieds and bulk wines, the Bleasdale production is about 30 000 cases, 20 000 of which is sparkling. The balance is 3000 cases of Shiraz/Cabernet, 2500 Malbec, 2000 cases each of Cabernet Sauvignon, White Burgundy and Reserve Port, and 1000 of Pioneer Port.

New Plantings

(Not yet yielding.) Some 15 hectares are being planted with Merlot, Cabernet Sauvignon, Oeillade(!), Chardonnay and Colombard.

Market

One third each for South Australia and Victoria, 30 per cent New South Wales and tiny amounts to other states.

Winery Visiting Details

Monday to Saturday 9 am to 5 pm. The address is just Langhorne Creek, 5255 Telephone (085) 377–1.

BOROKA

Boroka is a two part story, the second part of which is just begun. Established in 1969 by David McCracken of Stawell on cool, frost-free land only 5 kilometres from Halls Gap, Boroka was planted with Shiraz and Cabernet Sauvignon, together with smaller plantings of Rhine Riesling, Malbec, Trebbiano and a whimsical patch of Chasselas, Grey Riesling and Aleatico. For whatever reasons, all was not well with the venture. A small but adequately efficient winery was built, but the vines were poorly tended and the future of Boroka looked uncertain.

Enter Bernie and Cordelia Breen, who purchased the operation in July 1981, and part two of the story begins. Obviously the new management has not yet had time to make an impact on the wines, but there has been ample time for a substantial impact on the vineyard.

The Boroka range includes several wines which are not estate grown — indeed there is only one real Boroka wine in the range: Boroka Shiraz. This is because tardy development of the less than ideally nurtured vines meant that the vineyard was effectively marking time after the first batch of Shiraz came to bear. It would be most unfortunate if the quality and style of the pot-boiling tourist-trap wines were taken by the unobservant as an indication of Boroka's potential. One can hardly compare a pleasant and drinkable Colombard made from juice bought-in from Irymple with wine made from the embattled Shiraz fruit grown in the cool, low-yielding Halls Gap vineyard.

Bernie has already planted more vines — Rhine Riesling — and intends in the next couple of years to extend the plantings still further, with Chardonnay. He envisages a total area under vine of 12 hectares. He will then be looking at a range consisting of Shiraz, Cabernet Sauvignon, Rhine Riesling and Chardonnay: not a bad stable for any vineyard.

I don't know what he is going to do with those other varieties though. I mean to say: Grey Riesling? Aleatico?

Winemaker

Bernie Breen is by training and avocation an industrial chemist. His interest in wine is long-standing, in winemaking rather more recent. However, he has not gone into the Boroka venture with his eyes closed, and has already completed the Wine Science course at Riverina College of Advanced Education.

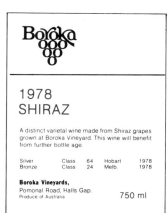

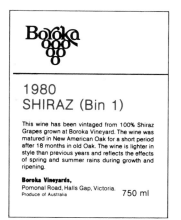

Range of Wines

Boroka Colombard (Irymple fruit)
Boroka Shiraz (Estate grown)
Other bought-in wines

Style

Boroka Shiraz

This has been the wine which alone has had to carry on its back the responsibility for Boroka's reputation. It has done this very well indeed, starting with the fine 1976, with its intense fruit and seductive flavour. Subsequent vintages did nothing to diminish the reputation won by the 1976, apart from an occasional minor winemaking fault. The common denominator has been the fruit intensity, together with the admirably long finish. It would seem inevitable, now that both the vineyard and the winery have been refurbished, that we can look forward to the further deepening and polishing of this aristocratic style.
Best years: 1976, 1979

Ownership

Boroka is owned by Bernie and Cordelia Breen.

Production

Ignoring bought-in juice, production is minimal at the moment: of the order of 600 cases. However, this should double almost immediately as the Cabernet Sauvignon is now coming on stream. Eventual full production will be about 5000 to 6000 cases.

New Plantings

(Not yet yielding.) Another 4.5 hectares of Chardonnay and Rhine Riesling is planned for the immediate future.

Market

All cellar door at the moment, but specialist merchants are being developed as Boroka stockists under Bernie Breen's new policy.

Winery Visiting Details

9 am to 5 pm Monday to Saturday, 1 pm to 5 pm Sundays (during holiday season only). The address is Pomonal Road, Halls Gap, 3380 Telephone (053) 56 4252.

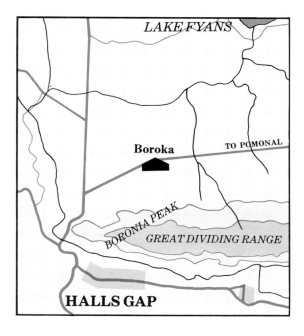

BOTOBOLAR

Gil Wahlquist, Bachelor of Arts, journalist and opter-out, determined to establish and entrench a viable and enjoyable lifestyle in keeping with his amiably conservationist principles. Not being a teetotaller, wine became an obvious choice and the beauty of the Mudgee area beckoned. Gil is an aficionado of what is for some reason called 'organic' growing (what other type of growing is there?) and brings his theories to bear with his viticulture, eschewing the use of whatever it is that organic growers eschew the use of. Cultivation is kept to a minimum so that a proliferation of myriad non-vine growth in the vineyard encourages the existence of a substantial and motley insect and bird population. These resident birds apparently frighten away the feathered tourists who turn up for a meal at vintage time, so there is no need for bird scaring devices.

Since the first wine was made in 1974 the winery (which began as an old woolshed) has developed along conventional lines. Gil's or-ganic preoccupations stop short of pedantry. Cultured yeasts are used, a modest degree of temperature control during fermentation is imposed, and sulphur dioxide is allowed a limited role sufficient only to prevent oxidation. Beyond this the Wahlquists prefer to let the wines make themselves.

The vineyard was established in 1970 and 25 hectares are under vine. Roughly another 25 hectares are grazed with Suffolk sheep which are allowed in to potter around the vineyard during the winter as part of the organic programme. Varieties planted comprise Crouchen, Chardonnay, Rhine Riesling, Trebbiano, Semillon, Traminer, Marsanne, Mataro, Shiraz and Cabernet Sauvignon.

Gil also keeps his journalistic muscles flexed by publishing a delightful quarterly, The Botobolar Bugle, which disseminates organic propaganda as well as local and vineyard news, and includes the relevant order forms for the season's wines.

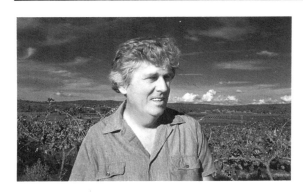

Winemaker

Gil Wahlquist makes the Botobolar wines. A self-taught enthusiast who has also attended many mini-winemaking courses, most of his expertise has nevertheless been acquired 'on the job'. His son Roland is also interested in winemaking and is a graduate of the Riverina College. The latter made most of the 1978 and 1979 wines and is now gaining experience with Lindemans at Coonawarra, so the future looks secure.

Range of Wines

Botobolar Budgee Budgee
Botobolar Cabernet Sauvignon
Botobolar Chardonnay
Botobolar Crouchen
Botobolar Hermitage (Shiraz/Cabernet)
Botobolar Marsanne
Botobolar Mataro
Botobolar Port
Botobolar Rhine Riesling
Botobolar Semillon/Traminer
Botobolar Shiraz
Botobolar Trebbiano

Style

Botobolar Budgee Budgee

A creation of Wahlquist whimsy, but for all that a popular and unique style. Made from Shiraz and Muscat grapes fermented away from the skins to produce a white wine, it is a semi-sweet but quite crisp style of no great pretensions but considerable charm.
Best year: 1981

Botobolar Cabernet Sauvignon

It would be a gross error for anyone to assume that the Wahlquists' organic predilections mean that their wines are what is politely called rustic. The Cabernet is probably the area's best red wine, with an absolutely enchanting bouquet like sweet violets and an harmoniously balanced palate to match. These are very good drinking even when quite young.
Best years: 1977, 1979

Botobolar Chardonnay

To date this has been a far less successful wine than the very fine Cabernets. Fruit character has been fairly variable, ranging from innocuous to belligerent, and the style generally lacks both balance and continuity. Nevertheless the better years show an agreeable attractiveness, albeit without great depth.
Best years: 1978, 1979

Ownership

Botobolar is a partnership between Gil and Vincie Wahlquist.

Production

11 000 cases, just over half of which is red. Shiraz dominates the reds and Crouchen the whites.

New Plantings

(Not yet yielding.) No further expansion is envisaged, although Gil is interested in purchasing area grapes from other organic growers.

Market

Mailing list and cellar door account for 80 per cent of the production, the balance being distributed to specialist merchants.

Winery Visiting Details

10.00 am to 5.00 pm Monday to Saturday, noon to 5 pm Sunday. The address is Botobolar Lane, Mudgee 2850 Telephone (063) 73 3840.

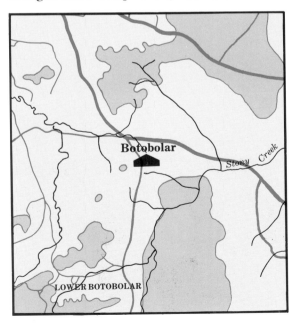

BOWEN ESTATE

Reading between the lines of the background information supplied to me by Doug Bowen about the creation and development of Bowen Estate, one senses that the earlier days of the project were times of considerable hardship, difficulty and work.

Doug and Joy Bowen purchased 16 hectares at Coonawarra in 1972 with the sole intention of developing the property into a vineyard and winery. At the time of purchase, 3 hectares were planted to the two Coonawarra reds — Cabernet Sauvignon and Shiraz — and a further 4 hectares were planted immediately. Doug was then working as a winemaker for Lindemans at Coonawarra, and had only the weekends to tend and rear his vines. One wonders what he did with his spare time.

This situation subsisted until 1977, when Doug's first vintage, the 1975, was released for sale. 'At that point in time I left Lindemans', Doug writes, but one can imagine he would have heaved an immense sigh of relief at being able to afford to be full-time on his own vineyard after 5 years of arduousness.

Until 1980 the Bowen Estate wines had been made 'in an old shed, and/or under the stars', so the building of a winery in 1980 must have been a further relief. If one bears in mind the conditions under which the vines were tended and the wines made and nurtured until very recently, the quality achieved, reputation earned and following generated by Bowen Estate wines is nothing short of remarkable. As David Dunstan points out in a recent issue of the Australian Wine Newsletter, 'He (Doug Bowen) now has better control over his winemaking operations and the ability to protect his wine. If you thought he made good wine then you haven't seen nothing yet.'

Varieties planted comprise Cabernet Sauvignon, Shiraz and Rhine Riesling (yielding), and Merlot and Chardonnay (not yielding). Doug Bowen knows where he is going.

Winemaker

Doug Bowen graduated from Roseworthy in 1971. He had previously worked with Chateau Tahbilk, Hungerford Hill and Reynella. He joined Lindemans at Coonawarra when he and Joy bought their own land there. At Lindemans he was fortunate to work with John Vickery at the Rouge Homme winery, a circumstance which must necessarily have left an indelible mark on Doug's white winemaking expertise.

Range of Wines
Bowen Estate Cabernet Sauvignon
Bowen Estate Rhine Riesling
Bowen Estate Shiraz

Style

Bowen Estate Cabernet Sauvignon
A powerful but urbane winestyle, both denser and less inky than the traditional Coonawarra Cabernet. Indeed, in many aspects some of the earlier wines are reminiscent of Hunter Valley Cabernets, but the style has since moved towards a more convincing area and varietal emphasis. The now complete 'new' winery should have a substantial impact on this wine, particularly with regard to eradicating oxygen-derived imperfections.
Best years: 1977, 1979

Bowen Estate Rhine Riesling
This is a wine quite out of character with some of the area's earlier austere, almost cadaverous Rieslings. Deeper, more generously flavoured, and honeyed to an extent that even the crisply acid 1981 cannot disguise, the style tends away from the standard Australian Rhine Riesling taste parameters, towards a more German voluptuousness, although lacking the latter's floral intensity.
Best years: 1980, 1981

Bowen Estate Shiraz
Emphatically Shiraz, and emphatically Coonawarra: these are wines of impressive stature and style. Like the Cabernets they will improve as the greater control made possible by the new equipment makes itself felt, but one hopes without sacrificing the attractive cigar undertone in the nose or the languorous strength of the palate.
Best years: 1978, 1979

Ownership
Wholly owned by Doug and Joy Bowen.

Production
Currently about 2600 cases, being Cabernet Sauvignon 1000 cases, Shiraz 1200 cases, Rhine Riesling 400 cases.

New Plantings
(Not yet yielding.) Cabernet Sauvignon 2 hectares, Merlot 2 hectares, Chardonnay 1 hectare.

Market
Cellar door accounts for 50 per cent, the balance being 20 per cent each to Melbourne and Sydney, and 10 per cent to Adelaide.

Winery Visiting Details
Monday to Saturday 9 am to 5 pm, Sunday by appointment only. The address is simply Coonawarra, 5263 Telephone (087) 37 2229.

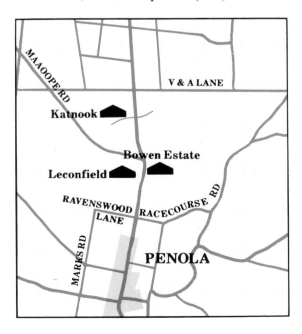

BRANDS 'LAIRA'

Coonawarra, SA

Brands 'Laira' could be called the Baileys Bundarra of Coonawarra. Not that I suggest that there is any similarity of style, but there are a great many points of similarity outside the bottle. Although Brands have existed as a visible label for only fifteen years, they have generated an immense respect and a loyal following, in spite of maintaining what is nowadays called 'a low profile in the market place'.

Like Baileys, Brands wines will only be found in specialist retailers' shops. Like Baileys, the label is unsophisticated to the point of naïveté. Like Baileys, it would be unthinkable to change that label.

Eric Brand worked for sixteen years in the baking, smallgoods and cooking industry (!) before moving to Coonawarra and working for Redmans. He and his family acquired Laira in 1950 and sold the grapes to other vineyards until 1966 when the first Laira wine was made. The vineyard, incidentally was established in 1896 and, many of the original vines are still thriving and bearing comparatively well. Wine was in fact made by Captain Stentiford, who established the vineyard, naming it after a ship which apparently evoked affectionate memories for him.

1966 was a fortuitous time to launch a new Coonawarra winery; the wine boom was just beginning; red wine was paramount; and Coonawarra was the superstar of Australian vignobles. Brands couldn't miss and they didn't. Within a remarkably short time a solid nucleus of devotees had accreted, and these have remained faithful despite minimal advertising and promotion by the winery.

Winemaker

Eric Brand developed his expertise working with Redmans prior to building his own winery. Recently the duties of winemaker have been assumed by the younger generation of Brands — Bill and Jim, both of whom have studied Oenology under the Croser/Jordan influenced Riverina College of Advanced Education. We can probably expect a consequent lightening but deepening of style in future vintages.

Range of Wines

Laira Cabernet Sauvignon
Laira Coonawarra Blend
Laira Rosé
Laira Shiraz

Style

Laira Cabernet Sauvignon

A big, hard, tight and deep-fruited dry red with intense Coonawarra overtones, this is a wine which even in poorer years is good for at least a decade of cellaring. Perhaps more so than with other Coonawarra reds, Laira Cabernet needs such cellaring to soften its austerity.
Best years: 1974, 1979

Laira Coonawarra Blend

Made from a blend of Shiraz, Malbec and Cabernet Sauvignon grapes, this is a notably successful wine of considerable charm; softer and more beguiling than the Cabernet and more complex than the Shiraz.
Best year: 1979

Laira Rosé

It is with Rosé that the oft maligned Grenache assumes a noble role. I have never been happy with the intense vinosity of the many Cabernet Rosé attempts, but Laira has that fresh, crisp lightness so essential to the Rosé genera.
Best years: 1980, 1981

Laira Shiraz

An uncompromising and straightforward dry red, emphatic both in its varietal nature and its Coonawarra provenance. Hard, almost harsh, when youthful, time softens and ameliorates the wine's impact and develops the complexity, if not the elegance, of the Redman clarets.
Best years: 1972, 1978

Ownership

Brands is entirely family owned.

Production

Average annual production is about 14 000 cases, being 2500 Cabernet Sauvignon, 8000 Shiraz, 3000 of the blend and 500 Rosé.

New Plantings

(Not yet yielding.) Half a hectare each of Malbec and, interestingly, Merlot have been established.

Market

Cellar door and mail order account for 35 per cent of the production; the balance is distributed by normal wholesale channels as follows: Victoria 25 per cent, New South Wales 20 per cent, South Australia 15 per cent, Queensland 3 per cent and Western Australia 2 per cent.

Winery Visiting Details

The winery may be visited from 9 am to 5 pm on Monday to Saturday and public holidays. The postal address is PO Box 18, Coonawarra 5263 Telephone (087) 36 3260.

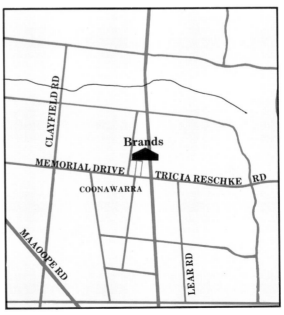

Brokenwood is a gentle legend. Gentle because there has been little or no attempt to create instant publicity for the label, all such efforts being devoted to generating respect for the concept. A legend because those same efforts have been entirely expended in an unremitting quest for the highest possible quality. Word spreads, and hence the legend.

In alphabetical order of surnames, Tony Albert, John Beeston and James Halliday were the three originators of the Brokenwood dream, in an era when Max Lake had just demonstrated to the most imaginative, creative and enthusiastic that dedicated consumers who were prepared to work hard as producers could revolutionize wine in Australia by achieving standards previously thought to be the sole preserve of the great classified growths of Bordeaux.

For that full story, or at least a fuller account, refer to the pages on Lakes Folly, but Brokenwood's striving for excellence has undeniably extended the consumer's gamut.

The vineyard is planted on heavy clay, and the yields are very low. Grapes are picked early and fermented in cooled open stainless steel. The 'cap' (the mush of skins forced to the surface by fermentation) is plunged by hand, an extremely tedious and arduous operation which is only feasible with small quantities of wine. Literally hand-made. Wood-aging is carried out in Nevers oak hogsheads, and the wine is bottled after only eight to ten months.

Brokenwood wines are released for sale to a fortunate few immediately after bottling, and should ideally be left to slumber undisturbed for a further decade before employing a corkscrew.

Winemaker

Who is the Brokenwood winemaker? With democratic modesty, any of the nine partners will insist that each vintage is a team effort and that no one partner's view or expertise overrides the others. I am personally inclined to regard this comradely asseveration as more credible than credible, while admiring the solidarity it embodies. My guess is no better than yours, but for what it's worth I suspect James Halliday, Nick Bulleid or John Beeston would be sorely missed at vintage time.

Range of Wines

Brokenwood Cabernet Sauvignon
Brokenwood Hermitage
Brokenwood Hermitage/Cabernet
Brokenwood 'Hunter Coonawarra' Cabernet/
  Hermitage

Style

Brokenwood Cabernet Sauvignon

These are wines which to a remarkable degree combine elegance and power. Even from poorer years like 1974 they are densely languorous and age slowly. Better years produce astonishing wines; fine, deep and intense.
Best years: 1975, 1979, 1981

Brokenwood Hermitage

Shiraz becomes almost a different grape in the Hunter, where a unique style has evolved; peppery, dark, vinous and tight. The Brokenwood version is atypical, being more in the mould of the old O'Shea dry reds, with an unexpected (here comes that word again) elegance.
Best years: 1975, 1979, 1981

Brokenwood Hermitage/Cabernet

A lesser wine than the above, and almost a 'second' label. Its existence, however, attests to the strenuously good intentions behind the two wines without which it would not exist. An urbane and fulfilling wine of what can only be called excellent parentage.
Best years: 1973, 1975, 1979, 1981

Brokenwood 'Hunter Coonawarra' Cabernet/Hermitage

Many are the Hunter/Coonawarra blends that have been made, and without exception I deprecate the lapse in taste which generates such shotgun weddings. To my considerable chagrin, this is a plangently successful wine. I wish it weren't, but pusillanimous congratulations to all concerned.
Best years: 1979, 1980

Ownership

The original three partners have grown, not merely in stature, but in number. They now list as follows: Tony Albert, John Beeston, Nick Bulleid, James Halliday, Ian Irwin, Tony Rees, Frank Rossetto, Peter Seville and Ray Soper.

Production

2500 to 3500 cases, of which about 10 per cent is Cabernet Sauvignon, 20 per cent Hermitage, and 70 per cent the two blends.

New Plantings

(Not yet yielding.) 1.5 hectares of Chardonnay have been established, and a further 2 hectares of Cabernet Sauvignon.

Market

By mail order, including wine merchant and licensed restaurateur orders.

Winery Visiting Details

Weekends only: 9 am to 5 pm Saturdays, 12 noon to 5 pm Sundays. The address is MacDonalds Road, Pokolbin Telephone (049) 98 7559.

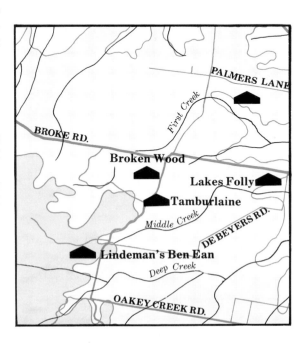

CAMBRAI

Even when Graham Stevens was working for somebody else — Hugh Lloyd at Coriole — his individual style brought a new dimension to the wines of the McLaren Vale area. Now that he has his own vineyard and winery he is going his own way with a vengeance.

Usually described as an innovator or even a rebel, Graham is more an intelligent individualist who is not really interested in breaking other people's icons, but in making his wine his way.

Clearly unhappy with the area's traditional 'double chin and paunch' red wines, his tenure at Coriole created a range of wines both finer and deeper, as we all know. His Cambrai venture appears to be adding further refinement and complexity to his established stylistic benchmark.

Cambrai's 8.5 hectares of vines began to be planted in 1975 at McLaren Flat on land whose marginally cooler micro-climate Graham felt to be appropriate to the furthering of his aspirations towards more elegance. The varieties he chose must have raised a few local eyebrows: in addition to the district's staples of Cabernet Sauvignon and Shiraz, he established Malbec, Merlot, Pinot Noir, Zinfandel, Chardonnay, Sylvaner, Traminer and Muller-Thurgau. He also planted Grenache, a variety of which most of the area's growers are now ashamed, and I doubt if anyone else would dream of planting the variety. But Graham believes that carefully grown and early picked Grenache is just what is needed to mitigate the vegemite blubber of

the area's reds. As a further act to remarkable individualism, he deliberately omitted Rhine Riesling, which many growers are short-sightedly planting as if the long-term future demand could be forecast by infinite extrapolation from the last decade's trends.

Another sacred cow given scant respect by Graham is the currently fashionable preoccupation with single variety wines. Nearly all of his wines are blends, or to use his word, combinations of grape varieties. He is experimenting, but doing so responsibly and competently. One could perhaps sum up Graham Steven's attitude to fashions, as distinct from tastes, as: never mind how 'interesting' a wine is, but how good is it?

Winemaker

Graham Stevens has had twenty years of winemaking experience. From 1962 to 1969 he worked closely with d'Arry Osborn at d'Arenberg before leaving to become the winemaker and to create the styles at Coriole. He remained there until 1979 when his Cambrai operation necessitated his full-time attention.

Range of Wines

Cambrai Burgundy
Cambrai Cabernet/Zinfandel
Cambrai Chardonnay/Chenin Blanc
Cambrai Chardonnay/Sylvaner/Chenin Blanc
Cambrai Hermitage
Cambrai Pinot Noir/Cabernet
Cambrai Private Bin Claret
Cambrai Traminer/Sylvaner
Cambrai Vintage Port

Style

Cambrai Chardonnay/Chenin Blanc

That a wine, not so much of this quality, but of this style can be made in the Southern Vale area is something I find remarkable. In its beauty, depth, breeding and finesse it more suggests a provenance like the Strathbogie Ranges in Victoria than the Vales. The version with Sylvaner included is even more powerful but perhaps less subtle, the obtrusive vanilla nose swamping the gentler Chardonnay characteristics.
Best year: 1981

Cambrai Pinot Noir/Cabernet

Another remarkable wine, atypical for the vignoble. Subtle hints of raspberry flavours underlie the Cabernet Sauvignon power, and there is an intensity (rather than a strength) of fruit on both the nose and the palate which lends the wine considerable conviction. It finishes with emphatic acid and good soft tannin.
Best years: 1978/1979

Cambrai Vintage Port

Perhaps Graham Stevens' most impressive achievement to date — a lovely, fine but dense, rich but dry-finishing Vintage Port ennobled with excellent brandy spirit. A completely convincing wine of great beauty and immense promise.
Best years: 1979, 1980

Ownership

Wholly owned by Graham Stevens.

Production

About 4200 cases, which comprise 2700 red, 750 white and 750 Tawny and Vintage Ports.

New Plantings

(Not yet yielding.) Muller Thurgau 1.2 hectares, Sylvaner 1 hectare, and small plantings of Merlot and Malbec.

Market

Dedicated enthusiasts everywhere manage to find the Cambrai cellar door or the postal address, as this is how all of the wine is placed apart from a few bottles in specialist merchants.

Winery Visiting Details

9 am to 5 pm seven days a week. The address is Hamilton Road, McLaren Flat, 5171 Telephone (08) 383 0251.

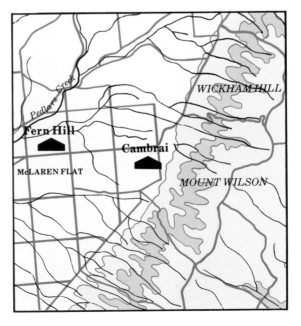

33

CAMPBELLS Rutherglen, Vic.

Campbells is as much a part of Rutherglen as the main street. One of a great many vineyards and wineries established in the area in the latter part of the 19th century, it is one of the comparatively few to have survived the wildly fluctuating vinous fortunes of the hundred and ten years which followed.

Little if any of the original plantings exist identifiably today. Indeed, only about 6 hectares of vines pre-date the massive replanting programme commenced in 1969.

As with the rest of the area, indeed, as with all traditional Australian wine areas with the possible exception of the Hunter Valley, the table wines of Campbells were, until the last decade or two, more bucolic than elegant. 'Wine for heroes' was the euphemism for the old style of big, fat Rutherglen reds; the whites

bore no such fanciful description (wine for cowards?). Sherries, ports and of course the fabled muscats were the area's staples, table wine merely filling out the range.

As we all know, the market changed totally from the mid-sixties onwards. Campbells adapted, but did so intelligently, creating a range of finer, more urbane table wines including their remarkable 'Chablis', but maintaining their superb fortified styles. The programme of replanting was rigorously followed, and substantial new equipment was installed, together with major building changes.

The annual crush is currently about 400 tonnes, roughly one-quarter each of which is dry red, dry white, fortified whites or muscats, and fortified reds.

Winemaker

Colin Bruce Campbell is the great grandson of John Campbell, who established the vineyard in 1870. After being educated at Scotch College, Melbourne, he studied Agriculture at Dookie and then took his diploma of Oenology at Roseworthy in 1967. He has personally been largely responsible for rationalizing the wine styles of Campbells and creating their unique 'Chablis'.

Range of Wines

Campbells 'Bobbie Burns' Shiraz
Campbells Cabernet Shiraz
Campbells Chablis
Campbells Empire Port
Campbells late picked Semillon
Campbells Light Mataro
Campbells Liqueur Muscat
Campbells Liquid Gold
Campbells Old Frontignac
Campbells Old Port
Campbells Old Tokay
Campbells Rutherglen Hermitage
Campbells Sauternes
Campbells Tawny Port
Campbells Trebbiano
Campbells Vintage Port
Campbells White Hermitage

Style

Campbells 'Bobbie Burns' Shiraz

A modern version of the traditional Rutherglen red, 'Bobbie Burns' Shiraz is a full bodied, mouth-filling wine of substance and character. While not porty or jammy like its vinous progenitors, it is nevertheless in the same earthy, alcoholic, long-living mould.
Best years: 1979, 1980

Campbells Chablis

Paradoxically for a wine which is so uncharacteristic of the area, this Chablis is becoming one of Rutherglen's 'flagship' wines. Made entirely from Pedro Ximenez, a variety which, when not used for Sherry, normally produces remarkably undistinguished white wine, Campbells Chablis has a flinty austerity which develops with bottle age to a unique and admirable complexity.
Best years: 1978, 1980

Campbells Liqueur Muscat

Campbells well-made version of the incomparable Rutherglen Muscats, which are virtually subsidized by the other wines. As a cost-efficient exercise, the making of Muscats would make an accountant shudder, but producers like Campbells see their role as Rutherglen winemakers as involving an essential responsibility to keep alive this amazingly rich, luscious and intense wine style.

Ownership

Campbells is a family-owned winery and vineyard.

Production

Average annual production is about 25 000 cases.

New Plantings

(Not yet yielding.) Three hectares each of Tokay (Muscadelle), Rhine Riesling and Pedro Ximenez, together with a total of ten hectares of experimental varieties including Chardonnay, Sylvaner, Ruby Cabernet, Durif, Tinta Cao, Touriga and Alvarelhao.

Market

Cellar door sales account for 50 per cent. The remainder is 35 per cent within Victoria, 10 per cent to New South Wales with small amounts to Queensland, Western Australia and export.

Winery Visiting Details

The winery may be visited from 9 am to 5 pm Monday to Saturday, and from noon till 5 pm on Sundays. The address is Murray Valley Highway, Rutherglen, 3685 Telephone (060) 32 9458.

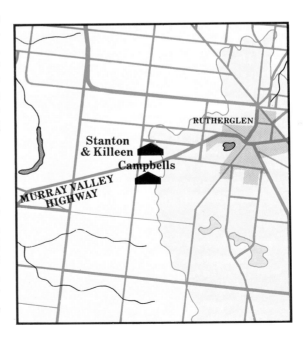

CAPEL VALE

One of the intriguing aspects of this book is that I have no light to shed upon the reason for Capel Vale's depiction of a male Mallard duck upon its label. This sort of mystery makes richer the world of wine.

Likewise, I can supply only a modicum of background information to the establishment of the vineyard and winery. Peter Pratten is a Bunbury radiologist who, one would imagine, wanted to plant a vineyard and make his own wine. He did both of these at Capel, near Bunbury, in what is known in the West as the South West Coastal district, some 50 kilometres north of Margaret River.

The grapes he planted were Shiraz and Cabernet, in the original plantings in 1974. Since then he has extended the vineyard with Rhine Riesling, Traminer and Chardonnay. A modern well-equipped winery was completed in time to deal with the 1979 vintage, the struc-ture being erected on a site dug into the river bank.

Peter has not been over-generous with the information supplied to me about his motivation in creating Capel Vale, but he does impart that his intention was and is to produce wines with 'intense fruit, and a light, elegant palate'. His aim is also to make small parcels of high quality wine bearing, and indeed creating, the stamp of his vineyard area. To date, these wines are largely experimental, in that he wishes to 'get to know the fruit' before adopting rigid styles.

The area is markedly different from the Margaret River vignoble in both climate and micro-climate, yet ultimately the expectable style could be similar. Everything depends upon results, and what we have to judge from to date is promising.

Winemaker

Peter Pratten is, as noted, a radiologist whose winemaking ambitions impelled the creation of Capel Vale. He states that his expertise is largely a matter of personal endeavour, by which one would imagine that a large proportion of his private time is spent in reading and study. With perceptive eloquence, he also pays full tribute to his wife's patience in facilitating his oenological competence.

Range of Wines

Capel Vale Cabernet Sauvignon
Capel Vale Chardonnay
Capel Vale Rhine Riesling
Capel Vale Shiraz
Capel Vale Traminer

Style

Capel Vale Cabernet Sauvignon

A medium-bodied wine of very considerable beauty, and elegance bordering on the seductive. The colour is fine, dark and exemplarily limpid; the nose is quite vinous — unexpectedly so for these days of ham-fisted over-use of oak — but quite deep and varietally faithful; and the palate's finely chiselled austerity does not mask the gently sweet fruit. A lovely wine.
Best years: 1980, 1982

Capel Vale Shiraz

Another remarkably attractive wine, notably similar in structure to the Cabernet. The more uncompromising nature of Shiraz as a variety lends the nose and palate an even greater vinosity, and almost humidity, which evokes aspects of Hunter Valley Shiraz. The finish is again firm and the acid again high.
Best years: 1980, 1982

Ownership

Capel Vale is owned by Peter and Elizabeth Pratten.

Production

When in full production, each vintage should generate about 4500 cases — 1000 cases each of Cabernet Sauvignon, Shiraz, Traminer and Rhine Riesling, and 500 cases of Chardonnay.

New Plantings

(Not yet yielding.) Nil, but the existing 9 hectares are not yet fully yielding.

Market

Not yet fully developed, but the wine already has a following in Melbourne and Sydney.

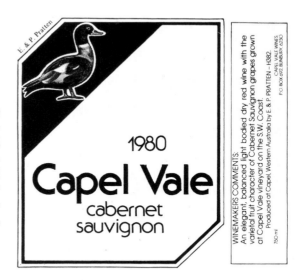

Winery Visiting Details

Monday to Friday 9 am to 5 pm, Weekends 10 am to 5 pm. The address (postal) is 12 Crowea Street, Bunbury, 6230 Telephone (097) 21 6404.

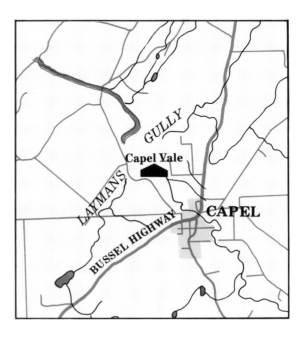

CAPE MENTELLE

There could scarcely be anything less romantic than a surgeon, a mining engineer and a pastoralist deciding to diversify their farming operation. But Leslie Le Soeuf, John Hohnen and Alan Salmon chose wine for their diversification, and Cape Mentelle was born. 1970 saw about one hectare of Cabernet Sauvignon planted on sloping land some six kilometres east of the mouth of the Margaret River. There are now some seventeen hectares established, mostly to Cabernet Sauvignon, Rhine Riesling, Shiraz and Zinfandel, with lesser plantings of Semillon and Chenin Blanc.

The winery was constructed of rammed earth, which is both aesthetically appealing and good insulation. (The somewhat hyperbolic information supplied to me describes the winery as 'timeless', from which I assume that the structure has no clock-tower.)

David Hohnen, who is now part owner of Cape Mentelle, was installed as manager and winemaker in 1976. He brought to the project a dedication which could only ensure the inevitability of extreme quality. The reds are aged in new oak Barriques which are imported direct from Bordeaux, and the standard of vineyard and winery hygiene is entirely adequate. David's Californian training and experience has engendered a laudable respect for the concept of the grapes' determining the character of the wines, with consequent acknowledgement of the importance of viticulture.

The nexus with California is maintained still, as in the last two vintages (1980 and 1981) David Hohnen has been assisted by two Californian colleagues, just as he himself assisted Bernard Portet at Clos du Val in the Napa Valley for the 1978 vintage.

Winemaker

David Hohnen has supervised the Cape Mentelle plantings, designed the winery and plant, and has made all the wines except the first vintage (1976). He studied oenology at Fresno State University in California and has worked as winemaker at Taltarni in Victoria and at Clos du Val in the Napa Valley.

Range of Wines

Cape Mentelle Cabernet Sauvignon
Cape Mentelle Hermitage
Cape Mentelle Rhine Riesling
Cape Mentelle Semillon/Chenin Blanc
Cape Mentelle Zinfandel

Style

Cape Mentelle Cabernet Sauvignon

It is difficult to know precisely what we are looking at in tasting young Cape Mentelle Cabernets. I believe it is possible that time — lots of it — could develop these into wines of world greatness: they are of stunning power, grace and promised longevity, yet lack the slightest hint of coarseness or truculence in their emphatic impact. But to taste them young is to stand next to a Colossus — you can't really see it properly.
Best years: 1978, 1979

Cape Mentelle Rhine Riesling

To say that this is a giantess of a Riesling sounds rather uncomplimentary, but it is a well-knit, superbly proportioned giantess of very considerable attractiveness. The fruit is heartily intense and densely floral, and the fullness of the palate is nicely offset by very substantial acid.
Best year: 1980

Cape Mentelle Zinfandel

I know of no other wines to which this style could be likened. At first contact there are evocations of Californian Zinfandels, but unlike the latter these are not porty, they lack the improbably high alcohol and the finish is much more tannic and crisply acid. A little residual sugar adds charm to the style. They will be very long-living, like their Napa Valley relations.
Best years: 1979, 1980

Ownership

Cape Mentelle Vineyards is a private company jointly owned by David Hohner and Margaret River Land Holding Ltd.

Production

6000 to 7000 cases, being Cabernet Sauvignon 2500, Hermitage and Zinfandel about 1000 each, Rhine Riesling 1500 and Semillon/Chenin Blanc 500 cases.

New Plantings

(Not yet yielding.) Nil.

Market

Limited distribution exists through specialist merchants in Perth, Sydney, Melbourne and Canberra, but cellar door and mailing list account for the lion's share.

Winery Visiting Details

Monday to Saturday 10 am to 4.30 pm, but telephoning first is recommended. The address is Wallcliffe Road, Margaret River, 6285 Telephone (097) 57 2070.

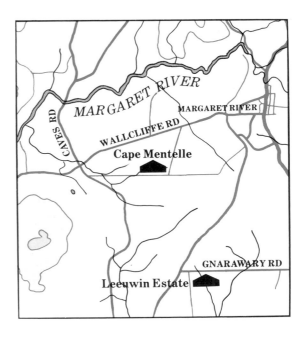

CHATEAU LE AMON Big Hill, Vic.

It is inevitable that any description of Chateau Le Amon will invariably dwell on similarities to and differences from Balgownie, its near neighbour. An indication of the high quality of Le Amon is that it does not suffer from such comparison, although the common denominator of the area's fruit characteristics serves only to highlight the essential differences in style between the two vineyards.

Philip Leamon was a rising star in the State Electricity Commission when promotion took him to a position where mundanity precluded interest. So he started a vineyard.

A concern for availability of adequate water led him, unlike Stuart Anderson, to select a property with a water right, and 1973 saw the planting of nearly 4 hectares of vines; one-third each of Cabernet Sauvignon and Shiraz, and one-sixth each of Semillon and Rhine Riesling.

Virtually starting from scratch, Philip studied textbooks, attended seminars, completed a course on inorganic chemistry and, just before his first vintage, attended the first of Tony Jordan's and Brian Croser's short winemaking courses at Riverina College.

Theoretical muscles thus flexed, he tackled the 1977 vintage. And produced a wine (Cabernet Sauvignon) which won a Gold Medal and the Small Makers Trophy at the first National Wine Show!

Subsequent vintages have generated considerable consumer respect for Chateau Le Amon (what execrable would-be French that is — worse than Rouge Homme instead of Homme Rouge. Oh, well). At a tasting I and one hundred and forty-eight other people attended a year or so ago twelve red wines were served masked (six top Victorian, five top 'other states' and one good Bordeaux) in an attempt to find out democratically which was the best wine. Chateau Le Amon Cabernet Sauvignon came out on top.

One might well observe that the answer was a Leamon.

Winemaker

Philip Leamon and his son Ian now make Chateau Le Amon wine. As has been mentioned, Philip is virtually self-taught, from textbooks and from attending every seminar he could, although prior to his first vintage he did a course at Riverina College. Ian's training is more formal, and at the time of writing he is about half way through the same College's Oenology course.

Range of Wines

Chateau Le Amon Cabernet Sauvignon
Chateau Le Amon Hermitage/Cabernet
Chateau Le Amon Semillon/Rhine Riesling

Style

Chateau Le Amon Cabernet Sauvignon

Stylish, slender, supple and notably attractive, Le Amon Cabernet is like a fashion model by comparison with the more generously endowed Balgownie version. Quite beguiling in their youth, the earlier vintages are now developing nicely, and augur very well for the future when both the vines' roots and the winemaker's experience grow deeper.
Best years: 1978, 1980, 1981

Chateau Le Amon Hermitage/Cabernet

In an average year a blend of 80 per cent Shiraz and 20 per cent Cabernet Sauvignon, this is a fine, crisp, delicately balanced but straightforward wine of considerable charm. It promises to live reasonably well in the medium term.
Best years: 1979, 1980

Chateau Le Amon Semillon/Rhine Riesling

This remarkable wine is a 60/40 blend of the two varieties. When young the wine is redolent of Riesling; full, flowery and elegant, but two years in the bottle see the emergence of deeper honeyed overtones as the Semillon stirs itself.
Best years: 1980, 1981

Ownership

Entirely owned by Philip and Alma Leamon.

Production

An average of 2500 cases per vintage, made up of about 500 cases of Cabernet Sauvignon and 1000 cases each of Hermitage/Cabernet and Semillon/Rhine Riesling.

New Plantings

There is no more land within the property which could be planted.

Market

Writing list and cellar door sales account for 40 per cent of the production. Melbourne retail outlets take all but 5 per cent of the remainder, the latter going to Sydney, Canberra and Brisbane.

Winery Visiting Details

10 am till 5 pm Monday to Wednesday, and the same on Friday. Saturday is 9 am to 6 pm and Sunday noon till 6 pm. The address is Big Hill (Calder Highway), Bendigo, 3550 Telephone (054) 47 7995.

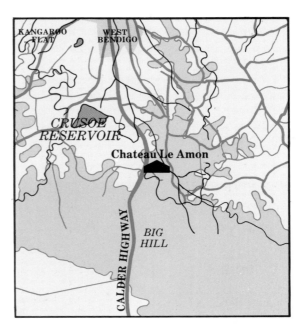

CHATEAU TAHBILK

Much indeed has been written about what is probably Australia's most beautiful winery, so that it is difficult to pen new words without raising the spectre of *déjà vu*. Historically the most ubiquitous piece of remarkably uninteresting information is that the first vine was planted in 1860 by R. H. 'Orion' Horne, a famous poet of whom nobody has ever heard except in the context of planting Tahbilk's first vine. Enough of all this.

Chateau Tahbilk makes an interesting contrast, in terms of image, with Bests, for example. The latter is in fact substantially bigger in both area and tonnage crushed than Tahbilk, but the Chateau's public profile has always been so strongly limned that the casual observer would be justified in thinking Tahbilk to be one of the industry giants. At 50 hectares, this is hardly the case.

Perhaps the most admirable past achievement of Chateau Tahbilk has been its success in continuing to market its wine in labelled bottles during those decades when Australian wine was almost entirely a bulk commodity. And also a similar success in maintaining a substantial traditional export programme while other makers withdrew from the collapsing export market, licking their wounds and muttering. To this day, the proprietors occasionally receive export orders of unthinkably large magnitude which are obviously impossible for them to supply.

Tahbilk wines have generated profound and firmly entrenched respect among the consumer — a respect which transcends the shorter term popularity of trendier vineyards (it is a little difficult to be trendy when you've been in busi-

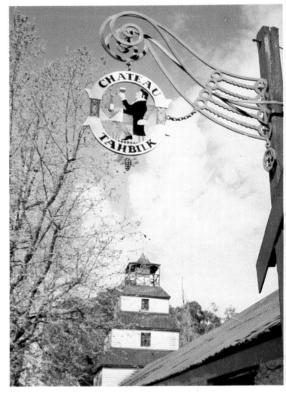

ness for 120 years). The quality of recent wines is if anything even better than before, and the creation of the 'Special Bin' reds is a laudable step. (Special Bin status is accorded to the best 4500 litre cask of red each year, be it Cabernet Sauvignon or Shiraz, the wine being bottled separately and released with six or seven years aging.)

Varieties planted are Cabernet Sauvignon, Shiraz, Marsanne, Rhine Riesling, Semillon, Chenin Blanc and Chardonnay.

Winemaker

Alister Purbrick is the third generation of Purbrick winemakers at Tahbilk, following his father John and grandfather Eric. He studied at Roseworthy Agricultural College where he gained his Diploma of Oenology in 1975. The next two vintages he spent with Mildara at Coonawarra before returning to assume oenological command in 1978.

Range of Wines

Chateau Tahbilk Cabernet Sauvignon
Chateau Tahbilk Chardonnay
Chateau Tahbilk Chenin Blanc
Chateau Tahbilk Marsanne
Chateau Tahbilk Rhine Riesling
Chateau Tahbilk Semillon
Chateau Tahbilk Shiraz

Style

Chateau Tahbilk Cabernet Sauvignon

Tahbilk Cabernet has an enviable place as one of the high quality staples of Australian wine. Recognition of this obvious fact is hardly a flash of insight, but how such place has been achieved is not quite so obvious. Over many years it has been reliably fine, but in certain vintages it assumes an authority, longevity and power which can astonish wine-lovers who had felt themselves familiar with the style.
Best years: 1962, 1965, 1966, 1968, 1971, 1976, 1978, 1980

Chateau Tahbilk Marsanne

When you consider that Marsanne is a minor Rhone Valley variety and that Tahbilk alone in Australia have paid it much attention, what an amazing wine this has been! Like the Cabernet it has been subject to severe vintage variation, but its continuity of style, its fresh charm when young, complex depths when mature, and fragile grace when old make it Australia's paramount Chablis style.
Best years: 1965, 1969, 1975, 1980, 1981

Chateau Tahbilk Shiraz

I believe I have been unfair to this wine as I found the four consecutive vintages from 1972 to 1975 both coarse and feeble, and thereafter either avoided the style or approached it with some prejudice. *Mea culpa*, for a closer inspection of these wines from 1976 onwards now convinces me that age could make them rival the magnificent 1971, the sensitivity of the fruit treatment in particular being exemplary. So, with the dramatic exception of the unpalatable years mentioned, I am happy to admit that this is very close to Shiraz at its best.
Best years: 1962, 1965, 1968, 1971, 1976, 1978

Ownership

Tahbilk Pty Ltd is entirely owned by the Purbrick family.

Production

About 35 000 cases, Marsanne leading with 15 000, then Shiraz 10 000, Cabernet Sauvignon 5000, Rhine Riesling and Chenin Blanc 1500 each, Semillon 1000 and a little Chardonnay beginning to come on stream.

New Plantings

(Not yet yielding.) These are considerable, being 10.5 hectares of Rhine Riesling, 8 of Cabernet Sauvignon, 6 of Chardonnay and 4 hectares of Shiraz.

Market

My request for market information was met with the response 'not applicable'(!)

Winery Visiting Details

Monday to Saturday 9 am to 5 pm, Sunday noon to 5 pm. The address is Tabilk (sic), 3607 Telephone (057) 94 2555.

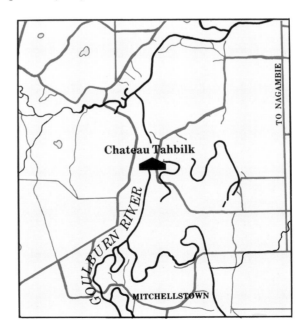

CHATEAU YARRINYA

To buy a property to fulfil a lifelong ambition to be a farmer, plant grapes almost as a matter of whimsy, learn a bit about winemaking, establish a label, and become the first Victorian winery to win the Jimmy Watson Trophy: it all sounds like the script for a Disney movie. But that has been what happened to Graeme Miller, who must wonder what other winemakers' fuss is all about.

Graeme's interest in wines evolved, as did mine, and probably yours, from being allowed a small glass as a child around the family table. As with other Yarra Valley growers, he was also impelled by a romantic interest in reviving the great nineteenth century vignoble.

The Yarrinya plantings total 14 hectares at the moment, but the total potential development is a substantial 56 hectares. Yielding varieties are Shiraz, Cabernet Sauvignon, Malbec, Merlot, Pinot Noir, Rhine Riesling and Traminer, and some Chardonnay is yet to come

to bear. Graeme's belief, with which there can be no argument, is that good wines can only be made from good grapes, and great wines from great grapes.

Chateau Yarrinya is sometimes criticized for bringing grapes into the area for processing. I feel this criticism quite unfair, as the label gives an honest attribution whenever this is done. Perhaps more importantly, Graeme Miller makes the point that he can afford to experiment with this bought-in fruit, to the greater benefit of his treatment of the home-grown premium grapes, whose yield is often sadly low (not much more than two tonnes per hectare in some years for the Cabernet Sauvignon).

Visitors should not be fooled by the frightful, mock castle facade of the winery. Behind it lies an efficient and modern plant well-adapted to the making of some of the Yarra Valley's most famous wine.

Winemaker

Graeme Miller studied Agriculture at Dookie College in line with his farming aspirations. For eight years he taught agriculture, mathematics and science before embarking on the Dixon's Creek venture which became Chateau Yarrinya. He has no formal oenological qualifications, being effectively self-taught.

Range of Wines

(Yarra Valley wines only)
Chateau Yarrinya Cabernet Sauvignon
Chateau Yarrinya Pinot Noir
Chateau Yarrinya Shiraz
Chateau Yarrinya Traminer/Riesling
Chateau Yarrinya Vintage Port

Style

Chateau Yarrinya Cabernet Sauvignon

The flagship of the Yarrinya fleet, and of course
the wine which carried off that infernal trophy
about which too much has been heard. These
are some of the biggest reds in the Yarra Valley,
extraordinarily intense in both flavour and
bouquet, with a mouth-filling richness com-
pounded of both plums and mint. Wood treatment is substantial, as is body (atypically so for
the area), and the style promises to be medium-
to-long-term aging prospects.
Best years: 1976, 1978, 1980

Chateau Yarrinya Shiraz

Expectedly, this is a less complex wine than the
Cabernet Sauvignon. Unexpectedly, it is not
that much less complex, showing a depth and
beauty remarkable for this variety, whose
popularity with the fickle public is fast fading.
The nose has coffee undertones in its sweetly
fragrant aroma, and the body is both profound
and elegant. A beautiful wine.
Best years: 1977, 1978, 1980

Chateau Yarrinya Vintage Port

This is an experimental wine of which only 600
bottles have been made to date (from the 1980
vintage). I include it here for two reasons: it is
almost certainly the first Vintage Port ever
made from Yarra Valley grapes; and it is of a
quality to render its exclusion irresponsible.
Entirely, indeed, enthusiastically Shiraz in
character, it nevertheless shares with the previous wine that soft sweetness of fruit which so
suits a Vintage Port. Full but fine, it has an
aristocratic dryness of finish and firmness of
grip that makes it one of the most impressive
young Ports I have tasted.
Best year: 1980

Ownership

The vineyards and wines are jointly owned by
Denise and Graeme Miller, and Jan and Don
Hall.

Production

Average production is 5000 cases, most of
which is red.

New Plantings

(Not yet yielding.) A little over 2 hectares each
of Chardonnay and Pinot Noir have recently
been planted.

Market

Virtually all by mailing list and cellar door.

Winery Visiting Details

Monday to Saturday 9 am to 6 pm, Sunday noon
to 6 pm. The address is Pinnacle Lane, Dixon's
Creek, 3775 Telephone (059) 65 2271.

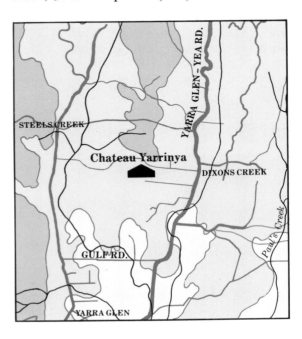

CHATTERTONS Lyndoch, SA

To refer again to a concern I expressed in my introduction: 'why include that producer when you leave this one out', Chattertons might seem an unexpected inclusion when one looks in vain for most other Barossa makers. The reason is twofold — the Barossa Valley has always been a tourist area and has subsequently been forced by commercial considerations to cater for the frequently unsophisticated tastes of the tourist market. The recent surge of interest among the more discriminating consumer (for whom this book is written) in high quality small vineyard wines, particularly from cooler climes, has forced many of the small Barossa makers to rely even more heavily on the tourist trade, with consequent diminution of quality. The larger companies with national distribution can of course afford to maintain a range of 'up-market' wines. The second reason is that I have a personal fondness for Chatterton wines.

Roland and Brian Chatterton took over their grandfather's firm in 1962. The property included some 18 hectares of vines, mostly Shiraz, Mataro, Grenache and a little Cabernet Sauvignon. It has been a painstaking and undercapitalized task to clean up, rationalize and indeed reduce the size of the vineyard, as well as to develop the wine styles. One style which was made for a few years was a massive, black and improbably atypical Grenache, normally a grape which produces apologetic and boring light reds, although this style has now been abandoned in favour of a tourist trap would-be Beaujolais. Another fascinating wine developed by the Chattertons is 'Obliqua', a white port made from Pedro Ximenez grapes and matured in Eucalyptus casks.

Eventually the old vineyard will be completely phased out as the newer plantings on a heavy loam soil come to bear. It has always been, and remains, the intention to make no more than 3000 litres of each wine in the small range, so that quality control, once the problems associable with small batch making are surmounted, does not present any difficulty.

Winemaker

Roland Chatterton is the chief winemaker. He qualified as an architect and practised for a time in that field before taking up winemaking as a hobby. He is largely self-taught, but has attended short courses at Riverina College. The services of a consultant, Robert O'Callaghan, are employed in the making of some wines.

Range of Wines

Chatterton Cabernet Sauvignon
Chatterton Crouchen
Chatterton Dry White
Chatterton Grenache
Chatterton Obliqua
Chatterton Shiraz
Chatterton Vintage Port

Style

Chatterton Cabernet Sauvignon

The floor of the Barossa Valley is probably not the place to grow quality Cabernet Sauvignon fruit and, attractive though the Chatterton version is, it adduces no unanswerable argument to the contrary. A wine of undoubted generosity and some unexpected finesse, it nevertheless shares with many of the area's Cabernets the triple demerit of being hot, strong and ropy in less kindly years. Better vintages show more depth with less strength and generally greater charm.
Best year: 1979

Chatterton Shiraz

It is with Shiraz that Chattertons achieve an admirable continuity of style quality, albeit without scaling the giddy heights of excellence. Honest, convincing Barossa Shiraz of some depth is what they annually produce — a style which is in danger of disappearing under the patchwork of tourist-trap wines, non-Barossa in area characteristics and tradition. Chatterton Shiraz is a rewarding wine of substance and grace, it ages well in the medium term; and it is a welcome reminder of what the area had produced for many decades.
Best years: 1977, 1979

Ownership

The winery operation is now set up as a separate company from the vineyards, but both are family owned.

Production

Only 1500 cases annually: Semillon, Crouchen and Shiraz 250 cases each, Grenache and Obliqua 200 cases each, Cabernet Sauvignon and Vintage Port (Shiraz) 150 cases each.

New Plantings

(Not yet yielding.) Cabernet Sauvignon 1.25 hectares, Shiraz 1.25 hectares, Rhine Riesling 1 hectare, Chardonnay 1.4 hectares, Cabernet Franc 0.4 hectares.

Market

Victoria 50 per cent, New South Wales 25 per cent, South Australia 20 per cent, other 5 per cent.

Winery Visiting Details

Monday to Saturday 9.30 am to 1 pm and 2 pm to 5 pm. The address is Barritt Road, Lyndoch, 5351 Telephone (085) 24 4082.

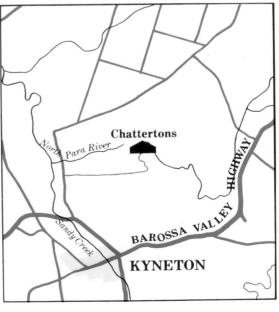

CONTI FOREST HILL

Over the last few years I have been increasingly impressed with the massive amount of intelligently conceived support given to the local wine industry by the Western Australian Government, in its various aspects. Yet another example of this was in the mid-1960s, when the South West was being evaluated as a new winegrowing area. The Government Viticulturist was Bill Jamieson, and it was his brainchild to establish a substantial but experimental planting of premium varieties on a property owned by Betty and Tony Pearse at Mount Barker. For the next decade the experimental growing programme involved Cabernet Sauvignon, Rhine Riesling, Traminer and Chardonnay. As is now history, the viability of this cool climate district for production of very high quality wine grapes was adequately demonstrated. End of experiment.

But not end of vineyard. By this stage the Pearses had their imaginations fired by winegrowing. But they did not see themselves as becoming winemakers, or building, staffing and managing a winery as well as maintaining the very considerable responsibilities imposed by their grazing and farming interests.

Enter Paul Conti, proprietor and winemaker of Conteville Wines of Wanneroo, west of the Swan Valley. Paul had already established quite a reputation with his Conteville wines and had aspirations, but no vineyard land, so far as the South West was concerned. The availability of premium fruit from Mount Barker was ideal for him, and access to his winemaking facilities and expertise was equally as ideal for Betty and Tony Pearse.

This fortunate fusion of complements has derived Conti Forest Hill wine, now a sought-after but comparatively scarce label. What must be borne in mind is that the vines supplying the fruit are for the most part some sixteen years old — unexpected vine maturity for a new area, and consequently profound and long-lasting fruit flavour.

Winemaker

Paul Conti has had no formal training in winemaking, but he has been making all of the Conteville wines since he took over from his father in 1968. For some years he was assisted by the consultant services of Dorham Mann, and he still avails himself of the facilities of the Department of Agriculture.

Range of Wines

Conti Forest Hill Cabernet Sauvignon
Conti Forest Hill Rhine Riesling

Style

Conti Forest Hill Cabernet Sauvignon

There is a notably consistent continuity of style discernible with all of the five vintages of this released to date, in spite of vintage variations. The fruit is of immense power and depth, and of midnight purple hue. Nose and flavour are both of sumptuous generosity, and all wines to date have shown significant oak treatment. I am less happy with two aspects of the series: elegance is not a strong point, the wine being almost furry in its lack of brilliance; and neither do I feel that the winemaking so far has succeeded in achieving the fruit's potential in terms of either complexity or sophistication. Nevertheless this is a rare and desirable wine, with an impressive future.
Best years: 1976, 1979, 1980

Conti Forest Hill Rhine Riesling

While lacking the intense varietal definition of the Cape Mentelle Rieslings of Margaret River, the Conti Forest Hill versions have considerable stylistic similarities. Massive in both nose and body, the finish may well be too hard for those who prefer more delicate styles, but will be appreciated by White Burgundy lovers, particularly as some wood treatment is readily noticeable.
Best years: 1979, 1981

Ownership

As described before, Conti Forest Hill as a label is jointly owned: the vineyard by Betty and Tony Pearse, and the winery by Conteville Wines.

Production

About 6000 cases of Conti Forest Hill wine are made each year, roughly 3000 cases each of Cabernet Sauvignon and Rhine Riesling.

New Plantings

(Not yet yielding.) 0.5 hectares each of Chardonnay and Traminer are just beginning to yield. There are no immediate plans for new plantings.

Market

Mostly Western Australia, including mailing list customers. Some specialist merchants in Melbourne and Sydney are also stockists.

Winery Visiting Details

The winery is open 8.30 am to 5.30 pm Monday to Saturday. The address is 19 kilometre peg, Wanneroo Resort, Wanneroo, 6065 Telephone (09) 409 9160.

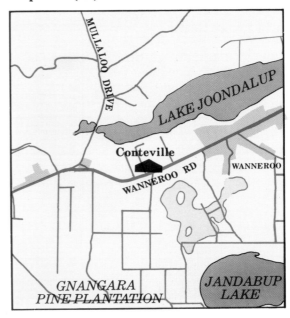

COOLAWIN ESTATE

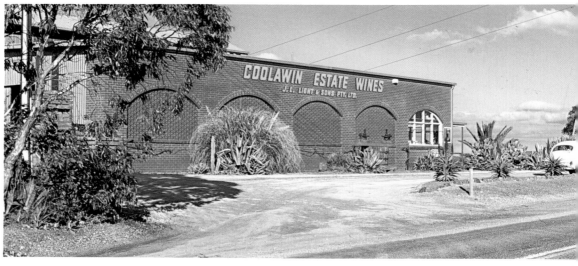

I remember a childhood playground joke about a man who had the unfortunate name of Tom Stench. His friends prevailed upon him to change the name by deed poll, so he did: to Fred Stench!

Well, 'Light Wines' was considered an inappropriate name for a wine-producer, particularly a few years ago when dry reds were frequently admired for sheer volume of flavour. It is arguable whether the new name, sounding as it does a compromise between Coolabah and Wynns, is much of an improvement.

I mention all this not to be flippant, but because this producer is making some notable inroads into national distribution with wines of respectable quality, and it would be a pity if the name caused identity problems amongst the consumer. Coolawin Estate has radically upgraded its image and its equipment during the 1970s, starting with the completion of a remarkably efficient winery which has the ca-

pacity to process a 1200 tonne crush with only three men. It was designed mostly for red wine production, so as the white wine cataclysm overwhelmed the market, they were forced to amend the equipment by the addition of drainers, refrigeration and earth-filtration.

At the same time a substantial planting programme was begun with the then super-star variety Rhine Riesling occupying the centre of the planting stage. Premium plantings, for which the owners must now be grateful, were of Cabernet Sauvignon and Shiraz. (For some years the Shiraz was incorrectly labelled 'Petite Syrah', which is in fact Durif and is not planted in their vineyards. 'Syrah' is Shiraz.)

Coolawin is not strictly speaking a small winery, crushing some 400 tonnes, but their image and place in the market is that of a 'smaller than medium' family-owned producer whose quality aspirations deserve both acknowledgment and respect.

Winemaker

Brian Light graduated dux of the Roseworthy Oenology course in 1973. He worked with Wynn Winegrowers at Coonawarra and Seaview Champagne Cellars until 1975, when he returned to the family company. Since then Brian has been sole winemaker for Coolawin Estate.

Range of Wines

Coolawin Estate Cabernet Sauvignon
Coolawin Estate Cabernet Shiraz
Coolawin Estate Cellarmaster Cabernet Port
Coolawin Estate Late Picked Rhine Riesling
Coolawin Estate Old Tawny Port
Coolawin Estate Rhine Riesling
Coolawin Estate Shiraz
Coolawin Estate Vintage Port
Coolawin Estate White Burgundy

Style

Coolawin Estate Cabernet Sauvignon

Quite a fine wine, but in the meaty style of Southern Vales Cabernet, which always lack the austerity and depth shown by this variety in cooler climes (and even some warmer climes — for example Pokolbin). Nevertheless the structure and balance are admirable, as is the generosity of the fruit. A pleasant and attractive wine for medium-term aging.
Best years: 1978, 1980

Coolawin Estate Rhine Riesling

Of recent years this area is starting to produce some much improved Rhine Rieslings, but of two disparate styles: one might well say Roseworthy or Wagga style. Coolawin is the former, and could perhaps be described as 'modernized traditional' — generously floral in both nose and palate, full but crisp in the mouth, and freshly acidic in the finish.
Best years: 1980, 1981

Ownership

. L. Light and Sons is a family-owned Proprietary Limited company.

Production

The annual average is a very substantial 25 000 cases, Rhine Riesling being the staple, closely followed by Old Tawny Port. Red wines account for some 4000 cases per year.

New Plantings

(Not yet yielding.) Nil.

Market

South Australia 40 per cent, New South Wales 30 per cent, Victoria 20 per cent, Western Australia 10 per cent.

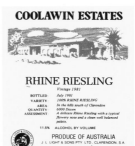

Winery Visiting Details

Monday to Saturday 8 am to 5 pm. The address is Windebanks Road, Happy Valley, 5159 Telephone (08) 383 6138

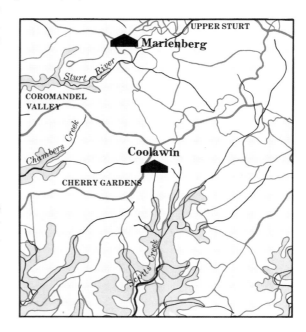

CORIOLE

Springtime visitors to the McLaren Vale area will be struck by the extraordinary beauty of almond orchards in full flower — seen from a distance from the higher ground, they smear a pale lilac wash across the view. Certainly Hugh Lloyd was thus romantically infected when he purchased a property in 1967 with the intention of fulfilling a lifelong ambition to grow almonds. But the property contained some 8 hectares of old vines as well as a derelict winery, and it rejoiced in the name Chateau Bon Sante. Crossroads for Hugh Lloyd.

With, one imagines, a philosophical shrug of the shoulders, Hugh accepted the dictates of fate and set about re-establishing the vineyard, re-planting vines and re-building the winery, and Coriole was born. Graham Stevens joined the project as manager and eventually winemaker, and the first Coriole wine, a Shiraz, was produced in 1970.

Coriole wines have always been a quite disparate style from the typical, traditional reds of the district, being lighter, finer and distinctively more elegant. Cool fermentation and annual new French and American oak were used to achieve this greater finesse, as well as total concentration on a small number of dry reds wines with an admirable continuity of style. Hugh Lloyd's stated aim was 'to make the highest possible quality red wines'. Most, if not all, wine producers would make the same claim, but their winery procedures are such that one must take this high-flown altruism with several grains of salt. Coriole, on the other hand, are demonstrably aiming high, and have always done so.

Varieties planted are Cabernet Sauvignon and Shiraz, with a few old Grenache vines remaining. Chenin Blanc and Rhine Riesling are also established and now yielding, and the Portuguese variety Touriga has just been planted. Perhaps we will be drinking a graceful Coriole Vintage Port at the turn of the century.

Winemaker

Mark Lloyd took over as winemaker from Graham Stevens in 1979. The son of Hugh Lloyd, Mark is a Science Graduate from Adelaide University who has worked in the wine industry in both Australia and Europe. His particular hobby horse is that Australian reds often lack freshness, and he has focused his attentions on producing clear, flavoursome wines.

Range of Wines

Coriole Cabernet Sauvignon
Coriole Cabernet/Shiraz
Coriole Chenin/Riesling
Coriole Shiraz
Coriole Shiraz/Cabernet

Style

Coriole Cabernet Sauvignon

The straight Cabernet from Coriole is not made every year and often alternates with the Cabernet/Shiraz blend. It is an atypical wine for this vineyard, being generally more turbid than the other reds, even those with a Cabernet content. Depth is not lacking, nor complexity, and there is more than a hint of the expected Coriole elegance. However this is not the style which made the winery famous.
Best year: 1978

Coriole Cabernet/Shiraz

It is a unique aspect of the McLaren Vale vignoble that Cabernet Sauvignon, normally a variety productive of wines of notable austerity, here produces wines which can often incline to flaccidness. It is also worthy of attention that Coriole make a clean and fine Shiraz. Perhaps for these combined reasons I prefer the blend to the 100% Cabernet. The wine is impressive in both substance and finesse, and it ages gracefully.
Best years: 1973, 1976, 1978

Coriole Shiraz

It is with this wine that I believe the Coriole winery makes a definitive statement. Shiraz is fast becoming an untrendy variety (memories being short, and 1953 Baileys, 1947 Mount Pleasants and 1959 Lindemans Bin 1590 being in shortish supply), but it has been, and still is, a vitally important grape for Australia. Coriole's version has ever been remarkably good: limpid, perfumed, vinous, tight and almost idiosyncratically elegant. A fine wine.
Best years: 1970, 1975, 1978, 1979

Ownership

Owned by seven members of the Lloyd family.

Production

Averages between 5000 and 7000 cases, and occasionally a little bulk for bottling by cheapskates.

New Plantings

(Not yet yielding.) One hectare of Touriga was planted in 1981.

Market

Cellar door sales often represent the culmination of a pilgrimage, such being this winery's following. Mailing list and selected merchants account for the remainder.

Winery Visiting Details

Monday to Saturday 10 am to 5 pm, Sunday 11 am to 5 pm. The address is PO Box 88, McLaren Vale, 5171 Telephone (08) 383 8305.

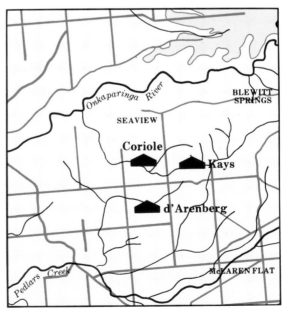

53

CRAIGMOOR

At more than 80 hectares of wines, it is perhaps arguable that Craigmoor cannot strictly be called a small winery. I agree. But by concept, marketing integrity and discreteness of style, it has developed the image and essence of the small maker. Besides, if you don't agree, you can always skip this page.

Craigmoor as we know it is a re-birth of a vineyard established originally in 1857. Re-birth, rather than re-establishment, because there has been unbroken continuity of production since midway through last century, but the visible profile of the maker underwent a century-long hiatus which ended with its acquisition in 1970 by Cyrille and Jocelyn Van Heyst.

Under the new ownership, gradual inroads were made into public consciousness of the label, at first from a local, then state and finally national standpoint. One of the unique winestyles created (which I do not intend to review in these pages) was 'Rummy Port', originally an accident brought about through the happenstance of aging some port by mistake in old rum casks. Hardly stuff to inflame the connoisseur's fervour, but substantially responsible for the vineyard's survival for three or four decades.

The Van Heysts modernized and rationalized the range, creating a new image for the table wines for the Sydney market, but maintaining the locally popular fortified styles which the area's tipplers traditionally expected from 'the Old Man of Mudgee'. During the 1970s Mudgee was being comprehensively planted with new vineyards, the publicizing of whose labels has finally convinced consumers that Mudgee is not just an understudy for the Hunter Valley, but a unique vignoble with its own style and intense pride as evinced by the very successful self-imposed 'Controlled Appellation'.

Winemaker

Although Cyrille Van Heyst maintains an overview of each Craigmoor vintage, the nuts and bolts winemaking is done by Barry Platt. Barry made wine in South Africa for five years before spending the period from 1970 to 1974 studying wine chemistry under Helmut Becker at Geisenheim. Returning to Australia, he worked as winemaker with Denman Estate and Hollydene/Richmond Grove in the Upper Hunter before joining Craigmoor in 1981.

Range of Wines

Craigmoor Cabernet Sauvignon
Craigmoor Cabernet Shiraz
Craigmoor Chablis
Craigmoor Chardonnay
Craigmoor Muscat
Craigmoor Port
Craigmoor Rhine Riesling
Craigmoor Rummy Port
Craigmoor Shiraz
Craigmoor Traminer Riesling

Style

Craigmoor Cabernet Shiraz

It is a most unfortunate semantic accident that many of the dry reds of Mudgee have been muddy, a fact which generated some consumer concern in the past. Craigmoor wines have never been guilty of such turbidity and the Cabernet Shiraz particularly is a clean, fine and powerful dry red which ages magnificently.
Best years: 1979, 1980, 1981

Craigmoor Chardonnay

Chardonnay has existed in reasonably substantial plantings at Craigmoor since 1959. Unfortunately no-one knew that the previously unnamed variety planted by Jack Roth in that year was Chardonnay until it was identified in 1970. The style has been very full and broad, without the taut balance seen in great Chardonnays.
Best years: 1979, 1980

Craigmoor Shiraz

As is so often the case when a maker produces a particularly fine Cabernet/Shiraz blend, the Craigmoor Shiraz is a much simpler, more basic style. One suspects that the best shiraz fruit is kept for the blended wine, thus impoverishing the quality of the remainder, and can only applaud the integrity implicit in this. Basic, but attractive and reasonably elegant drinking.
Best years: 1972, 1974, 1979

Ownership

Cyrille and Jocelyn Van Heyst now have a private company which has owned Craigmoor since 1980. For the preceding decade the Van Heyst family had a controlling interest.

Production

Annually 22 500 cases are produced, being Chardonnay 1500, Semillon Chardonnay 4000, Traminer Riesling 3000, Chablis 3000, Rhine Riesling 2000, Moselle 1400, Shiraz 2600, Cabernet Sauvignon 1000, Cabernet/Shiraz 1500, Pinot Noir 500, Rummy Port 1500 and Vintage Port 500 cases.

New Plantings

About 4 hectares of Chardonnay and Merlot have yet to come to bear.

Market

New South Wales 50 per cent, Victoria 25 per cent, Queensland 10 per cent, other states 5 per cent, export 10 per cent.

Winery Visiting Details

10 am to 5 pm Monday to Saturday. The address is simply Mudgee, 2850 Telephone (063) 72 2208.

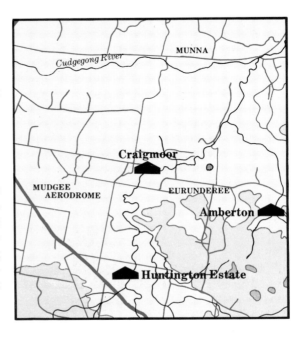

CULLENS WILLYABRUP

Cowaramup, WA

The Willyabrup story really begins back in the 1960s when agricultural scientist John Gladstones, a friend of Kevin and Diana Cullen, did a thesis on microclimates. As a result of some of the investigations in the district which had led to this, John advised the Cullens to plant grapes on their Cowaramup property rather than mess about with cattle.

They did just that, and 1971 saw the first grapes being planted. A fair range of varieties have been established on the undulating 21 hectare property, including Cabernet Sauvignon, Merlot, Malbec, Rhine Riesling, Chardonnay, Semillon and Sauvignon Blanc.

The soil type varies through the vineyard, but most of the Cabernet Sauvignon is planted on granitic soil, with the other varieties on gravelly loam over a clay base. Heavy winter rains evanesce as summer encroaches, and the district is very dry from December to April. Were it not for the almost certain predictability of wet conditions becoming set in mid-April, botrytis could produce some magnificent very late-picked styles, particularly with the Sauvignon Blanc. Perhaps a freak year may make this possible in the future.

Cullens Willyabrup wines tend to have a slumbrous power which makes even the whites candidates for some years' aging. The Rhine Rieslings for example can be notably innocuous when young, but unsuspected depths appear when time is allowed to do its work. The reds age slowly but well, and are subject to considerable vintage variation, depending among other things on the intensity of the ravages annually wrought by the spring winds.

Winemaker

Diana Cullen is the Willyabrup winemaker, although husband Kevin lends valuable assistance. Diana has a background in physics and biochemistry, the latter in particular being of considerable value from an oenological standpoint. As is the case with other Margaret River makers, much advice and support is freely given from certain of the other wineries, notably Leeuwin Estate.

56

Range of Wines

- Cullens Cabernet/Merlot/Malbec
- Cullens Cabernet Sauvignon
- Cullens Cabernet Vintage Port
- Cullens Chardonnay
- Cullens Dry Rosé
- Cullens Rhine Rieslings (Dry, Spatlese and Auslese)
- Cullens Sauvignon Blanc
- Cullens Semillon

Style

Cullens Cabernet/Merlot/Malbec

As might be expected, this is a subtler wine than the 100% Cabernet, the Merlot adding gentleness and the Malbec voluptuousness to the uncompromising Cabernet Sauvignon. The colour has the characteristic depth shown by most reds of the area, with good clarity; the nose is emphatic but of fair complexity; and the palate is almost challenging in its depth and strength. A fine wine.
Best year: 1979

Cullens Cabernet Sauvignon

It could be said that this wine suffers a little by comparison with its prettier sister above. For all that it is a big, strong but tightly assembled wine which will take many more years than the blend to achieve maturity, after which time its frequent slight turbidity will have thrown as a crust, and the slow moving complexities of this noble grape will have stirred themselves.
Best year: 1976

Cullens Sauvignon Blanc

As a 'new' wine area develops, theories quite properly begin to yield to empirical evidence, and it must be said that the quality of the Sauvignon Blanc fruit from this vineyard cannot be ignored as an indicator for the future. Never apologetic, innocuous or stinting in bouquet and flavour, Sauvignon Blanc can nevertheless be frequently coarse and obvious. The Cullens Willyabrup is subtle, beguiling and honeyed, a delightful wine, and a credit to the area.
Best year: 1981

Ownership

Entirely owned by the Cullen family (Kevin, Diana and six children).

Production

About 5500 cases, being 1000 cases of Cabernet Sauvignon, 500 cases each of Cabernet/Merlot/Malbec, Cabernet Vintage Port, Dry Rosé, Dry Rhine Riesling, Spatlese Rhine Riesling and Sauvignon Blanc, 750 cases of Semillon and smaller lots of 'Spatlese Cabernet' and Chardonnay.

New Plantings

About 5 hectares are yet to bear, being of all the varieties already established except Malbec, and with the addition of Pinot Noir.

Market

Half of the production is sold through cellar door and mailing list, 25 per cent in Perth, 5 per cent in the Australian Capital Territory, and the balance in the three eastern states.

Winery Visiting Details

Willyabrup goes to some trouble to welcome visitors. The hours are 10.30 am to 4.30 pm Monday to Saturday. The address is Cowaramup, 6284 Telephone (097) 55 5277.

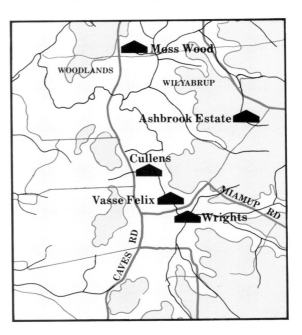

d'ARENBERG

In 1912 Francis Ernest Osborn purchased a 22 hectare vineyard from the Milton family who had established it late last century. He named it 'Bundarra', meaning on a hill, which fact was many years later a source of distress to the Baileys of Glenrowan, and doubtlessly generated a sabre-rattling exchange of solicitors' letters. It is an interesting aside that F. E. Osborn must have decided that it would have been too repetitious if he had been yet another doctor to go into wine, as he dropped out of medicine for the vineyard after three years of study.

His wife was born Frances Helena d'Arenberg, and died giving birth to her third child, Francis d'Arenberg Osborn, whom we all know as d'Arry. It was d'Arry who developed the d'Arenberg red stripe label when he assumed control of the company after his father's death in 1957.

The vineyard area is now 60 hectares, planted to Shiraz, Grenache, Cabernet Sauvignon, Palomino, Crouchen, Rhine Riesling and Pedro Ximenez. The average rainfall is 520 mm, and supplementary water is available to a large part of the plantings. Soil type is sandy over ironstone subsoil, with portions of limestone.

The winery has been modernized in recent years to include bulk handling facilities, refrigeration and auto-fermenters, and still uses an hydraulic press. Like many other traditional

makers, d'Arenberg had to undergo substantial expense in extending the premises to cope with the dramatic increase in the consumer demand for quality table wines. Such extensions included the installation of a bottling plant, with warehousing and bottle storage facilities to be able to deal with d'Arry's insistence on releasing red wines with substantial bottle age.

Winemaker

d'Arry Osborn is the d'Arenberg winemaker. When asked for his background and qualifications, he replied: 'I started making wine in 1943 and have been doing so ever since'. Fair enough.

Range of Wines

d'Arenberg Amontillado
d'Arenberg Burgundy
d'Arenberg Cabernet Sauvignon
d'Arenberg Claret
d'Arenberg Dry Red
d'Arenberg Moselle
d'Arenberg Muscat
d'Arenberg Muscat of Alexandria
d'Arenberg Rhine Riesling
d'Arenberg Shiraz
d'Arenberg Shiraz/Cabernet
d'Arenberg Tawny Port
d'Arenberg Vintage Port

Style

d'Arenberg Burgundy

This remarkable wine is a product of d'Arry Osborn's individualism and independent attitude towards winemaking. When others were blushing guiltily about their Grenache plantings, d'Arry blended his Grenache with Shiraz and Shiraz pressings, gave the wine old wood and bottle age, and created one of the area's most attractive wines: soft, mature and unexpectedly harmonious.
Best years: 1975, 1976, 1978

d'Arenberg Cabernet Sauvignon

An agreeable style, without overmeasure of the Southern Vales softness but nevertheless owing little to the Bordelaise for its breeding. The fruit is generous as always for this maker and the wine is always in most pleasant balance. It ages with dignity.
Best years: 1975, 1976, 1977, 1978

d'Arenberg Vintage Port

I have always been an admirer of this area's Vintage Ports, the soft generosity which characterizes the district's fruit being particularly felicitous for the style. This is big, dark, strong, long-living and has that tight richness so appreciated by lovers of the genera.
Best years: 1973, 1976, 1977

Ownership

A family-owned company with d'Arry Osborn as the 'chief executive'.

Production

Average production is of 10 000 cases, being 75 per cent dry reds, 15 per cent fortified wines and 10 per cent whites.

New Plantings

(Not yet yielding.) 2 hectares of Rhine Riesling and a little more of Chardonnay are planted.

Market

South Australia 40 per cent, Victoria 35 per cent, New South Wales 15 per cent, others 10 per cent.

Winery Visiting Details

9 am to 5 pm Monday to Friday, Saturday 10 am to 5 pm. The address is simply McLaren Vale, 5171 Telephone (08) 383 8206.

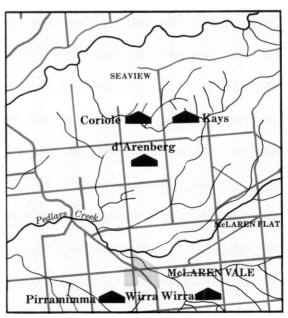

DRIDAN SKOTTOWE ESTATE

I am not an art critic, and this is not a book on Australian painters, so David Dridan's pre-eminence in the field of depositing paint on to virgin canvas is not germane to these pages. Suffice to say that his good taste gave him the inclination and his artistic success supplied the wherewithal for this delightfully self-indulgent and eccentric venture.

Dridan Skottowe is one of the smallest commercial wineries in Australia, producing about 1300 cases in an average year. The tasting room is a large port barrel, and the heads of the puncheons and hogsheads in the winery are heavily decorated, not with carved Bacchus's in the teutonic manner, but individually painted by some of David's friends; John Olsen, Kenneth Jack, Clifton Pugh, Ray Crooke, Frank Morris, Charles Blackman et al. The view from the front of the tasting barrel is one of the Southern Vales' finest.

The wines are made by David, who controls his naturally impetuous insouciance to the extent that they are made both with skill and care to achieve a remarkable quality. It is probably true to say that Dridan Skottowe has the highest proportion of 'non-wine' customers of any small winery in Australia, due to three factors; David's artistic fame; the extreme rarity of bottles from such a small production enhancing the wine's desirability; and the fact that the labels are undoubtedly amongst the most attractive ever seen in Australia. It is equally true, however, that the quality of the product behind those labels is such as to justify the eagerness with which these wines are sought after.

It might be worthy of note (and worthy of mention by David should anyone ever pass a disparaging remark about the small size of his vineyard) that, at a little under 2 hectares, Dridan Skottowe is exactly the same area as Romanee Conti.

Winemaker

David Dridan makes all the Dridan Skottowe wines as a labour of love and the challenge of achievement. He has had no formal training whatsoever, but has been given, as he puts it, 'a bloody lot of help and advice from many of the local winemakers'. Such entirely creditable assistance from these good people leaves unexplained why David's wines are substantially better than those of most Southern Vales makers.

Range of Wines

Dridan Skottowe Estate Cabernet Sauvignon
Dridan Skottowe Estate Rhine Riesling
Dridan Skottowe Estate Shiraz/Cabernet
Dridan Skottowe Estate Tawny Port

Style

Dridan Skottowe Estate Cabernet Sauvignon

Made from grapes grown at Hackham (a little south of Clarendon), this is an urbane and sweet-fruited wine of some depth and charm. It is made to be quite light and fresh, without the full-bosomed flaccidity which so often characterizes the Southern Vales area.
Best years: 1977, 1978

Dridan Skottowe Estate Rhine Riesling

A fresh, clean, naively perfumed and entirely captivating dry white whose surprisingly Germanic depth is rather mitigated by a lack of complexity. But somehow the wine is so pretty that such uncomplicated directness seems almost a virtue. Good acid balance, and again sweet fruit.
Best years: 1979, 1981

Dridan Skottowe Estate Shiraz-Cabernet

Probably the finest wine in the range, this wine has some of the best Shiraz fruit one could wish for in the area. Dark-hued and limpid, with an almost 'coffee and cigars' nose and a rich but fine palate with perhaps a suspicion of liquorice character at the finish.
Best year: 1978

Dridan Skottowe Estate Tawny Port

This is not made by David Dridan, but blended by him from five different Ports ranging in age from four to seventeen years. The wine is generous and full-flavoured, but with the finesse and length of finish imparted by the elderly components in the blend.

Ownership

Entirely owned by 'Old Clarenden Winery Pty Ltd.'

Production

Average annual crush yields 500 cases each of Rhine Riesling and Cabernet Sauvignon, and about 400 cases of the Shiraz blend.

New Plantings

(Not yet yielding.) Nil.

Market

Entirely cellar door and mailing list, with South Australia accounting for some 75 per cent, New South Wales and Victoria 10 per cent each, and Queensland about 5 per cent.

Winery Visiting Details

Monday to Saturday 11.00 am to 7.30 pm, Sundays 11.00 am to 6.00 pm. The address is Main Street, Clarenden Telephone (08) 383 6056.

ENTERPRISE WINES

Clare, SA

When the H. J. Heinz organization gulped down the Stanley Wine Company like an elephant taking an aspirin, winemaker Tim Knappstein decided that it would be more fulfilling to own his own vineyard. 'Grapes for fun and profit' is the way he puts it, intending as he did merely to sell the fruit to other makers. Accordingly he planted 37 hectares of vines and remained as the Stanley winemaker. By 1976 he had experienced very little fun and could foresee negligible profit, so in partnership with his mother Olive, he created a winery.

A picturesque stone building, erected in 1878 as the Clare Enterprise Brewery, was purchased and converted, and modern equipment was installed in time to process the 1977 vintage. (Small batches of '75 and '76 wine had been made by Tim anywhere he could find a bucket, and stored in various cellars in the Clare district, but such wines were strictly part-time hobbyist stuff.)

The 1977 wines had instant success in the wine circuses — sorry, wine shows — and enthusiastic consumers rapidly became conscious of a desirable new label.

Since then the winery has been progressively extended and upgraded, and as more vineyard came to full bear the annual production has climbed to 10 000 cases. The vines are planted some three kilometres south-east of Clare at an altitude of 450 metres. Varieties are Cabernet Sauvignon (8.2 hectares), Shiraz (6.8 hectares), Rhine Riesling (11.8 hectares), Sauvignon Blanc and Gewurztraminer (3.3 hectares each), Chardonnay (1.2 hectares), Cabernet Franc (0.8 hectares) and Merlot (0.6 hectares). In the past two years some 2 hectares of Shiraz have been grafted to Merlot and Cabernet Franc.

In July 1981, 18 hectares of land were purchased in the Adelaide Hills near Lenswood. This is the site of a cooler climate Enterprise vineyard, to be planted mainly with the Burgundian varieties Pinot Noir and Chardonnay. When this comes to full bear the annual production will be about 16 000 cases, which will be the limit of the company's growth.

Winemaker

Tim Knappstein is the Enterprise Winemaker. He joined Stanley Wines, then his family company in 1962 after leaving school. After attending Roseworthy College in 1964 and 1965, winning the Gold Medal for Oenology, he returned to Stanley and took over as winemaker later in 1966. During the period 1967 to 1976 he created the Leasingham range of wines, and from then on, obviously, the Enterprise range.

Range of Wines

Enterprise Wines Cabernet Sauvignon
Enterprise Wines Cabernet/Shiraz
Enterprise Wines Fume Blanc
Enterprise Wines Gewurztraminer
Enterprise Wines Late Picked Rhine Riesling
Enterprise Wines Rhine Riesling
Enterprise Wines Shiraz

Style

Enterprise Wines Cabernet Sauvignon

Clare Valley deserves its measure of renown for production of generously full-flavoured fruit, and Tim Knappstein's sensitivity with its handling is outstanding. His Cabernet is both denser and finer than the area's norm, and is probably as good as the area is capable of, which is saying something. The greater complexity which will be imparted as the Cabernet Franc and Merlot come into full yield will make the style even more elegant.
Best years: 1978, 1980

Enterprise Wines Fume Blanc

Tim was the first Australian winemaker to produce this style: a dry, wood-aged Sauvignon Blanc. Lightly golden in colour, the wine has a convincing smokiness to the bouquet although hardly of the Bombay Duck intensity of the Loire Valley versions; a peach-soft but dry palate; and an agreeably long finish. A very pleasant and welcome style, now being copied by other makers.
Best years: 1979, 1980

Enterprise Wines Rhine Riesling

The man who created the Leasingham range and played his part in the production of the superb 1971 and 1972 Rhine Rieslings of that range could be expected to generate an exemplary style for his own Rieslings, and rightly so. The wine is densely floral, fine and crisp, with a touch of lusciousness in the fruit. In some years, Tim also makes an Auslese, and a successful experience in 1980 with a Beerenauslese from botrytis affected fruit will be repeated when the conditions are suitable.
Best years: 1977, 1979

Ownership

Enterprise Wines is a family-owned Proprietary Limited Company.

Production

Around 10 000 cases currently: 4000 Rhine Riesling, 1000 each Late Picked Rhine Riesling, Gewurztraminer, Cabernet Sauvignon, Cabernet/Shiraz and Shiraz, and a little over 1000 of Fume Blanc.

New Plantings

(Not yet yielding.) Chardonnay 0.6 hectares at Clare and 1.5 hectares at Lenswood. At Clare more grafting of Merlot and Cabernet Franc to Shiraz vines is continuing, and at Lenswood a further 12 hectares will be planted.

Market

30 per cent New South Wales, 25 per cent Victoria, 20 per cent South Australia, the balance being Tasmania.

Winery Visiting Details

Monday to Friday 9 am to 5 pm, Saturdays and Public Holidays 10 am to 5 pm. The address is 2 Pioneer Avenue, Clare, 5453 Telephone (088) 42 2096.

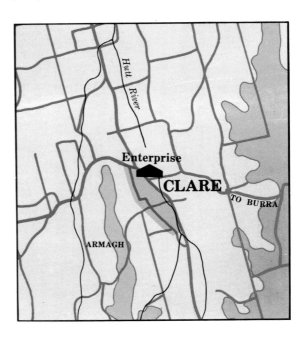

EVANS AND TATE

For an industry whose newer participants have so often been amateurs, albeit enthusiastic and frequently of extreme competence, the Evans and Tate operation has been remarkable for its sheer professionalism. Ever since we consumers all had our eyebrows lifted in disbelief on first encountering the extreme quality of the 1975 Gnangara Shiraz, the company has not put a foot wrong.

There are three Evans and Tate vineyards whose wines are identified by the particular vineyard name: Gnangara, Bakers Hill and Redbrook. Gnangara, in the Swan Valley, was the first planted. Of surprisingly modest size, considering its reputation, Gnangara has a mere 4.6 hectares of vines: 3.6 of Shiraz and 1.0 of Cabernet Sauvignon. The area has 865 mm rainfall, almost all of which falls during the winter months. In spite of this, no irrigation whatsoever is used, so yields are low (and quality is high).

Bakers Hill, where the Evans and Tate vineyard rejoices in the name 'Côte de Boulanger', has 2 hectares of Cabernet Sauvignon planted in the shallow gravel soils of the Darling Ranges some 60 kilometres east of Perth. To date none of the wine has been released, but I understand it is quite intense, with deep colour, full flavour and firm tannin.

Redbrook is the major vineyard, both in quality and size. Twenty-one hectares of premium varieties are established at Willyabrup, near Margaret River, on soil types which vary from sand to gravelly loam.

All production is carried out at the Gnangara winery, using traditional open fermentation with plunged cap, and temperature controlled to 15° Celsius. Temperature control is also used in the French oak wood storage (12 to 18 months in hogsheads), and the bottle storage is air-conditioned. To date, white wine production is both minimal and experimental.

Winemaker

Bill Crappsley has had no 'formal' training, but since 1964 has worked with Houghtons, d'Arenberg and Redmans (two vintages each), Tullochs, and Renmano. Then in 1972 he became the winemaker at Basedows, until joining Evans and Tate in 1977.

Range of Wines

Evans & Tate Rose Cabernet
Gnangara Shiraz
Redbrook Cabernet Sauvignon
Redbrook Hermitage
Redbrook Semillon

Style

Gnangara Shiraz

A fine, big, Rhone style wine of a quality quite improbable for the Swan Valley (bearing in mind that there are only two hotter wine-producing areas in Australia: Alice Springs and Mildura). The wine is notable for its depth and elegance, its convincing fruit, its soft tannin and its length of finish. Gnangara Shiraz is not a wine to consider for lengthy aging.
Best years: 1977, 1979, 1981

Redbrook Cabernet Sauvignon

A clean, fine and extremely chic Bordeaux style which adds still more to the already massive array of evidence of the Margaret River area's admirable potential. The wine is limpidly clear and handsomely coloured, with excellent varietal aroma and generous but profound fruit in the palate. One of the West's best wines.
Best years: 1979, 1980

Redbrook Hermitage

If Shiraz is to survive as an important variety for quality red wine in Australia, then this is the style in which it will have to be made: tight, light, graceful and fragrant, instead of truculent and implacably vinous. Evans and Tate are among the forefront of those talented makers who are finding a new role for our traditional red variety.
Best year: 1979

Ownership

The operation is owned by John Evans, John Tate and their wives.

Production

We are only a couple of years away from full production from all vineyards, at which time the estimated maximum will be 16 000 cases, the bigger part of which will be Gnangara Shiraz, 5000 cases, and Redbrook Cabernet Sauvignon, also 5000 cases.

New Plantings

(Not yet yielding.) 3.6 hectares of Chardonnay, 1.8 of Merlot, 1.0 of Sauvignon Blanc and 1.0 of Traminer are yet to bear (all planted at Redbrook).

Market

Sydney, Melbourne and Canberra account for 30 per cent, cellar door and mailing list 15 per cent, and the balance goes to Perth.

1979
EVANS & TATE

GNANGARA
SHIRAZ

PRODUCE OF
WESTERN AUSTRALIA
750ml.

Winery Visiting Details

Monday to Saturday 9 am to 5 pm. The address is Gnangara Road, West Swan, 6055 Telephone (09) 296 4329.

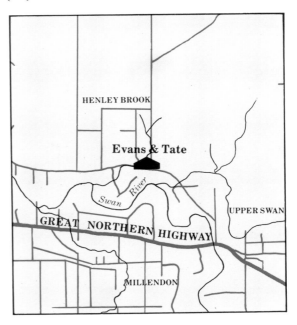

FAREHAM ESTATE

I remember some four years ago being retained to advise on wine selection for a well-known 'negociant label'. About 40 Rhine Rieslings were lined up for me to taste, identified by number only. Some of them were very good indeed, but the one I chose as clearly the best turned out to be a Fareham Estate. This was a matter of some embarrassment to me, as I had never heard of them. (By the way, nothing ever came of the negociant's venture, but that is another story.)

Not a great deal has changed since then so far as the low-profile of Fareham Estate is concerned, nor indeed so far as the impressiveness of their wines is concerned. The brainchild of winemaker Peter Rumball and Adelaide engineer Stephen Elliott, the venture was established with two definite aims. One was the sound business sense operation of contract bottling for other producers — initially intended as a Clare Valley small maker service, but now grown to such a scope that the greater proportion of the work is from outside the Clare district. Clearly a successful project, and doubtless one which is able to fund the less profitable but more absorbing aim: winemaking.

When the property was purchased in 1975 it contained a partly developed vineyard. The altitude is over 400 metres which makes the Fareham Estate plantings among the higher, and therefore better, in the area. The soil is reddish brown loam over limestone, and the rainfall in excess of 600 mm. Plantings to date are a little less than 8 hectares, comprising 3.3 of Rhine Riesling, 2.3 Sauvignon Blanc, 1.6 of Traminer and 0.5 Cabernet Sauvignon. The estate grown fruit is supplemented with grapes from a vineyard, Gully View, owned by Stephen Elliott's parents, only one kilometre distant, where there are Rhine Riesling, Shiraz and Cabernet Sauvignon yielding, and Chardonnay yet to bear.

Fareham Estate, like Allandale, Redbank, Yeringberg and a few others around the country, has been conceived and specifically designed for small parcel, high quality production. In summary, they are highly professional specialists.

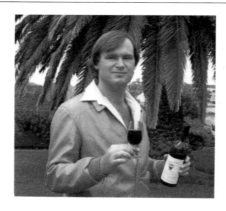

Winemaker

Peter Rumball must be one of the very few Adelaide born winemakers who can claim no previous family wine associations. Nevertheless the romance of the grape beckoned, and he graduated from Roseworthy in 1973, by which time he had gained practical experience working under Brian Barry at Berri Cooperative. His post-graduate experience was with Stanley under Tim Knappstein, where among other things his extreme competence in the specialized sterile bottling field was achieved.

Range of Wines

Fareham Estate Cabernet Sauvignon
Fareham Estate Gewurztraminer
Fareham Estate Rhine Riesling
Fareham Estate Sauvignon Blanc
Wan So (commercial semi-sweet white).

Style

Fareham Estate Cabernet Sauvignon

If not actually experimental, this wine is certainly still in the developmental stages. Peter Rumball is too much a perfectionist to be happy with either the finesse or the fruit intensity of any of his Cabernet Sauvignon since the 1976, and it is very much to his credit that he makes no secret of this. So as the '76 is close to his desired style, it would seem fair to describe it alone: rich, deep, fine, intense and very well-proportioned, with admirable balance and finish.
Best year: 1976

Fareham Estate Rhine Riesling

This is the wine for which this maker has some degree of renown amongst the comparatively few winelovers who are familiar with the style. All the crisp floral intensity which might be expected from well-made Clare Rhine Riesling is readily discernible, together with a less expectable lazily honeyed opulence which permeates the long finish. These are wines which need a year or three in the bottle to develop their languorous power.
Best years: 1977, 1978, 1980

Ownership

Fareham Estate is a private company the majority of whose shares are held by Stephen Elliott and Peter Rumball.

Production

Taking account only of the Fareham Estate and Gully View plantings, 3000 cases are produced annually, most of which is Rhine Riesling.

New Plantings

(Not yet yielding.) One hectare of Chardonnay has been established recently at Gully View.

Market

Some cellar door, and the balance in limited distribution to Victoria and South Australia.

Winery Visiting Details

The winery is open, 8 am to 4 pm Monday to Friday, 10 am to 5 pm most weekends (you are advised to ring first). The address is Main North Road, Leasingham, 5451 Telephone Auburn (088 493) 98.

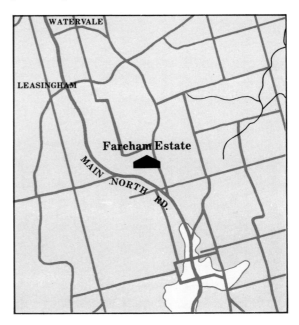

FERGUSSON

Peter Fergusson is an easy-going, relaxed, personable young man (well, fairly young anyway) whose light-hearted, almost flippant attitude blinded many people to the underlying deadly seriousness with which he set out to fund, establish and develop his vineyard and winery.

Initially, it must be admitted, the vines surrounding his picturesque and incredibly informal restaurant were almost cosmetic, or at least secondary to the restaurant in commercial importance. Perhaps it really was Peter's original intention merely to go through the motions of winemaking to justify the attractions of a winery restaurant set amongst the vines. He would be crazy to admit this now that he is making some of Victoria's better wines.

Enough of the early days: Fergussons is now 8 hectares of bearing vines with another 3 hectares planted but not yet yielding. Varieties bearing are Rhine Riesling, Marsanne, Chenin Blanc, Cabernet Sauvignon and Shiraz. The winery is completely equipped to handle fermentation and storage efficiently. I am particularly impressed that the wood-storage area is now air-conditioned, so that it is possible to use new oak for 18 months without harshly extractive shackling of the fruit character.

This book is about wineries, not restaurants, but it would be remiss of me not to mention the charm and unique character of the 'winery restaurant', with its huge spit-roasting facilities and its pleasant front courtyard, usually littered with a herd of stuporose, amiable, giant Rottweiler dogs.

Fergusson wines have grown dramatically in stature, elegance and quality since his first vintages in the early 1970s. Peter's ability and undeniable, if undetectable, determination is such that we can look forward to further growth.

Winemaker

Peter Fergusson is responsible for the winemaking. Having said that, it is also true that the technical know-how is increasingly supplied by Andrew Forsell. Peter studied applied chemistry and medical technology and his oenological qualifications are practical rather than formal. Andrew, on the other hand, is in the process of completing the Wine Science course at Wagga.

Range of Wines

Fergussons Cabernet Sauvignon
Fergussons Chenin Blanc
Fergussons Marsanne
Fergussons Nouveau Shiraz
Fergussons Rhine Riesling
Fergussons Shiraz
Fergussons Vintage Port

Style

Fergussons Cabernet Sauvignon

After a degree of stylistic indecision with the earlier Cabernets, some of which leaned towards flaccidness and others towards trucu-lence, the style is now growing finer, deeper and more convincingly elegant, with the supple fruit and cedar nose which typifies the best Cabernets of the area, and have become very good wines indeed.
Best years: 1979, 1980, 1981

Fergussons Rhine Riesling

This has been a remarkably successful wine at virtually every level of consumer competence. All of the desirable attributes of Rhine Riesling are present: floral nose; fresh, passionfruit pal-ate; sweetness of fruit and crisp, clean finish — in short, all of those characteristics so often as-cribed to many wines, but usually being a pol-ite exaggeration.
Best years: 1978, 1979, 1981

Fergussons Shiraz

This has not been this maker's most impressive wine, and is still not. However the same in-creasing elegance referred to with the Cabernet Sauvignon is also overtaking the Shiraz, to the wine's greater benefit. An attractive, almost Burgundian rather than Rhone, soft but tight wine which lacks the scope and complexity, but not the grace, of the Cabernet.
Best years: 1979, 1980, 1981

Ownership

The complex is owned by Peter and Michael Fergusson, 'with sympathetic funding by the A.N.Z. Bank'.

Production

The average annual production is about 5000 cases.

New Plantings

(Not yet yielding.) Two hectares of Chardonnay and one of Marsanne are not far off yielding. It is planned to plant some Merlot and Sauvignon Blanc in the near future.

Market

Mailing list and cellar door customers receive preference, leaving very little for the occasional specialist merchant.

Winery Visiting Details

Monday to Saturday 9 am to 5 pm, Sunday noon to 6 pm. The address is Wills Road, Yarra Glen, 3775 Telephone (059) 65 2237.

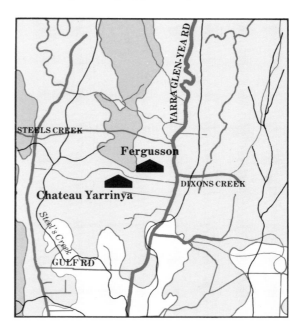

FERN HILL ESTATE

Along with Graham Stevens' Cambrai, the Johnston family's Pirramimma and Greg Trott's Wirra Wirra, Wayne Thomas is quietly playing a significant role in the current McLaren Vale quality revolution. Intriguingly, he started with literally nothing — quite literally, like no vines and no winery, buying in the fruit and fermenting open. Sounds rather rustic, to say the least, but Wayne is a competent oenologist who knew exactly what he was doing, and the results were surprising. The wine, a 1975 Shiraz, was precisely the style Wayne sought to produce: big but balanced, and maintaining the good points of the area's Shiraz while eradicating the bad.

There is now a winery, and even some vines (one hectare of Cabernet Sauvignon) although the major part of Fern Hill production is from carefully selected fruit bought-in from the McLaren Flat area.

But it is Shiraz — and McLaren Flat Shiraz at that — which is Wayne Thomas's particular enthusiasm. Every year since his first 'invented' vintage appeared he has produced a Shiraz of a quality and style to make quite an impact on those winelovers who are able to obtain a bottle or two of it from the extremely small production.

Now Fern Hill Estate is beginning to move into white wine production, but, as with the reds, the wines are of a quality and sophistication unparalleled for the area.

Wayne Thomas sees his chosen role as developing the idea of making a number of different wines of very high quality in small parcels. To this end, although his winery is theoretically capable of handling a crush of 100 tonnes, he currently produces less than half of this, and does not see himself exceeding 80 tonnes in the future. The operation is a very valuable adornment to the Southern Vales.

Winemaker

Wayne Thomas has been making wines for 22 years, working with Stonyfell, Saltram and Ryecroft before becoming a freelance consultant in the mid 1970s. He studied Oenology at Roseworthy College back in 1964, and now finds the Fern Hill operation an opportunity to make his own vinous statements.

Range of Wines

Fern Hill Estate Cabernet Sauvignon
Fern Hill Estate Chardonnay
Fern Hill Estate Rhine Riesling
Fern Hill Estate Shiraz

Style

Fern Hill Estate Rhine Riesling

Whether this is the ultimate Southern Vales Rhine Riesling remains to be seen as the area's quality revolution develops. (In any case, the fruit is grown at Middleton, which is closer to Victor Harbour than to McLaren Vale, so it is not from an area traditionally encompassed by the term 'Southern Vales'.) Certainly it is currently the best, by a long chalk. Beautiful, lightly floral nose with the barest hint of spice, soft, warm but gently crisp flavour, and lazily long finish: those are the rarely encountered hallmarks of superb Rieslings, and they can be seen in this wine with crystal clarity. A wine to be proud of.
Best years: 1979, 1981

Fern Hill Estate Shiraz

The Fern Hill flagship, and rightly so. This is a big, full but not soft, tight, mouthfilling wine of generosity and some muscle. Its major points of disparity from other Southern Vale Shiraz are its sophistication and taut balance. The wine is matured in American oak for 15 to 18 months and released when bottled. It might well be termed the Southern Vales' answer to Gnangara.
Best years: 1975, 1978, 1980

Ownership

Fern Hill Estate is owned by Wayne and Patricia Thomas.

Production

Only about 40 tonnes (2500 cases), and unlikely ever to exceed 80 tonnes.

New Plantings

(Not yet yielding.) About 0.5 hectares of Cabernet and still to yield. Most fruit is bought-in, and this will remain the case.

Market

Mailing list and cellar door account for virtually all of the limited production. A few bottles find their way to good merchants.

Winery Visiting Details

Monday to Saturday 10 am to 5 pm. The address is Ingoldby Road, McLaren Flat, 5171 Telephone (08) 383 0167.

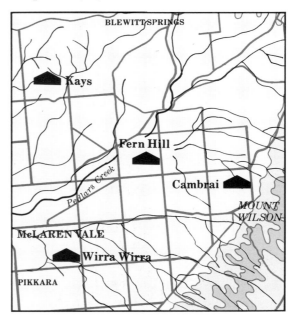

GOLVINDA

I remember Walter James writing in one of his books that there is not a square metre of France where one can stand and pronounce with confidence that 'a vine has never grown here'. Well, Australia is certainly not like France in that regard, yet in Victoria particularly there are many vineyards being established in areas which we consumers regard as 'new' but which saw their fair share of both viticulture and winemaking during the nineteenth century.

One such is Gippsland, which for the latter half of last century was a significant vignoble, climatically similar to the Geelong area. The turn of the century saw the tail end of Gippsland winemaking, as it did several other areas where yield was low and quality high.

We now skip a life-span to 1970, and vines begin to be grown again inland from the Ninety-Mile Beach. The second, but the biggest, of the new plantings was Robert Guy's Golvinda. Robert took immense pains to analyse climatological data from virtually every likely spot in the country before settling on the land he then acquired, some 16 kilometres west of Bairnsdale. He planted 10 hectares with Rhine Riesling, Semillon, Chenin Blanc and small quantities of Sauvignon Blanc and Chardonnay, with Cabernet Sauvignon as the main red variety and experimental patches of Merlot, Pinot Noir and Shiraz.

Robert Guy's approach is both painstaking and enthusiastic, but cautious withal. He believes that the total lack of recent experience of Gippsland as a wineproducing area will necessarily mean perhaps as much as a twenty-year period of experimentation and development before the maximum desirable quality and optimal style can be achieved. One hopes that this view is exaggeratedly pessimistic, but the results will speak for themselves anyway with whatever voice they possess, and all 'new' areas should be allowed to make their mistakes before they start blazing away with publicity so perhaps Robert is as wise as he is prudent

The first Golvintage (?) was 1975, and yields since then have suggested that production while quite viable, will always be low. And quality high.

Winemaker

Robert Guy comes from a grape growing back ground in South Australia. His introduction to the winemaking world began when he worked at an Adelaide winery during school holidays This prompted an interest which led to his graduating in Oenology from Roseworthy College in 1965, after which he worked with winemaking and winery design both in Australia and overseas.

Range of Wines

Golvinda Cabernet Sauvignon
Golvinda Chenin Blanc
Golvinda Rhine Riesling
Golvinda Rhine Riesling Auslese

Style

In deference to Robert Guy's eloquently manifested concerns regarding the still experimental and developmental nature of Golvinda and indeed the other Gippsland plantings, it seems hardly fair to expound on the quality and style of the wine to date. Having said that, however, it should be made quite clear that this is not because quality has been disappointing — if anything the reverse is the case. But if, as seems possible, Gippsland wines are to achieve any dizzy heights of excellence once the development phase is over, any well publicized assessments of the 'undeveloped' styles could be both counter-productive and quite inapplicable within a couple of vintages.

Ownership

Entirely owned by Robert Guy.

Production

Currently a mere 1500 cases a year. This will probably peak at 3500 to 4000 cases as the vines mature.

New Plantings

(Not yet yielding.) None, but the existing 10 hectares are not yet yielding fully.

Market

Entirely by cellar door and mailing list.

Winery Visiting Details

Monday to Saturday 9 am to 6 pm, Sunday by appointment only. The address is R.M.B. 4635, Lindenow, via Bairnsdale, 3865 Telephone (051) 59 1480.

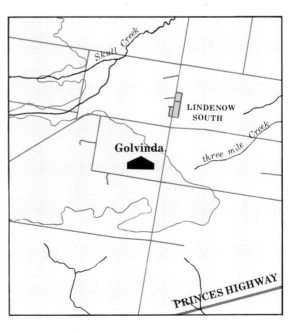

73

HEEMSKERK

Information about Heemskerk is both sparse and almost grudgingly divulged by the proprietors. What follows is all I could muster.

In 1966 Graham Wiltshire of Launceston established a small vineyard at Legana on the Tamar river. The potential of the wines he made attracted the attention and interest of two men in particular: Bill Fesq of the Sydney wine and spirit merchants Fesq & Company, and Colin Haselgrove, who had recently retired as managing director of Walter Reynell & Sons Limited.

All of this devolved in the formation of a consortium to seek and acquire a vineyard site adequate for the extreme quality aspirations of the participants in the venture. They chose 92 hectares at Pipers Brook, and planted 20 hectares with Cabernet Sauvignon, their main variety, Traminer and Chardonnay, with smaller plantings of Pinot Noir, Rhine Riesling, Sylvaner and a few experimental varieties. The original Wiltshire vineyard at Legana was brought into the operation as well, although it is now only one hectare of Cabernet Sauvignon.

The soil at Heemskerk is what geologists call tertiary basalt, and winelovers call terra rossa. The southerly latitude (41°) means both very cool climate and a long ripening day, both of which are factors which potentiate the depth of colour and the intensity of varietal character.

Winemaker

Graham Wiltshire is the Heemskerk winemaker. He would not supply a photograph of himself or any information regarding his qualifications and experience, on the very tenable grounds that from a quality standpoint winemakers are much less important than viticulturists, so he opposes the superstar cult among modern winemakers. Fair enough.

Range of Wines

Heemskerk Cabernet Sauvignon
Heemskerk Chardonnay
Heemskerk Pinot Noir

Style

Heemskerk Cabernet Sauvignon

To date we have seen only wines which are entirely or predominantly fruit from the Legana plantings. This fruit quality has been disappointingly furry, and the '78 in particular, as to a lesser extent the '77, has been marred by an unpalatable level of oxidation. It is with the '79, with its component of Heemskerk fruit, that we begin to see greater depth and finesse. The 1980 vintage (not tasted at the time of writing) should make a more emphatic statement on the potential inherent in the Heemskerk operation.

Best years: 1979, 1980

Heemskerk Chardonnay
Heemskerk Pinot Noir

Not tasted, but I understand that the 1980 vintage is shortly to be released. Both wines are entirely Heemskerk grown.

Ownership

The venture is now a private company 'Fesq, Haselgrove, Wiltshire and Company Pty. Ltd.'

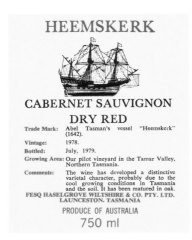

Production

Currently about 50 tonnes, but with mature vines 100 tonnes are expected. This will mean about 7000 cases, about half of which will be Cabernet Sauvignon.

New Plantings

(Not yet yielding.) None as such, but the existing plantings have yet to reach full bear.

Market

About 80 per cent to Sydney and Melbourne, 20 per cent within Tasmania (all retail).

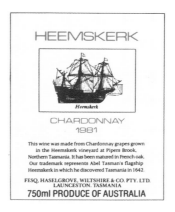

Winery Visiting Details

None. Nor is there any mailing list facility.

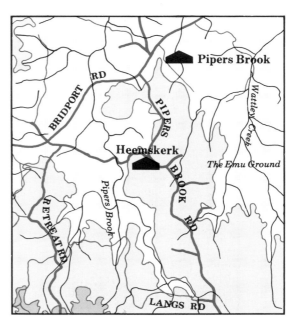

HENSCHKE

It is intriguing to read in a potted history of the Henschke family that Johann Christian Henschke established 'seven acres of vines from which he hoped to make enough wine for his family requirements' in the 1850s. Must have been a large family with a drinking problem.

As decades ticked by the original vineyard grew in size and several more were planted under the Henschke umbrella. It is difficult for us in the 1980s to realize that the wine industry for most of this century was such that it was nearly 1950 before the first bottling of Henschke wine, all previous sales being in 5 or 10 gallon demijohns.

It was Cyril Henschke who effectively revolutionized the winemaking concepts of the family company during the 1950s and 1960s, developing the dry table wine styles which supplanted the sweet fortifieds of the first halfcentury. These included the now famous Hill of Grace and Mount Edelstone reds as well as a range of delicate and supple white wines

which did much to create the reputation of the Eden Valley.

Today there are more than 100 hectares of Henschke vineyards and the company still maintains its established associations with other growers. Their own holdings are at about 500 metres altitude and range from Springton to Keyneton. The entire production is now of table wines, produced by traditional methods in the charming old stone winery. The cellar capacity is 700 000 litres, plus 250 000 bottles in the deep underground bottle storage.

After Cyril's death in 1977, his son Stephen assumed control, becoming the fifth generation of Henschke winemakers to guide the company. Although it is fair to say that it was fortuity rather than foresight that the whole vineyard venture was based one hundred and twenty years ago on the Eden Valley, the current sensible preoccupation with cooler climate wine areas must be causing a few envious looks from Henschke's Barossa Valley neighbours.

Winemaker

Stephen Henschke graduated with a Bachelor of Science degree from Adelaide University in 1973, majoring in Biochemistry and Botany. After working for a year or so on the family winery, he studied for two years under Helmut Becker at Geisenheim before returning to take over the reins as winemaker in 1977.

Range of Wines

Cyril Henschke Cabernet Sauvignon
Henschke Cabernet/Shiraz
Henschke Chenin Blanc
Henschke Dry White Frontignac
Henschke Hill of Grace
Henschke Keyneton Estate
Henschke Malbec
Henschke Mount Edelstone
Henschke Rhine Riesling (Dry, Spatlese and
  Auslese)
Henschke Semillon
Henschke Ugni Blanc
Henschke White Burgundy

Style

Henschke Hill of Grace

This is one of the most respected Shiraz wines
in South Australia. Traditionally a fine, elegant
style, it is nevertheless notable in its youth for
an almost pungent nose suggestive of cooking
cabbages, rather like the Bailey wines of the
1950s and 1960s. Candidly, I like this aspect of
the wine, which matures to more immediately
attractive characteristics.
Best years: 1977, 1978, 1980

Henschke Mount Edelstone

Another traditional Eden Valley Shiraz, but
from a different vineyard and a little more to
the taste of those who are taken aback by the
uncompromising nature of the Hill of Grace, in
whose shadow it has been Mount Edelstone's
perennial fate to remain. Both wines age with
unhurried grace.
Best years: 1977, 1978, 1980

Henschke Rhine Riesling

Back in the days when only Burings and
Orlando were producing good South Australian
Rieslings, Henschke improved and developed
this style to share the honours with the two
giants. Always crisp and delicate, the wine has
created an army of admirers with its gentle
depths and beautiful young fruit.
Best years: 1979, 1980, 1981

Ownership

Henschke is a family company.

Production

30 000 cases, about half of which is Shiraz and
a little under a quarter Rhine Riesling.

New Plantings

(Not yet yielding.) Nil.

Market

The major proportion is through merchants
and restaurants in Sydney and Melbourne, with
the remainder from mailing list and cellar door
sales.

Winery Visiting Details

Monday to Friday 9 am to 4.30 pm, Saturday
9 am to noon. The address is just Keyneton
5353 Telephone (085) 64 8223.

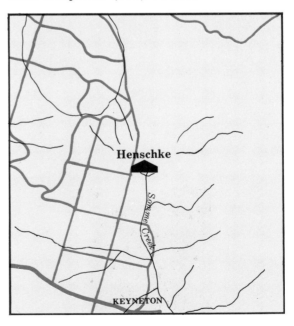

HOLMES ESTATE

Most pharmacists I speak to treat their professional life as a gaol sentence. If this seems a little extreme, bear in mind that unlike milk bar proprietors, pharmacists are required by law to stay in their shops every second the shop is open, or employ another qualified pharmacist to do so. Must be a dreadful life.

Anyway, Leon Holmes decided he had had enough of the above, so he planted a vineyard on land he purchased at Mount Pleasant in the Eden Valley. The year 1974 saw the establishment of 5 hectares of Rhine Riesling and 2.5 each of Shiraz and Cabernet Sauvignon, but he and his wife Leonie began making wine immediately from bought-in grapes. (They are now just reaching the stage where their own yield is adequate for the self-imposed limit of their crush, so the use of the word 'Estate' is, perhaps belatedly, justified.)

Initially the winemaking equipment and procedures were both a little rustic, and so was the wine, but Leon and Leonie have exorably if slowly upgraded the appointments. Their annual crush is 40 tonnes, and they see no reason to increase this.

Leon and Leonie are promotionally innovative and imaginative, and an unusual aspect of their marketing is to offer their mailing list customers the opportunity of prepurchasing wine: paying for it as it is made, but accepting delivery 12 months later and benefiting from a 50 per cent discount by so doing. Their access to the tourist market has been considerably enhanced by their acquisition of a romantically attractive old stone blacksmith's shop in the main street of Springton. This has been converted into a tasting, 'cellar door' facility.

A new winery at the back of the Springton cellars is in the planning stages, and will include underground bottle storage area. It seems likely that the Holmes' access to cooler grown fruit and their continual improvement of the equipment will eventually devolve in the emergence of an individual and admirable style.

Winemaker

Leon Holmes has no formal training, but his original interest in pharmacy was obviously impelled by a desire to be involved with scientific knowledge. He finds much more outlet for such as a winemaker than he did selling perfume and relabelling tablets. He reads and studies winemaking tomes avidly.

Range of Wines

Holmes Estate Cabernet/Merlot
Holmes Estate Rhine Riesling
Holmes Estate Vintage Port

Style

Holmes Estate Cabernet/Merlot

A light, fine and attractive dry red with an admirable intensity of Cabernet fruit showing the
quality advantages of a 450 metre altitude
vineyard. The Merlot, only 10 per cent, is
bought in from Langhorne Creek. At the moment the wine lacks weight, but this will no
doubt correct itself as the vines mature.
Best years: 1980, 1981

Holmes Estate Rhine Riesling

This has not been the best of Rieslings in its
vintages to date, fermentation in old wood having developed some curious off-flavours. However as I write, the 1982 version is fermenting
away cosily in stainless steel, so we may look
forward to a far better style from now on. Certainly the fruit quality contains the potential for
fine wine.
Best years: 1982 onwards.

Holmes Estate Vintage Port

A very good port style indeed, and a far cry
from the burnt plum jam Ports too frequently
found from the Barossa. Made from 100%
Shiraz grown on the Estate, this is a firm, tight
and spirituous wine with an intense bouquet
and almost dry finish. Very good indeed.
Best years: 1980, 1981.

Ownership

Wholly owned by Leon and Leonie Holmes.

Production

About 3000 cases, half of which is white.

New Plantings

(Not yet yielding.) Nil.

Market

Almost entirely by cellar door and mailing list,
with very little even in specialist merchants.

Winery Visiting Details

Seven days a week: 10 am to 5 pm. The address
is Main Street, Springton, 5235 Telephone
(085) 68 2203.

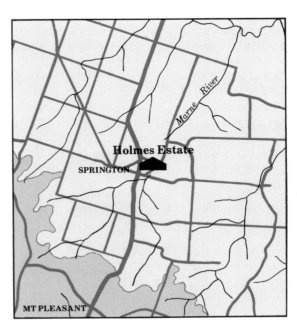

HUNTINGTON ESTATE

Sydney solicitor Bob Roberts and his wife Wendy were seduced by the beauty of Mudgee and the romance of wine into establishing the Huntington Estate in 1969. Not one to do things by halves, Bob now has 41 hectares of vines on his undulating property. The proportions he chose were 18 hectares of Shiraz, 10.5 of Cabernet Sauvignon, 4 each of Chardonnay and Semillon, 2 each of Pinot Noir and Merlot, and half a hectare of Sauvignon Blanc.

The winery followed in 1972/73, designed by Bob and Wendy and constructed of concrete blocks. In concept it was in keeping with Bob's purist approach, having the capacity to cope with the longer fermentation period imposed by his use of cold fermentation for both red and white wines, and also the wood storage to allow two years of cask maturation for the red wine prior to bottling.

It was always intended to market the wines through cellar door sales, and the tasting area is incorporated with the winery so that visitors may stroll through the complex at their leisure.

The concept behind the establishment was originally and still is that of an estate which grows and processes its own fruit. Grapes are not bought in from other growers under the official Huntington Estate label, although recently some Trebbiano wine was purchased and marketed as Chablis under a distinctly different label.

Increasingly Bob Roberts' wines are tending to be regarded by other growers in the area as the ones to beat in the local shows and in the competition for the high regard of the district's devotees.

Winemaker

Bob Roberts is heavily qualified for most contingencies, being a solicitor who has also obtained a Diploma in Agriculture at Wagga and a Diploma in Oenology from the Oenological Research Institute in Surrey. He has also had the not inconsiderable experience of making to date eleven vintages of Huntington Estate wines.

Range of Wines

Huntington Estate Cabernet/Merlot
Huntington Estate Cabernet Sauvignon
Huntington Estate Cabernet Shiraz
Huntington Estate Chablis
Huntington Estate Chardonnay
Huntington Estate Pinot Noir
Huntington Estate Rosé
Huntington Estate Semillon
Huntington Estate Semillon/Chardonnay
Huntington Estate Shiraz
Huntington Estate Shiraz/Cabernet
Huntington Estate Sweet White Semillon
Huntington Estate Vintage Port

Style

Huntington Estate Cabernet/Merlot

Deep coloured if slightly turbid wines, the nose of which I find slightly unprepossessing in their humid earthiness. The fruit is powerful and profound, and the wines have a most attractive finish with a tannic firmness, acid crispness and fruit sweetness nicely combined.
Best years: 1978, 1979

Huntington Estate Chardonnay

These are far and away the area's best Chardonnays: quite without coarseness, beautifully sweet-fruited, ideally coloured and with considerable depth of flavours. Remarkably for Chardonnay of such quality, it owes little, if anything, to France or California. An excellent style of very agreeable wine.
Best years: 1979, 1981

Huntington Estate Pinot Noir

Still a developing style, with some lack of continuity of characteristics. The common denominator seems to be the admirable quality of the fruit with its classic strawberry overtones, but the 1979 for example has an unpalatable stalky bitterness in the finish, a quality I could not detect in the quite attractive 1980.
Best year: 1980

Ownership

Entirely owned by Bob and Wendy Roberts.

Production

13 000 cases, being: Cabernet Sauvignon 3000, Cabernet Merlot 3000, Shiraz 3000, Pinot Noir 300, Shiraz Cabernet 600, Rosé 700, Semillon 700, Chardonnay 500 and Port 500 cases.

New Plantings

Nil, but 3 hectares of Semillon and 4 of Chardonnay are being grafted to existing vines.

Market

All cellar door and mailing list.

Winery Visiting Details

Monday to Friday 9 am to 5 pm, Saturday 10 am to 5 pm, Sunday noon to 4 pm. The address is Cassilis Road, Mudgee, 2850 Telephone (063) 73 3825.

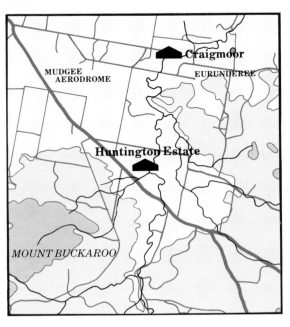

IDYLL VINEYARD

Geelong, Vic.

Nini and Daryl Sefton are delightfully amiable enthusiasts with a penchant for hard work. They established Idyll Vineyard in 1966, with three aims clearly in mind. First, they wanted passionately to re-establish the viticultural areas of Geelong, and encourage others to follow their lead. Daryl's great-grandparents, Rosina and Jacob Just, had been part of the Swiss community who made Geelong a great wine-producing area in the 19th century, and he had grown up with his imagination fired by stories of the old Swiss wine days.

Second, they wanted their vineyard to be totally purist in its concept. All the Idyll wine was to be made from grapes grown on the property, matured, bottled and sold from Idyll. This was a daunting programme in view of their limited capital resources.

Third, they planned to integrate the vineyard, winery complex, home and gardens into an aesthetically pleasing and harmonious whole, making Idyll a place of beauty and tranquillity.

It is clear to any visitor that they have achieved their three primary aims. Other vineyards have followed their lead, and the Geelong area is now recognized as an important viticultural area. Idyll now has 20 hectares of grapes, an 80 square winery complex, with bottling line and cask room, storage areas, and an attractive tasting and sales room, all built by Daryl. The wine is now sold all over Australia, and more recently to the West German market.

Daryl and Nini richly deserve the ultimate reward of sitting overlooking their beautiful valley while they drink their own wine, lapped by a sea of vines.

Winemaker

Daryl Sefton, who by qualification and avocation is a Doctor of Veterinary Science, turned to winemaking to fulfill a lifelong dream of owning his own vineyard, and as an escape from continually peering up various orifices of cows and horses. He has enhanced his sixteen years of practical winemaking experience by attending courses and seminars at Roseworthy and Wagga, and has further increased his knowledge and feel by travelling extensively throughout the wine-growing districts of the world.

82

Range of Wines

Idyll Blush
Idyll Cabernet Sauvignon/Shiraz
Idyll Gewurztraminer

Style

Idyll Blush

One of the country's finest Rosé styles, Idyll Blush is made from sensitively handled Shiraz fruit. The wine is far from inconsequential, unlike many of the genera, being a graceful, delicate but tightly balanced Rosé without that hard vinosity which so often attends attempts to construct Shiraz Rosés.
Best years: Blush should be drunk after about 12 months in the bottle, regardless of vintage.

Idyll Cabernet Sauvignon/Shiraz

A supple, fine and stylish dry red without quite the power or sweetness of fruit of our top Cabernets, but aristocratic withal. The wine tends to deep red rather than dark purple when young, and it ages with charm and urbanity.
Best years: 1976 (Shiraz/Cabernet), 1979, 1980

Idyll Gewurztraminer

This is a wine which polarizes critics. Some find it hard, coarse and pungent. Let them write their own books. I regard it as a unique style: unsubtle it is true, but powerful, substantially complex, voluptuously generous, long living and admirably different from the lolly-water slosh which so often masquerades as Traminer in this country.
Best years: 1975, 1976, 1977, 1980

Ownership

Idyll is an equal partnership between Dr Daryl and Mrs Nini Sefton.

Production

Average is: Cabernet Sauvignon/Shiraz 3000 cases, Gewurztraminer 1500 cases, Blush 1000 cases.

New Plantings

Gewurztraminer 2 hectares, Cabernet Sauvignon 2 hectares, Chardonnay 2 hectares.

Market

Cellar door, apart from a small quantity to specialist merchants and export.

Idyll Wine

Gewurztraminer

1980 Vintage, Seventh Release

Estate Bottled

This wine was made from 100% Gewurztraminer grapes grown on the vineyard and bottled in the winery at Idyll. This vineyard lies in the Moorabool Valley, one of the famous old wine-growing areas of Geelong.

Daryl & Nini Sefton,
Idyll Vineyard, Moorabool,
VICTORIA

MADE IN AUSTRALIA   750ml

Winery Visiting Details

10 am to 5 pm Tuesday to Saturday. The address is Ballan Road, Moorabool, 3221 Telephone (052) 76 1280.

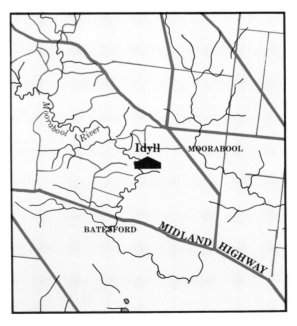

KATNOOK ESTATE Coonawarra, SA

To hark back to the concern I expressed in the introduction about what I should make the parameters for inclusion in a book on 'small wineries', where does this leave Katnook? As viticulturists and bespoke vineyard managers, the owners are among the largest in Australia, having some 219 hectares of their own vines (and enough land to plant another 143 hectares); they are contract suppliers of fruit to Orlando, Stanley and Krondorf, and recently have even sold fruit to other Coonawarra grower/makers.

Certainly not small, you say. But Katnook as a label represents a small — extremely small — production, albeit with the capacity to expand astronomically. With almost a quarter of a square mile of premium fruit from which to select their grapes, the minuscule Katnook crush is obviously assured of the very, very best indeed. Combine this utopian fruit availability with the heavily used consultancy of Tony Jordan's and Brian Croser's Oenotec

organization and throw in the money to afford unstinted winery equipment, and you have a recipe for painless production of extreme quality wine.

In any event, this has been the case with the few Katnook wines released to date. But all of the above does not mean that Katnook can do no wrong — the 1981 releases contained minor disappointments amongst the impressive array of their virtues, but it would be an unromantic world if all that was needed to make great wine were money and grapes.

The entire Katnook exercise is a prestige venture for a comfortably entrenched and thriving, low-profile organization whose quality aims are high. As consumers you and I benefit from this sort of 'state of the art' product, and want only some reassurance of both continuity and maintenance of standards to espouse the cause of a new Australian wine superstar.

Winemaker

Wayne Stehbins, son of the vineyard manager Ray Stehbins, worked for several years on the company's (Coonawarra Machinery's) vineyards before studying oenology at Riverina College. He gained practical cellar experience with Denman Estate (under Tony Jordan), Wynns at Yenda and Lindemans at Coonawarra before assuming the role of Katnook winemaker in 1979, working closely with Oenotec.

Range of Wines

Katnook Chardonnay
Katnook Cabernet Sauvignon
Katnook Gewurztraminer
Katnook Rhine Riesling
Katnook Sauvignon Blanc

Style

Katnook Chardonnay

At the time of writing, only one release of this has been made, but it is a wine of improbable beauty and power. Paler and finer than the Hunter Valley Chardonnays with which most of us are familiar, it nevertheless shows superb strength of fruit and complexity, and rivals the Leeuwin Estate and Moss Wood versions for sheer impressiveness. A wine to be sought out.
Best years: 1980, 1981

Katnook Rhine Riesling

The Katnook staple, and one which bears a very close resemblance to Petaluma Rhine Riesling in both style and character. Again, density of fruit is a notable attribute, as is the wine's intense floral aroma and elegant balance. A valuable gem of a wine, and a welcome relief from the proliferation of boring mediocrity of this over-produced but under-perfected genus.
Best years: 1980, 1981

Katnook Sauvignon Blanc

It has given me no little pleasure to serve this wine to unsuspecting wine-buff friends and watch their reactions on first encountering the incredible bouquet. Sauvignon Blanc grown at Coonawarra can produce an amazing nose, sweet and strong, but quite without the smoky overtones of the Loire Valley or the lusciousness of the Sauternes regions. For all that, the finish of the Katnook offering has to date been disappointingly abrupt.
Best years: 1980, 1981

Ownership

Katnook is the label name for 'Coonawarra Machinery', a division of the pastoral company Rentier Pty Ltd.

Production

Full Katnook production is not envisaged as exceeding 10 000 cases — roughly 2000 each of the five wines.

New Plantings

(Not yet yielding.) Nil.

Market

Nationally available in dribs and drabs. Twist a specialist merchant's arm, or write to the winery.

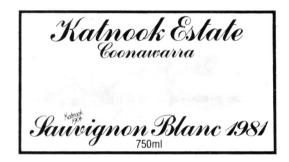

Winery Visiting Details

By appointment only, at the moment. The address is PO Box 6, Coonawarra, 5263 Telephone (087) 37 2391.

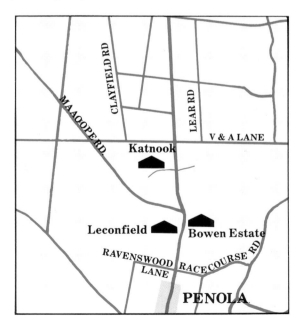

KAYS 'AMERY'

The Kay family progenitors purchased the 'Amery' property in 1890 and immediately planted Shiraz and some Cabernet Sauvignon. Five years later saw the first vintage, and by 1900 there were some 40 hectares under vine. The wine was big, busty, soft dry red mainly for the British bulk trade.

This market grew steadily for the next sixty years until the backside suddenly fell out of export. It was as late as 1970 before Kays wines started seeing the inside of bottles bearing the Kays label.

Changes in winemakers so often mean changes in wine styles as distinct from the much more gradual evolution of styles within a winemaker's tenure. So it was with Kays, with Cuthbert ('Cud') Kay refining and lightening the style during the 1940s, 1950s and 1960s, and his son Colin seeking still greater elegance over the last decade.

The Amery vineyard now has about 65 hectares, and is planted to Shiraz, Cabernet Sauvignon, Pinot Noir, Rhine Riesling, Frontignan, Sauvignon Blanc, Traminer and Grenache (the latter being reserved for the tawny port styles).

In the midst of a chaotic winemaking revolution as we are, it is reassuring to see a wholeheartedly traditional producer in a traditional area maintaining the characteristic styles which made the area famous, allowing intelligent adaptation to the realities of the present, it is true, but without breaking their nexus with the past. In a few years time, the more thoughtful consumers will be grateful for the Kays of this country.

Winemaker

Colin Kay made his first wine when he was six years old — one of the advantages of growing up on a vineyard. He graduated from Roseworthy in 1963, winning the gold medal for that year. He worked at Kaiser Stuhl until late 1966, then spent some years wandering around the world until he returned to take over the Amery reins in 1970. From this time on he also worked as consultant to other vineyards in the area, many of whom now acknowledge a considerable debt to him.

Range of Wines

Kays Amery Auslese Riesling
Kays Amery Cabernet Sauvignon
Kays Amery Dry Red
Kays Amery Late Picked Rhine Riesling
Kays Amery Late Picked White Frontignan
Kays Amery Pinot Noir
Kays Amery Rhine Riesling
Kays Amery Sauvignon Blanc
Kays Amery Shiraz
Kays Amery Shiraz/Cabernet
Kays Amery Tawny Port
Kays Amery Vintage Port

Style

Kays Amery Auslese Riesling

McLaren Vale is not famed for the crispness or delicacy of its white wines, yet the area's attempts at 'Auslese' styles have been remarkably successful, the normal fullness of body mitigating the lack of botrytis character. Rich in hue, age will deepen it further to gold. The nose is sumptuous rather than profound, and the palate hints at lusciousness while still maintaining a tight acid balance.
Best years: 1978, 1979

Kays Amery Shiraz

The most traditional of the Kay winestyles, still redolent of that soft, warm McLaren Vale fruit, but lighter and finer than the wines which established this area's reputation as a vignoble. Enjoyable basic drinking at any age, it is nevertheless advisable to maximize the wine's rather limited complexity by letting it sleep in the bottle for five years or so.
Best years: 1971, 1976, 1977, 1980

Kays Amery Cabernet Sauvignon

Cabernet behaves oddly in McLaren Vale, making wine of depth, colour, power and sweetness of fruit, but quite without the austerity and subtlety which should be the hallmark of the variety. Kays version is no exception; full and generous, but astringent rather than austere, and enjoying a sweetly floral if rather straightforward bouquet. It ages well in the medium to long term.
Best years: 1976, 1978, 1981

Ownership

The vineyard is 100 per cent family-owned.

Production

Currently, annual vintage represents Shiraz 4500 cases; Shiraz Cabernet 4500 cases; Cabernet Sauvignon 1500 cases; Rhine Riesling 3000 cases; Late Picked Rhine Riesling 1500 cases; White Frontignan 1500 cases; together with another 30 000 gallons of odds and sods, much of which is sold in bulk.

New Plantings

2.5 hectares of Pinot Noir and 3 hectares each of Traminer and Rhine Riesling.

Market

Cellar door 20 per cent, New South Wales 25 per cent, Victoria 20 per cent, South Australia 10 per cent, export 10 per cent, bulk 25 per cent.

Winery Visiting Details

Monday to Saturday 10 am to 5 pm. The address is Amery Vineyards, McLaren Vale, 5171 Telephone (08) 383 8211.

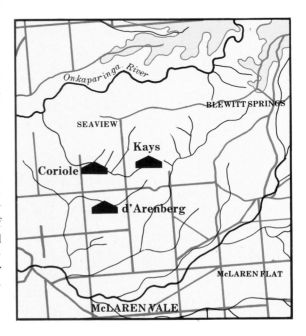

KIDMAN

Ken and Sid Kidman are farmers who have lived and farmed in the Coonawarra area all their lives. One can well imagine that for two such people in the late 1960s the idea of planting grapes on the famed red soil must have been both obvious and attractive. Anyway, plant they did — with an establishment pro-gramme which has now led to 23 hectares of Cabernet Sauvignon, 22 of Shiraz and 7.5 of Rhine Riesling.

But everything was not quite so easy. As the wine started to come on stream the market situation had changed dramatically from the heady days, full of promise, of 1969. Red was in the doldrums, and to make matters worse the infamous 'discounting' practice began to blotch the face of wine marketing like acne.

Enter Melbourne wine merchant Dan Murphy, who is one of the most committed of Coonawarra admirers in the country. He acquired an interest in the venture — incidentally fulfilling a lifelong dream — and of course undertook Kidman distribution through his very large outlets in Melbourne. A second label was created, Terra Rossa Estate, so that lesser quality wine could still be marketed in years where it was felt the Kidman label was not justified. In fact there have been only three releases of the Kidman reds to date: 1975, 1976 and, by the time you read this, 1980.

The winery has a crush capacity of 200 tonnes, but this is being extended over the next two years to double this figure. Capital has been raised by the formation of a public company, Terra Rossa Wines Limited, and an experienced winemaker, Ken Ward, retained. It remains only to mitigate the boastfulness of the red label ('Great Red Wine of Coonawarra', a rubric which sits rather more embarrassingly than 'Grand Vin de Chateau Latour') and to develop the style with a little more purism, and the project will undoubtedly begin to fulfil some of its undeniable promise.

Winemaker

Ken Ward is now the Kidman winemaker. One of the most experienced winemakers in South Australia, Ken was for many years with Wynn making their Coonawarra wines including the 1972 Cabernet Sauvignon, which won the 'double gold' at Bristol, and the 1976 Cabernet Sauvignon, which won the Jimmy Watson Trophy.

Range of Wines

Kidman 'Great Red Wine of Coonawarra'
Kidman Rhine Riesling

Style

Kidman 'Great Red Wine of Coonawarra'
Behind this cumbersome and pretentious label lies an honest Coonawarra Cabernet/Shiraz blend. At the time of writing, only the 1975 and 1976 have been released and the 1980 is imminent. Generally I have found them more substantial than elegant, and I understand that it is not intended to lighten the style but rather to deepen and intensify the fruit. Quite clearly the aim is to create a very long cellaring big Coonawarra red, and not a bad idea at that. I do hope they change that label, though.
Best years: 1975, 1980

Kidman Rhine Riesling
An attractive but extremely straightforward wine in its only release to date. I am certain that Ken Ward will bend his very considerable oenological talents towards the production of more stylish, profound and complex wines in future vintages. Up to now the wine has been made by 'one of the leading wineries' under contract. I venture to suggest that this is unsatisfactory.
Best years: 1981, 1982

Ownership

Terra Rossa Wines Limited is a public company, but a sizeable proportion of the shares are owned by the Kidman and Murphy families.

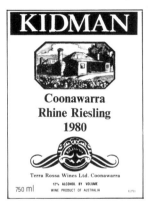

Production

Annually 10 000 cases are produced, comprising 8500 red and 1500 white.

New Plantings

(Not yet yielding.) Nil.

Market

Kidman wines are nationally available through normal outlets except for Melbourne, where Dan Murphy's Cellar has the lion's share.

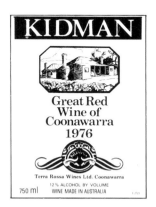

Winery Visiting Details

By appointment only. The postal address is PO Box 25, Coonawarra, 5263 Telephone (087) 36 5094.

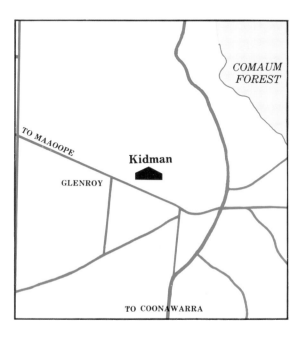

LAKES FOLLY

It was twenty years ago when Max Lake started planting Cabernet Sauvignon and Shiraz on a volcanic slope in the Pokolbin area. Remember the period; there was no 'wine boom' to justify the venture economically, and his was the first new family-owned small vineyard to be established in Australia this century. His friends thought it insanity; Max demurred, but conceded that it was folly. Thus the name was born, and so was the first of an entirely new breed of winemaker; the dedicated, painstaking, intelligent amateur with immense consumer experience and an international palate.

From these beginnings, wine in Australia was revolutionized, and the era of the small winemaker had arrived. Almost simultaneously the Californian industry was being similarly penetrated by perfectionist amateurs whose concern was quality rather than profit. In the two countries the good ones achieved both.

Although an admirer of the traditional Hunter styles, humid Hermitage and nutty 'Rieslings' (Semillon), Max was interested only in making Bordelaise type reds, incurring a few raised eyebrows from his sceptical neighbours.

1966 saw the first vintage, and its release eighteen months later was like a drop of water on parched soil. Such has also been the case with all subsequent vintages, as the sceptics grew silent and started planting Cabernet.

Thinking to save himself the cost of French Champagne, Max then established Chardonnay,

intending to make an extreme quality bottle fermented sparkling wine from it. Which led to the incredible first vintage, 1974 Lakes Folly Chardonnay, a wine of Montrachet stature, and bubbles were forgotten. Lake had done it again and another revolution was under way, the Chardonnay phenomenon. (Credit here must be shared with Tyrrells, who had already made their magnificent, but Californian rather than French, 1973.)

Lakes Folly is one of the important vineyards of the world, and son Stephen Lake's sensitivity with winemaking is a comforting assurance for the consumer. At least as long as the aluminium smelters, the biggest threat since phylloxera, permit the area to survive as a vignoble.

Winemaker

Obviously, Dr Max Lake has been the winemaker at Lakes Folly since its inception. Less obviously, son Stephen is now winemaker. Max is a unique figure; a man of immense intellect and intense enthusiasms, with boundless creativity. His friendship with the world's leading wine scientists; Andre Tschelitscheff and Maynard Amerine, led to his own oenological skills being of an order which surpasses the need. Stephen has vinicultural brilliance which is now becoming apparent, and the thumbprint of Max Lake on Lakes Folly wines is annually becoming less essential.

Range of Wines

Lakes Folly Cabernet Sauvignon
Lakes Folly Chardonnay
Lakes Folly Dry Red

Style

Lakes Folly Cabernet Sauvignon

In its best years, this is one of the great wines of the world: Cabernet's iron hand encased in a velvet glove, with gentle Pomerol cigar-box overtones, fine, supple and deeply powerful fruit, and a lingeringly eloquent finish. A wine quite without dissonances.
Best years: 1969, 1972, 1978, 1980

Lakes Folly Chardonnay

Another great wine, and one of the very few Australian Chardonnays with roots in the Cotes de Beaune rather than the Napa Valley. Of beautiful hue, it hints at peach and apricot nuances as a toddler, but these deepen to overtones of ripe quinces when the wine matures to a lissom seductress.
Best years: 1974, 1978, 1980, 1981

Lakes Folly Dry Red

A complex blend of Shiraz, Cabernet Sauvignon, Merlot and Malbec, 'Folly Red' suffers from being in the perpetual shadow of its big brother, the Cabernet Sauvignon. For all that, it is a stylishly graceful and harmoniously assembled wine which grants improbable rewards to those prepared to cellar it for five years after release.
Best years: 1969, 1976, 1980

Ownership

Lakes Folly is family-owned.

Production

Total average Lakes Folly 3500 cases, 1400 cases Cabernet Sauvignon, 1200 cases Folly Red, 900 cases Chardonnay and Hunter Valley Estate 3000 cases.

New Plantings

Nil.

Market

Entirely by mailing list, and then on a 'first come, first served' basis, except that tastings are always available and a small quantity is kept back for long distance travellers with touching stories.

Winery Visiting Details

Weekdays 10 am to 4 pm or by appointment. The address is Broke Road, Pokolbin, 2321 Telephone (049) 98 7507.

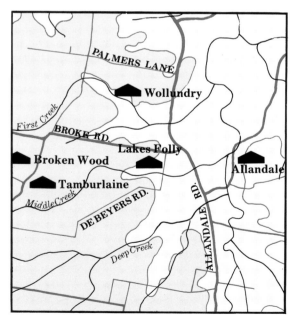

LECONFIELD

The Hamilton family's connection with wine in Australia spans the country's entire vinicultural history, without the slightest break in continuity since Richard Hamilton planted some vines in 1838. The company which grew from those vines became one of the wine-producing giants of the twentieth century before its star waned and it was eventually absorbed by the Mildara/Grants empire, leaving just a name on a label.

But by the time this happened, two members of the family had struck out on their own — separately at the time, but as we shall see, their interests are becoming conjoint. Syd Hamilton retired, after a distinguished career in wine, a decade ago. So what does a retired wineman do to fill the afternoon of his life with some challenge and interest? I don't know what others do, but Syd established a vineyard and winery at Coonawarra: Leconfield.

He planted 12 hectares of Cabernet Sauvignon and Rhine Riesling and began to make honest, hand-crafted Coonawarra wines of perhaps rather traditionalist style, but convincing in their integration and individualism. This situation obtained until late 1980, when Syd decided to make a second attempt at retiring, so he sold Leconfield to his nephew Richard Hamilton.

Richard was the other Hamilton family member to have trodden his own vinicultural path. A doctor of medicine, his wine interests were too strongly ingrained to be satisfied by mere hobbyism, so he established his own vineyard, winery and label at Willunga, just south of McLaren Vale. A fuller account of that venture is given on pages 134 and 135, but it can be seen that the Hamiltons are riding again, with a vengeance.

With Richard Hamilton's enthusiasm and the current (second) renascence of Coonawarra's popularity as a wine-producing area as plus factors, Leconfield looks to be heading for a very good run.

Winemaker

Dr Richard Hamilton is now the winemaker for both his Willunga vineyard and the newly acquired Leconfield. His interest is wine and his training is medicine — a marriage which is apparently not just made in Heaven, but mass produced there. He is one of many who have found the disciplines of medical science of immense benefit in winemaking endeavours.

Range of Wines
Leconfield Cabernet Sauvignon
Leconfield Rhine Riesling

Style

Leconfield Cabernet Sauvignon
This has been a variable wine over the years: not so much variable in quality, but in style. The two extremes are probably best evinced by the 1978 and the 1980, the former being a Rabelaisian wine: lusty but eloquent, with both cedar and violets on the nose, and a full, deep and complex palate which is enthusiastically Cabernet. The 1980 on the other hand is more Louisa May Allcott than Rabelais: light, soft, feminine and gentle. It seems probable that under Richard Hamilton's hand future vintages will show more consistency, hopefully without sacrifice of either muscle or grace.
Best year: 1978

Leconfield Rhine Riesling
It is a source of personal pleasure for me that there is a small, widely dispersed but uncompromising knot of makers who refuse to join Rhine Riesling's stylistic mainstream. The wine world can stand a few more individualist wines like Leconfield's unashamedly wood-aged Rhine Rieslings, with their greater density, power and firmness, achieved at the expense of slight volatility, and White Burgundy finish. Unusual, and unusually fine.
Best years: 1978, 1980

Ownership
Leconfield is now owned by Dr Richard Hamilton.

Production
After a little viticultural tidying up is accomplished, the Leconfield production should peak at about 5000 cases, two-thirds of which will be the Cabernet.

New Plantings
(Not yet yielding.) Nil.

Market
Cellar door, mailing list and a few specialist merchants currently take care of the annual release. It is to be hoped that there will be a greater general availability of Leconfield wines in the next couple of years.

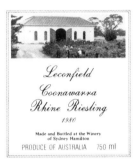

Winery Visiting Details
Monday to Friday 9 am to 5 pm. The address is Main Penola Road, Coonawarra, 5263 Telephone (087) 37 2326.

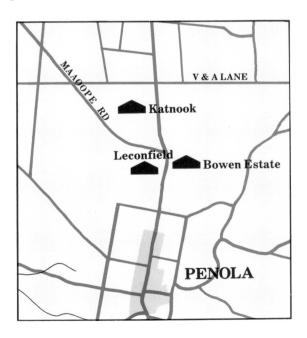

LEEUWIN ESTATE

To describe Leeuwin Estate as the most important wine venture in Australia for the last decade will probably involve me in lusty argument with some of my co-scriveners in the wine world. Nevertheless, I believe it is just that, for one quite simple reason: the Leeuwin project is designed ultimately to produce large quantities (40 000 cases annually) of wine of extreme quality. In a country whose very best wines — whether produced by a large or a small maker — have always been in limited quantity, this is nothing short of revolutionary.

Perth businessman Denis Horgan had owned the property which is now Leeuwin Estate for a number of years before deciding, in the early 1970s, to establish his own vineyard. His consultant in the project has been the legendary Napa Valley winemaker Robert Mondavi. The first 34 hectares were planted in 1975 and expansion continued until 1980, when the target size of 90 hectares was reached. The area under vine now comprises, in hectares: Rhine Riesl-ing 3, Cabernet Sauvignon 2, Chardonnay 18, Pinot Noir 5, Traminer 3, Malbec 2 and Sauvignon Blanc 4.

The nexus between Margaret River and the Napa Valley is maintained by the proprietors, not merely by winemaker Bob Cartwright's forays into the Mondavi winery at vintage, but also in the image and even style of the wines produced. Berry-setting has been a problem at Leeuwin Estate because of wind damage in mid Spring, but this has affected quantity rather than quality, and the problem is expected to abate as the wind-breaks grow.

Some Leeuwin Estate wines are among the most expensive in Australia (the 1980 Chardonnay came on the market at $15 to $17 a bottle) but they compare extremely well with French wines at the same price. These are released bearing a special label in years where the quality is judged to be worthy of such livery and price. Other Leeuwin wines bear a simpler label, and command a lower price.

Winemaker

The chief winemaker is Bob Cartwright. Bob completed his degree at Roseworthy College in 1967, and gained extensive experience in both the Barossa and Swan Valleys before joining Leeuwin Estate in 1978. Since joining the company he has completed a vintage at the Robert Mondavi Winery in the Napa Valley.

94

Range of Wines

Leeuwin Estate Cabernet Sauvignon
Leeuwin Estate Chardonnay
Leeuwin Estate Gewurztraminer
Leeuwin Estate Late Harvest Rhine Riesling
Leeuwin Estate Pinot Noir
Leeuwin Estate Reserve Bin Rhine Riesling

Style

Leeuwin Estate Chardonnay

This is a glorious wine, in world class. The colour is rich but fine pale gold; the magnificent nose hints at rather than shouts all of the fig, apricot and peach nuances which make up the complexity of good Chardonnay; and the palate is both densely generous and graceful. To round off a superb wine, its presentation is very impressive, the label bearing a specially commissioned Australian painting which will be changed every year, *à la* Mouton-Rothschild. A remarkable and desirable wine, at any price.
Best years: 1980, 1981

Leeuwin Estate Cabernet Sauvignon

Deep, dark and fine reds which are strongly characteristic of the variety. Generally the style has a more velvety lusciousness than is typical for the area, but is still in tight and controlled balance. The nose is almost voluptuous — a quality also found in the palate — but the wine's finesse stops it from straying into either coarseness or flaccidness.
Best years: 1979, 1980

Leeuwin Estate Rhine Riesling

A well-made and attractive style of some considerable elegance. The earlier versions have lacked the density and varietal conviction which might have been expected from this maker, but the recent wines have much greater power. It seems probable that development of the style will see the wines incline towards a Californian intensity of fruit and flavour, particularly in the 'Late Harvest' instances.
Best years: 1980, 1981

Ownership

Despite rumours to the contrary, Leeuwin Estate is entirely owned by Denis Horgan, Robert Mondavi's role being that of consultant.

Production

Currently the average production is about 20 000 cases. This will double as the vines come to full yield.

New Plantings

(Not yet yielding.) Some 12 hectares of Chardonnay and 4 of Sauvignon Blanc are yet to yield.

Market

At the time of writing, only the Rhine Riesling has any substantial history of availability, but it is fair to say that Leeuwin Estate wine will have national distribution through specialist outlets.

Winery Visiting Details

Monday to Saturday 10 am to 4.30 pm from September to March. From April to August the winery is open at these same times every day. The address is Gnarawary Road, Margaret River, 6285 Telephone (097) 57 6253.

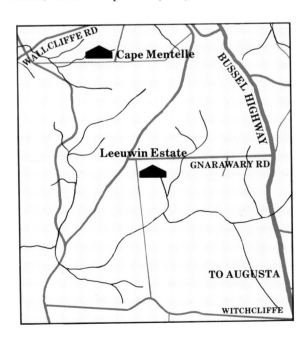

LESCHENAULT

A casual or even a close look at a map of Western Australia would give no indication of any common geographic denominator between Paul Conti's Wanneroo vineyard, some few kilometres north of Perth, and the Leschenault vineyard about 200 kilometres further south, past Bunbury. There is such, however: a fertile strip of sandy soil, rarely more than one kilometre in width, runs from about 30 kilometres north of Perth all the way down to Ludlow near Busselton. (Perhaps some promotionally minded Western Australian wine marketer should invent the phrase Terra Arena, à la Coonawarra's Terra Rosa.)

On this Tuart sand, as it is called, are grown market gardens, Tuart gums (said to be the hardest wood in Australia) and vines. The Leschenault plantings are all on Tuart sand, and comprise 16 hectares of Cabernet Sauvignon, Shiraz, Pinot Noir, Zinfandel and Traminer.

The vineyard was established in 1974 by Dr Barry Killerby (by my count, 18 of the 90 wineries in this book were started by doctors!). Barry's interest in wine was generated from his medical students days in Adelaide, and the dream of owning his own vineyard and making his own wine grew. He is not fond of pretentious descriptions of wine — goodness knows what he will think of my verbal excesses in this book — and his own labels carry an ultimately basic style description: 'Cabernet Sauvignon, a fruity, light-bodied dry red wine', 'Traminer, a spicy dry white wine', and even 'April Red, light and sweet for those who think they don't like red wine'. A refreshing approach, to say the least, and one which probably wins new winedrinkers, particularly among cellar door tourists.

It would be a mistake to assume from these simple descriptions that the wines are merely basic or bucolic (with the possible exception of the 'April Red'). Leschenault is a significant winery with the potential to enhance the already swelling reputation of the area.

Winemaker

Barry Killerby's qualifications as a medical practitioner are, as always, of immense advantage in winemaking. He has worked with two other wineries at vintage during the time his own vineyard was growing, and, beyond that, he attends seminars, reads numerous oenological textbooks and makes wine.

Range of Wines

Leschenault April Red
Leschenault Cabernet/Hermitage
Leschenault Cabernet Sauvignon
Leschenault Dry Rose
Leschenault Hermitage
Leschenault Pinot Noir
Leschenault Traminer

Style

Leschenault April Red

An enchanting and attractive wine made from Shiraz and Zinfandel grapes fermented until there is 1% of residual sugar. The colour is bright and translucent; the nose light but generous; and the palate is fresh-fruited but surprisingly deep.
Best years: 1980, 1981

Leschenault Cabernet Sauvignon

A wine of considerable depth and finesse, and one of which the area can be proud. Dark garnet in colour, the Cabernet has a hint of the cut-grass smell associable with good versions of this variety, and in the mouth there is an understated depth of flavour which belies the light-to-medium body. A fine wine.
Best years: 1978, 1980

Leschenault Traminer

There are two versions of this, the Traminer and the 'Traminer Pressings'. While one may understand why a maker may wish to try a pressings version of this variety, I feel that the increased flavour of the latter is more than offset by a concomitant coarseness. The 'ordinary' Traminer is most attractive: light and spicy as might be expected, but soft and crisp with good balance.
Best years: 1980, 1981

Ownership

A partnership between Barry and Betty Killerby.

Production

About 1500 cases, most of which is Cabernet Sauvignon, Hermitage or a blend of the two.

New Plantings

(Not yet yielding.) Two hectares each of Chardonnay and Semillon have yet to produce.

Market

Around 90 per cent of Leschenault wines are sold within Western Australia, most of this being through cellar door and mailing list.

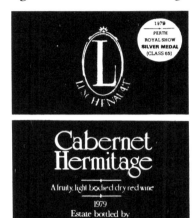

Winery Visiting Details

Monday to Saturday 10 am to 6 pm. The address is Lakes Road, Bunbury, 6230 Telephone (097) 21 2985.

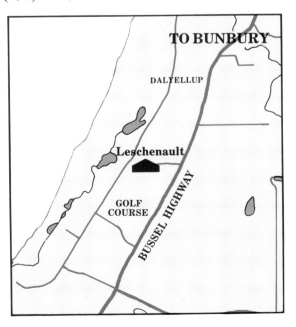

LINDEMANS 'BEN EAN' WINERY   Pokolbin, NSW

Before readers' eyebrows are raised too high at seeing the name of Australia's biggest selling wine in a book on small wineries, let me hasten to explain that Ben Ean is the name of a small, high quality vineyard in Pokolbin. Other vineyards owned by Lindemans in the area were Porphyry, Coolalta, Sunshine, Kirkton and Cawarra, each of which has been commemorated by the giant producer in the names of popular wines made from grapes grown elsewhere.

The Ben Ean winery is of modest size, annually crushing a mere 600 tonnes — about the same crush as Leeuwin Estate, or Chateau Tahbilk — and the total production capacity is only 1000 tonnes. The vineyard was first planted in 1870 and was acquired by Lindemans in 1912. It is now the centre of the company's Hunter Valley operations, and as such it has been the cradle of the fabled '4 figure Bin number' wines which have so ex-

tended the quality gamut of Australian wine. In this context it behoves the thoughtful consumer to acknowledge a debt of gratitude to Ray Kidd whose hand has been at the Lindemans helm during the time these wines were developed.

The grapes crushed at the Ben Ean winery come from the company's four major vineyards in the area: Sunshine, Steven, Broke and Ben Ean. The varieties are mostly Semillon and Shiraz (both of course traditionally misnamed 'Hunter River Riesling' and 'Hermitage'), together with some Chardonnay, Pinot Noir and Verdelhao. With all of the wines there is a remarkable continuity of style which varies very little even when there has been a change of winemaker.

Visitors to the area would be well advised not to miss the fascinating 'permanent exhibition' of historic winemaking equipment in the museum within the winery's grounds.

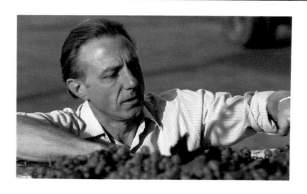

Winemaker

Karl Stockhausen came to Australia from Germany in 1955 and studied accountancy. By the time he graduated in 1961, his 'casual' job with Lindemans had grown to that of their Hunter Valley winemaker. Twenty years of producing wines of such quality renders formal qualifications rather unnecessary. For two years, 1980 and 1981, Karl was in charge of the Tanunda winery of Leo Buring, but has now returned to Pokolbin and Ben Ean.

Range of Wines

Lindemans Hunter River Burgundy
Lindemans Hunter River Chablis
Lindemans Hunter River Chardonnay
Lindemans Hunter River Hermitage/Pinot
Lindemans Hunter River Porphyry
Lindemans Hunter River Riesling
Lindemans Hunter River Steven Hermitage
Lindemans Hunter River White Burgundy

Style

Lindemans Hunter River Burgundy

A beautiful traditional Hunter Valley style with a noble history. The wine is densely coloured, not especially limpid but perfectly clean, notably grapey in its youthful aroma but much more vinous when mature, and full, fine and muscular in the palate. In its best years it is nothing short of magnificent.
Best years: 1959, 1965, 1970, 1975, 1980

Lindemans Hunter River Chablis

One of the classic wines in Australia, and uniquely Pokolbin in style. Made from Semillon grapes, the young wine is light, fresh, fragrant and extremely attractive, but age deepens it to a golden colour, nutty bouquet, complex honeyed palate and lingering finish.
Best years: 1965, 1968, 1970, 1979, 1980

Lindemans Hunter River White Burgundy

There are many points of similarity between this wine and the Chablis. However the White Burgundy is a wood matured wine whose greater substance is particularly noticeable when it is young. Age brings the two styles closer together, notably in the creamy nutty depths of the opulent palate.
Best years: 1965, 1978, 1980, 1981

Ownership

Lindemans Ben Ean winery is of course owned by Lindemans Holdings, which is in turn owned by the Philip Morris Company.

Production

About 40 000 cases annually, most of which is Semillon under various guises.

New Plantings

(Not yet yielding.) Seven hectares each of Chardonnay and Semillon and six of Verdelhao have yet to bear.

Market

Nationally available through specialized outlets and good restaurants.

Winery Visiting Details

Monday to Friday 9 am to 5 pm, Saturday 10 am to 5 pm, Sundays, September to May only, noon to 5 pm. The address is McDonalds Road, Pokolbin, 2321 Telephone (049) 98 7501.

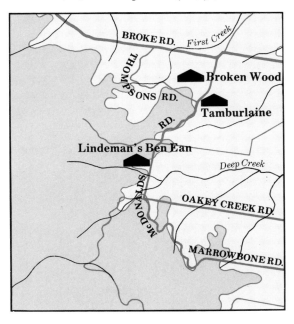

MARIENBERG

Ursula Marie Pridham was brought up on her family's vineyard at Steiermark, then in south-eastern Austria (now in Yugoslavia). After the border 'adjustment', the vineyard was lost so the family emigrated to Australia. In the mid 'sixties Ursula and her stockbroker husband Geoffrey purchased a seven hectare vineyard in Coromandel Valley on the southern outskirts of Adelaide. It was not intended as a commercial venture, and initially Ursula made wine purely as a hobby.

The hobby grew, and so did the production which now exceeds 100 000 litres per vintage. Much replanting has been carried out at Marienberg, varieties such as Grenache being replaced by Rhine Riesling, Cabernet Sauvignon, Shiraz and Gewurztraminer.

Originally Ursula matured her Rhine Rieslings in oak, a variation from normal practice which soon developed for Marienberg a reputation for 'over-oaking' its wines — particularly among some of the local winemakers who had not realized the importance of oak in viniculture. To still the ghosts of such gossip, let it be said that Marienberg Rhine Rieslings have not seen oak since the 1974 vintage. It is used, however, for the Chablis and White Burgundy styles.

In the late 'seventies, the Marienberg gamut was extended by the addition to the range of Auslese and Trockenbeerenauslese, depending of course upon the season. Try though I may, I can find no evidence of any botrytis character, even in the 'Trockenbeerenauslese' but for all that they are attractive and interesting wines.

It is not feasible to increase the size of the Coromandel Valley vineyard, but the Pridhams are developing another vineyard at Bethany, in the foothills a few miles east of McLaren Vale. Vines planted here comprise Rhine Riesling, Cabernet Sauvignon and Semillon.

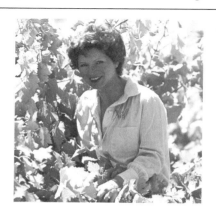

Winemaker

Ursula Pridham abandoned her profession as an electronics engineer to become Australia's first woman winemaker. Her family background of a couple of centuries of vintages in Austria was her starting point, and intelligent, painstaking study together with a dozen or so vintages has completed the job.

Range of Wines
Marienberg Alicante
Marienberg Auslese
Marienberg Cabernet Sauvignon
Marienberg Cabernet Shiraz
Marienberg Chablis
Marienberg Gewurztraminer
Marienberg Rhine Riesling
Marienberg Rosengarten
Marienberg Shiraz
Marienberg Trockenbeerenauslese
Marienberg Vintage Port
Marienberg White Burgundy

Style
Marienberg Cabernet Sauvignon
The style is now blended from grapes grown on both the Coromandel Valley and Bethany blocks. Like most of this maker's reds they have a fine translucency unexpected for the area, convincing if unemphatic Cabernet character and great elegance. The wines' tightness helps them to live remarkably well.
Best years: 1971, 1976, 1977

Marienberg Rhine Riesling
This has always been close to the best Rhine Riesling in the Southern Vales area. Ursula Pridham's sensitivity with fruit annually achieves, for this style, a wine of delicacy as well as depth, without sacrifice of the uniquely floral character of the variety.
Best years: 1972, 1977, 1979

Marienberg Trockenbeerenauslese
This is a unique and admirable style which extends the range covered by Australian wine. Made from Semillon grapes grown at Bethany, the wine has the limpid golden colour one might expect. The first surprise comes with the nose which contains almost lemony undertones, lifting considerably the usually unprepossessing flatness of South Australian Semillon. The second surprise is on the palate: much cleaner and prettier than expected for the Tockenbeerenauslese style, which usually depends upon a combination of slightly 'off'

flavours for complexity. Aging is of course essential.
Best years: 1978, 1980

Ownership
Marienberg is a partnership between the Pridhams.

Production
Total production is 12 500 cases, the major wine component being Cabernet Sauvignon 2500 cases, Rhine Riesling 2500 cases, Chablis 2500 cases, Trockenbeerenauslese (if made) 250 to 500 cases.

New Plantings
(Not yet yielding.) Nil, but grafting programme continues.

Market
Cellar door accounts for 25 per cent, Victoria 30 per cent, New South Wales 15 per cent, other states 20 per cent and export 10 per cent.

Winery Visiting Details
Monday to Saturday 9 am to 5 pm, Sunday noon to 5 pm. The address is Black Road, Coromandel Valley, 5051 Telephone (08) 270 2384.

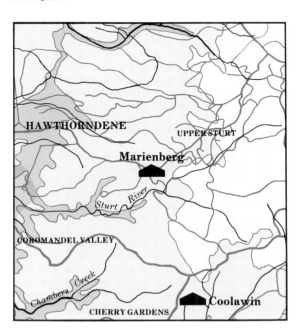

MARSH ESTATE

A few idle thoughts on the Lower Hunter Valley: it is closer to the equator than Baghdad (although not so close as the Swan Valley, whose latitude is comparable with Tel Aviv's), it has a mean January temperature of just under 23° Celsius (almost as hot as Griffith), and yield is appallingly low on the better vineyards (sometimes less than one tonne per hectare in a bad year). As a vignoble it would be disastrous were it not for one remarkable feature: humidity. The cloud cover over Pokolbin limits the average daily sunshine hours to just over seven — about the same as Launceston! Climatologically the area is unique.

And because of this so are the wines. Hunter Hermitage (Shiraz) and Hunter Riesling (Semillon) are remarkably traditional styles quite unlike wines anywhere else in the world. Among those to fall under their spell was Dr Quentin Taperell, who planted Shiraz and Semillon in 1971, and built a winery in time for

the 1976 vintage. The wines were impressive and made some initial impact when first released, but other considerations interposed and the operation was sold in 1978 to Peter Marsh a Sydney pharmacist.

By this stage the vineyard had grown to 18.5 hectares, and Cabernet Sauvignon and Traminer had been added to the two Hunter stalwarts originally established. Peter increased the area under vine to 21 hectares with Chardonnay and a little Pinot Noir, and Marsh Estate was off and running.

Peter does not irrigate at all, relying entirely on the fractious caprices of Pokolbin rainfall, like all of the better Hunter vineyards. Years like 1981 make life unpleasant for a Hunter winemaker, but quality usually mitigates lack of quantity, and sooner or later a more bounteous vintage relieves the pressure (as has happened with 1982).

Winemaker

Peter Marsh qualified a pharmacist at Sydney University in 1962. He has augmented his winemaking knowledge by reading, study and of course by the invaluable method of a continuing exchange of ideas with other winemakers. He has a deeply rooted respect for the traditional styles of the Hunter Valley and overtly aims to continue making these, while exending the gamut somewhat by his introduction of a Cabernet based Port.

Range of Wines

Marsh Estate Cabernet/Shiraz
Marsh Estate Hermitage — Vat R
Marsh Estate Hermitage — Vat 3
Marsh Estate Moselle (Semillon)
Marsh Estate P.M./Private Bin Hermitage
Marsh Estate Riesling (Semillon)
Marsh Estate Rosé
Marsh Estate Semillon
Marsh Estate Traminer
Marsh Estate Traminer/Riesling
Marsh Estate Vintage Port
Marsh Estate Wood Matured Semillon

Style

Marsh Estate Hermitage

Much is written about Hunter Valley Shiraz being reminiscent of all sorts of unlikely things such as sweaty saddles, athletes' armpits, wet dogs and pepper. Wine writers have fertile imaginations. In fairness to them, it is undeniable that many Hunter Shiraz wines do have an intriguing and unusual 'humid' smell when young, but this is not an aspect of coarseness. Marsh Estate in particular produce medium-bodied reds of some elegance, redolent of the area's style but attractive even when comparatively young. The 'P.M. Private Bin' version is bigger, and a longer term aging prospect than the other two: Vats R and S.
Best years: 1979, 1980

Marsh Estate Semillon

Very Hunter and very Semillon, but in spite of the maker's respect for the paradigmatic 'Hunter Rieslings' I do not think his own versions are exemplary. To date they are both softer and fruitier than might be regarded as ideal, and lack the tightness and elegance of the style's finest exponents. Nevertheless they are attractive and generous wines which make for enjoyable drinking.
Best years: 1980, 1981.

Ownership

The operation is owned by Peter and Robyn Marsh as a partnership.

Production

Average annual production is 5000 cases, most of which is Hermitage and Semillon.

New Plantings

(Not yet yielding.) Nil, but 2 hectares of Chardonnay and 0.5 hectares of Pinot Noir have just begun to yield.

Market

Entirely cellar door, with about 25 per cent going to interstate customers.

Winery Visiting Details

Monday to Friday 9 am to 5 pm, Saturday 10 am to 5 pm, Sunday noon to 5 pm. The address is Deasy's Road, Pokolbin, 2321 Telephone (049) 98 7587.

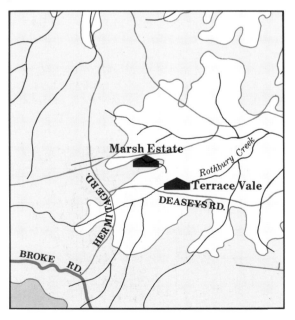

MIRAMAR

There could be no more enthusiastic and committed devotee of the Mudgee area than Ian MacRae. He first came to the district to be the winemaker for Sydney architect Ken Digby, who had planted the 15 hectares of Miramar vines in 1974. Ian's dedication culminated in his acquiring the operation, in association with two other partners, in 1981. He tells me that long before he came to the district he had decided that Mudgee was potentially the best area in Australia to make good wine — a conviction with which I would find it impossible to agree, much as I respect the vignoble's wines. But one must admire the intense loyalty which infects all Mudgee makers.

The first vintage was in 1977 when 25 tonnes were crushed. Cash flow pressures were such that there is hardly a bottle of the vintage left at the winery. The following year saw a 92 tonne crush which unfortunately included some fruit from other areas, and there were few wines to be proud of. From '79 onwards the style of Miramar wines began to be established, and the experience of 1978 ca now be forgotten.

Capital is still a problem for the Miramar ven ture, and a permanent winery is sorely needed Under Ian's intelligent guidance, availabl monies have been expended on adequatel sophisticated equipment rather than Taj Mah buildings. An interesting development is tha the IBM company, who are developing thei own vineyard in the area, has built much of thi equipment including wine pumps, he exchangers and stainless steel tanks.

Apart from the '79 vintage, fortune has n smiled upon Miramar, the next two year wines being of fine quality but miserable quar tity, and as I write the 1982 vintage looms. S far all is well, and a bumper year of 200 tonne would catapult the operation forward. Good ir tentions alone cannot make good wine, but ar nevertheless quintessential if such is to b made. Clearly, the stage is set for Ian MacRa and his beloved Miramar.

Winemaker

Ian MacRae has a background of bot winemaking and engineering. Born at Berri i the Riverland, his interest in wine was in grained, and he graduated from Roseworthy i 1962. He has worked as a winemaker wit Penfolds, Hardy's, Loxton Cooperative, Kaise Stuhl and Wolf Blass, as well as having had substantial hand in the designing of winerie for Hungerford Hill and Krondorf.

Range of Wines

Miramar Cabernet Sauvignon
Miramar Chardonnay
Miramar Dry White
Miramar Moselle
Miramar Muscat
Miramar Rhine Riesling
Miramar Rosé
Miramar Semillon/Chardonnay
Miramar Shiraz
Miramar Shiraz/Cabernet
Miramar Traminer
Miramar Vintage Port
Mudgee Shiraz

Style

Miramar Shiraz

This is what Ian describes as a 'cellar style' as distinct from his 'Mudgee Shiraz' (a softer, less complex, more traditional style). When young, which is the only way they exist at the moment, the Miramar Shiraz is big, tight, fairly profound and well oaked — a wine with a muscular handshake. The style will need some years to develop and come into balance.
Best years: 1979, 1980

Miramar Chardonnay

Although only one 100% Chardonnay has been produced to date — the 1981 — it is of such quality and power to suggest it could become a major style for the winery. The 1981 is a big wine but quite without coarseness, and redolent of the variety's characteristics. Richly golden in hue, it is a wine of Californian strength and intensity and is in splendid balance.
Best year: 1981

Miramar Semillon/Chardonnay

This has been such a successful style that one hopes that shortage of Chardonnay fruit will not mitigate against its continuing availability. Mudgee Semillon does not make the most interesting of wines, and the added complexity gained from its admixture with Chardonnay is highly desirable. Since 1980 German oak is used in maturing this wine.
Best years: 1980, 1981

Miramar Vintage Port

First made in 1978, this is big and spirity, with full, fat fruit but a strongly tannic impact and acid finish. Ian MacRae is unconcerned about what he described as 'this Portuguese or Australian nonsense' and would probably reply that it is Mudgee. The wine is given one year in secondhand Cognac casks, which adds appreciably to its depth.
Best years, 1979, 1980

Ownership

Owned by Ian MacRae, Maartin Velzeboer and Dr Gordon Packham.

Production

Variable to date, but expected to average around the 10 000 case mark in the future.

New Plantings

(Not yet yielding.) Nil.

Market

Nearly all cellar door and mailing list. Recently an export order was gained from Japan, and USA is being investigated as a market.

Winery Visiting Details

Monday to Saturday 9 am to 5 pm, Sunday noon to 5 pm. The address is Henry Lawson Drive, Mudgee, 2850 Telephone (063) 73 3874.

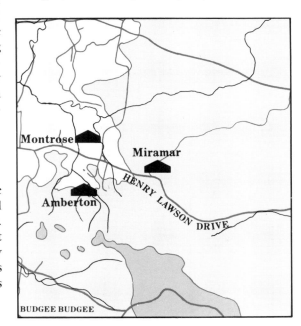

MITGHELLS

I suppose it is indicative of the increasing sophistication of the average wine lover that it is no longer enough in giving the provenance of a wine to name the general area: Clare, Southern Vales, Yarra Valley etc. People now want to know just where within the particular area the grapes are grown (an interest which some of the major companies would be well-advised to recognize and satisfy, albeit belatedly). A case in point is Mitchells.

Andrew Mitchell has two vineyards — one at Watervale, and the other around his winery a few kilometres from the township of Sevenhill. The Watervale plantings are at an altitude of 300 metres, but the Sevenhill Vineyard is at 450 metres. Climatologically this is a very significant difference, the major factor involved being an extra three weeks in the ripening period of the higher vineyard, with consequent notable gains in both depth and complexity of the fruit.

The project commenced in 1975 with Andrew acquiring the properties and establishing the plantings. These are now 12 hectares of Rhine Riesling at Watervale, and 8 hectares of Cabernet Sauvignon and 4 of Rhine Riesling at Sevenhill. The winery (at Sevenhill) was created from an old stone apple-storage shed which now houses one of the two most modern and well-equipped wineries in the area (the other being Tim Knappstein's Enterprise winery), refrigerated tanks, Wilmes press and all.

Andrew grew up in the Clare Valley and has an abiding respect for the area's fruit quality and its winegrowing potential. He believes, and will get no argument from me, that Rhine Riesling and Cabernet Sauvignon have been amply demonstrated to be the district's best varieties and this is all he makes, although he has planted Chardonnay on both of his vineyards

The red wine is matured in hogsheads mostly of American oak although there are some French, and 50 per cent of the wood is new each year. The Rhine Riesling is given no wood.

Difficult though it is to keep up with all the new producers currently abounding, the extreme quality for the area being achieved by Mitchells means that if you don't know these wines then you don't know just how good the Clare Valley can be.

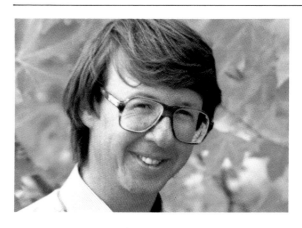

Winemaker

Andrew Mitchell grew up on his parents' vineyard in the Clare area. After gaining a degree in Economics at Adelaide University, his vinicultural aspirations led him to start his vineyard and do the Wine Science course at Riverina. His wife Jane did a course in Wine Production at Roseworthy, so each of Australia's seats of oenological learning holds some sway at Mitchells.

Range of Wines

Mitchells Cabernet Sauvignon (Sevenhill)
Mitchells Rhine Riesling (Sevenhill)
Mitchells Rhine Riesling (Watervale)

Style

Mitchells Cabernet Sauvignon

Andrew Mitchell's stated aim with this wine is to achieve a fully-ripened, intense flavour with very clean fruit. For him this is not just paying lip service to a few attractive-sounding attributes, but a painstaking and deadly serious effort to achieve a desideratum. The profile of the 1980 version attests to the success of his efforts, the wine being of great beauty and power, redolently Cabernet, and both clean and very long-finishing.
Best years: 1980, 1982

Mitchells Rhine Riesling (Sevenhill)

Whether in the late-picked or standard versions, this is a lovely wine which eloquently demonstrates Andrew's extreme adeptness, if not virtuosity, with the variety. The style has strength but grace, with the exemplary fruit quality commanding respect on both the nose and the palate.
Best years: 1977, 1980

Ownership

Entirely owned by Andrew and Jane Mitchell.

Production

About 6000 cases currently, the major part of which is Rhine Riesling.

New Plantings

(Not yet yielding.) A total of 7 hectares, mostly Chardonnay but with some Cabernet Sauvignon, is being established during 1982.

Market

Some cellar door and mailing list, the remainder going fairly equally to Adelaide, Melbourne and Sydney, with a little sent annually to New York.

Winery Visiting Details

The winery is open 10 am to 4 pm seven days a week, but only while wine is available, so ring first. The address is Hughes Park Road, Sevenhill, 5450 Telephone (088) 43 4258.

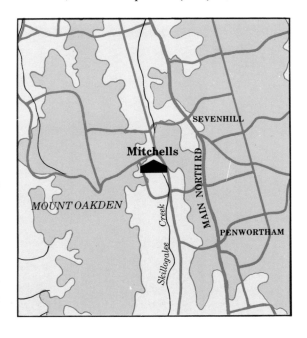

MONTROSE

Montrose Wines and Spirits Pty Ltd was a blending and marketing wholesale company in 1973 when it was acquired by two successful Italian engineers, Franco Belgiorno-Nettis and Carlo Salteri. The idea of establishing a vineyard and winery grew out of this acquisition, rather than vice versa. Nevertheless there was no 'toe in the water' aspect to the venture — on the contrary, a mere two years later very substantial plantings had been made and a modern winery built.

Initial plantings were of Shiraz, Cabernet Sauvignon, Traminer, Chardonnay and some experimental Italian varieties. Since then additional plantings have occurred on a regular basis over three vineyards, increasing the areas of the above varieties and adding Rhine Riesling and Semillon to the stable. The total plantings are now an impressive 45 hectares, comprising Chardonnay 12, Cabernet Sauvignon 11, Rhine Riesling 5, Shiraz 4.5, Traminer 4 and Pinot Noir 3 hectares, together with 3 hectares of San Giovese, Nebbiolo and Barbera. (San Giovese is the main grape used in red Chianti; Nebbiolo makes the fine Barolo and Barbaresco wines; and Barbera, a respected grape in Northern Italy, has now been widely established in California to the tune of over 9000 hectares!)

Intriguingly, re-grafting is already under way at the Montrose vineyards, Rhine Riesling being grafted to the existing Cabernet Sauvignon,

and Pinot Noir to Shiraz. One sees the wisdom of the latter, but the proprietors may well have cause to regret decreasing the area of Cabernet if the demand for quality red wine behaves as some vinous futurologists suggest. However the winemaker, Carlo Corino, feels that the particular patch of soil in question is more suited to Rhine Riesling anyway.

It is refreshing to see that the Montrose project brings a touch of both marketing professionalism and capital to an area where the norm is undercapitalization mitigated by enthusiasm.

Winemaker

Carlo Corino graduated from the Institute of Oenology at Alba in Italy in 1959. For the next few years he worked with Noilly Pratt in Turin until he left to become winemaker for a winery in Ethiopia. He returned to Alba and made wine there until 1976, when he came to Australia to join Montrose Wines.

Range of Wines

Montrose Barbera
Montrose Brut N.V.
Montrose Cabernet Sauvignon
Montrose Chardonnay
Montrose Frontignac
Montrose Pinot Noir
Montrose Rhine Riesling
Montrose Sauternes
Montrose Semillon
Montrose Semillon/Chardonnay
Montrose Shiraz
Montrose Traminer/Riesling
Montrose Vintage Port

Style

Montrose Barbera

I must confess to being inadequately familiar with the Barbera wines of Italy to recognize stylistic similarities in the Montrose version. Be that as it may, this is a beautifully attractive, light to medium bodied dry red with a lovely translucent ruby colour; gently vinous but sweet nose; and prettily balanced palate. Delightful drinking, and a welcome new facet to Australian wine.
Best year: 1979

Montrose Chardonnay

A very impressive wine: austerely dry, almost chalky in the finish, yet with the rich generosity of peaches suffusing the palate. A wine of considerable merit and elegance and quite different in style from the somewhat homespun Chardonnays of the area.
Best years: 1980, 1981

Montrose Sauternes

First made in 1978 as a non-botrytized 100% Semillon of massive proportions and convincing power, subsequent versions in 1980 and 1981 (there was no 1979) are softened considerably by being made from 30% Sauvignon Blanc. Certainly this is the best Sauternes in the area, and needs only a touch less volatility in the style to be very hard to match within Australia.
Best years: 1978, 1980

Ownership

The company is owned by Bemmosa — a partnership between Franco Belgiorno-Nettis and Carlo Salteri.

Production

After two severe drought years it is expected that normal production should be about 400 tonnes (30 000 cases) plus bought-in grapes.

New Plantings

(Not yet yielding.) All yielding, but planting programme for Semillon, Rhine Riesling and Pinot Noir is planned.

Market

New South Wales 75 per cent, Victoria 10 per cent, other 15 per cent.

Winery Visiting Details

Monday to Friday 8 am to 4 pm, Saturday 11 am to 4 pm, Sunday noon to 4 pm. The address is Henry Lawson Drive, Mudgee 2850 Telephone (063) 73 3853.

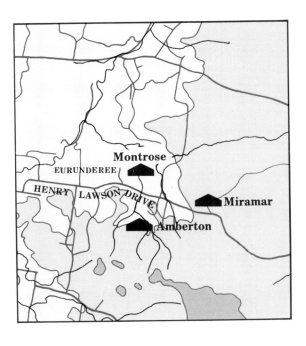

MOORILLA ESTATE

Berriedale, Tas.

'The prejudice that Tasmania is too cold for viticulture arises from the fact that most Australian vineyards are planted in areas much warmer than Tasmania. Like most prejudices, it is based on a fallacy.' So reads a statement published by Claudio Alcorso in 1975. Typically, he is too gentle. What he could have said, without overstatement, was that all but a tiny handful of Australian vineyards are planted in areas which are much too hot for quality.

But Claudio Alcorso is a gentle man in whose statements about Moorilla Estate it is impossible to detect any undertone of bitterness. Incredible, if you consider how much gratuitous advice he must have been given to abandon his Hobart vineyard project. He is also a man of enduring loyalties; loyalty to Italy, which gave him his love of wine; loyalty to the textile industry, in which his successful career supplied the finance to create his vineyard (all Moorilla Estate wines have cloth labels); loyalty to

Tasmania, the ubiquitous vineyard logo bears a Tasmanian aboriginal design of *trompe d'oeil* impact; and above all loyalty to his vineyard, continuing as he does to make small quantities of wine at crippling cost.

As he points out; if by some quirk of history the Derwent Valley had been colonized by a Mediterranean people, the slopes would all be covered with vines. So he bought 8 hectares of land at Berriedale and dappled them with plantings of Cabernet Sauvignon, Pinot Noir and Rhine Riesling. The length of summer and the length of the ripening days are two factors of immense quality importance in those cool climate vignobles which are distant from the equator (as distinct from areas much closer to the equator which are cool because of altitude), and the depth, elegance and nobility of the fruit quality are the rewards. Frost and low yields are the penalties.

Winemaker

Julian Alcorso is the winemaker. A graduate in economics, Julian attended oenology courses, studies continuously and works closely with consultants, both at vintage and between vintages. He says he does not wish to become a 'general' winemaker, but a very good specialist in the production of the two wines or possibly even one wine, which will eventually be the output of Moorilla Estate.

Range of Wines

Moorilla Estate Cabernet Sauvignon
Moorilla Estate Pinot Noir
Moorilla Estate Rhine Riesling

Style

Moorilla Estate Cabernet Sauvignon

Fine, light, dry, slender but languorously deep and supple, these are a superb series of wines at the very forefront of Australian Cabernet flavour, although in a distinctly unique style. If one can have such a thing as an 'intense hint', then there is an intense hint of coffee in the nose, and myriad noble nuances in the palate. A great wine, in miniature.
Best years: 1977, 1979

Moorilla Estate Pinot Noir

Enchantingly attractive, but delicate to the point of fragility, the Pinot Noir has been marred by inadequate colour and lack of firmness. Still comparatively experimental, it is now being found that older vines and canopy control are leading to wines with a more muscular handshake, without sacrifice of the extreme quality of the fruit.
Best years: 1975, 1981

Moorilla Estate Rhine Riesling

If we take the finest of the dry Rheingau wines as the paradigms, this and Pipers Brook would have to be acknowledged the best two Rieslings in Australia. It is a wine of delicacy but power, with flinty depths within the sweet fruit, and compares with most of the mainland Rhine Rieslings as does a sunset with a neon light.
Best years: 1974, 1979, 1981

Ownership

Moorilla Estates Pty Ltd is a family company.

Production

Currently only about 2500 cases, but expect to rise to a maximum of 3500 cases by 1985.

New Plantings

Some new plantings of Pinot Noir have been established, and considerable grafting of this variety to less suitable varieties is continuing.

Market

Entirely by mailing list, surprisingly mostly to South Australia, Victoria and New South Wales.

Winery Visiting Details

By appointment only, the address being 655 Main Road, Berriedale, 7011 Telephone (002) 49 2487.

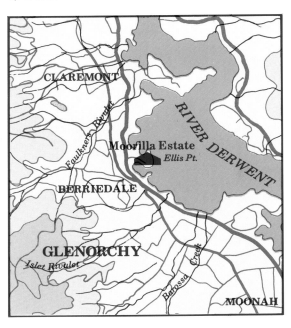

MOSS WOOD

Moss Wood is the acknowledged superstar of the West, having in a comparatively short time achieved a national reputation rivalling that of Lakes Folly, Balgownie *et al*. Indeed there are many who regard Moss Wood Cabernet Sauvignon as Australia's best red wine.

Bill and Sandra Pannell began planting the vineyard in 1969, giving them until 1973 to establish the winery. Much had been theorized about the suitability of the Margaret River area for production of extreme quality wine grapes ever since an entry speculating such was found in Maurice O'Shea's diary after his death in 1956. As an aside, it is significant to note that in spite of this theorizing the area had to await the arrival of the era of small makers before a vine was planted. So much for the then attitude of the large producers, whose place in the market is now fast becoming the bottom end. But enough of such bitchiness.

The vineyard is now of nine hectares, most of which is in full bear. This comprises some five hectares of Cabernet Sauvignon, a little over one hectare of Semillon and just under one hectare of Pinot Noir and Chardonnay. Obviously the latter two are of extremely limited availability.

It is not easy to write about Moss Wood without having to moderate one's language, lest the implied approbation should appear too fulsome. Nevertheless it would be unfair not to emphasize that the existence of this vineyard has appreciably extended the quality range of Australian wine, to the greater benefit of you and me.

Nothing seems to have gone wrong for Bill and Sandra, at least 'from the outside, looking

in'. Their choice of site, their tasteful label, their romantic and evocative vineyard name, and above all their achievement of extreme quality have their fairytale aspects. They must be doing something right.

Winemaker

Dr Bill Pannell is the Moss Wood winemaker. He is unforthcoming about his training and his qualifications so far as oenology is concerned, but then again I suppose all he has to do to answer such inquiries is point wordlessly to his wine. Max Lake has certainly been unstinting in his advice to Bill, as has Stuart Anderson.

Range of Wines

Moss Wood Cabernet Sauvignon
Moss Wood Chardonnay
Moss Wood Pinot Noir
Moss Wood Semillon

Style

Moss Wood Cabernet Sauvignon

It borders on the incredible that this wine is so good. The colour is deep, although not dark, and limpid, with hints of blackberry. The latter fruit is also gently suggested amidst the myriad complexities of the nose, which include suspicions of coffee, cedar and butter (by which last, would-be wine chemists please note, I do *not* mean some witches' brew of higher lactates). The palate is as long as anyone could wish, and is charged with sweet fruit, tightly controlled. Balance is exemplary, and the sheer quality of the Cabernet soars above normal longevity parameters so that a fortunate few could well be drinking 1970s Moss Woods in excellent condition in twenty years time. A great wine.
Best years: 1974, 1975, 1980

Moss Wood Chardonnay

I have seen only one of these — the 1980 — and it is a wine of staggering merit. The colour is rich straw, and it is limpid as a trout-stream; the nose has all the obvious peaches/figs/apricots components expected of the variety, but also contains complex smoky undertones of very great beauty; the palate is gently overwhelming: sweet without sugar, tight without austerity, crisp without sharpness. Unbelievable.
Best year: 1980

Ownership

Totally owned by Dr Bill Pannell and his wife Sandra.

Production

About 3000 cases, most of which is Cabernet Sauvignon.

New Plantings

(Not yet yielding.) 1.3 hectares of Pinot Noir and 0.4 of Chardonnay have yet to yield.

Market

40 per cent to New South Wales, 30 per cent Victoria, 20 per cent Western Australia, and 10 per cent for mail order and cellar door.

Winery Visiting Details

9 am to 4 pm Monday to Saturday, but only when an appointment is made by 'phone. The address is Cowaramup, 6284 Telephone (097) 52 1926.

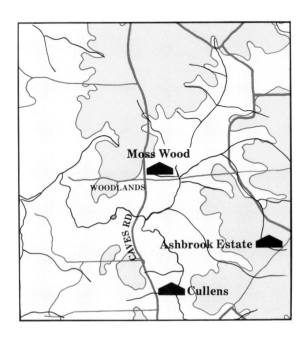

113

MOUNT AVOCA

It is most agreeable for me to discover that the writings of Walter James originally inspired John Barry to embark on a course of action which culminated in the Mount Avoca vineyard. For it was Walter whose first slim volume 'Barrel and Book' seduced me from the paths of (comparative) temperance. But I merely sip and scribble: John purchased 80 hectares of outstanding 'cool climate' vineyard land in the Pyrenees Ranges just 5 kilometres west of Avoca. This was in 1970, and the next three years saw 16 hectares planted on the gravelly soil: 4 hectares of Cabernet Sauvignon, 11 of Shiraz, and bits and pieces of Trebbiano and Semillon which we can ignore.

The winery is both modern and well equipped, and was finished in 1978 to deal with the first 'commercial' vintage. (One assumes that the not inconsiderable amount of grapes picked before 1978 must have been sold to large makers somewhat to mitigate the mediocrity of their wine stews.)

John Barry is justifiably proud of his wood storage, as he imports made-up barriques from the Bordeaux coopers who supply Chateau Lafite. (Gratuitous information: 'barrique' is the French term for what the English call a hogshead. With understandable swank, Australian winemakers reserve the word for those casks which are imported in an assembled state. Under either name, they hold about 250 litres.)

Essentially Mount Avoca is a red wine vineyard, reflecting the preference of John Barry, although 1981 saw the planting of Chardonnay and Sauvignon Blanc. Somewhat of a purist, he prefers to market the two reds unblended, although commercial considerations sometimes dictate the necessity to create some quantities of a blend between the two. As the styles are developing, it is becoming apparent that there is no reason why this vineyard should not produce some of Victoria's (and therefore Australia's) best reds.

Winemaker

Guy Stanford, a graduate in wine science at the Riverina College, met John Barry when the latter enrolled in the course in Oenology and Viticulture. John is a stockbroker and the size of the vineyard is far beyond the capacity of a weekend hobbyist to maintain, so Guy became the Mount Avoca winemaker in late 1980. To a considerable degree, however, the actual winemaking is a co-operative effort.

Range of Wines
Mount Avoca Cabernet Sauvignon
Mount Avoca Hermitage

Style

Mount Avoca Cabernet Sauvignon
This is an unusual style, of tremendous depth and power with substantial grape tannin. The colour is intense, the nose aggressive but far from straightforward, and the palate rich with some glorious fruit and a touch of almost stalky bitterness on the finish which I find very attractive in young Cabernets. Not one of those Victorian King Kong Cabernets which terrified us all a few years ago, but broad-shouldered withal.
Best years: 1979, 1980

Mount Avoca Hermitage
It is difficult to assess the Hermitage at the moment because a substantial style change has been affected with the 1980 vintage. The 1979, for example, is a fairly turbid wine with a fat and vinous nose, rich but bland palate and to my mind unsatisfactory integration. The semi-experimental 1980, on the other hand has a fine, profound nose with multiple components; a lighter colour; far better balance with considerable complexity and grace; and long-finishing sweet fruit. The 1981 is still in wood at the time of writing, and was a drought year anyway, so we must look to the future in awaiting the establishment of a continuity of style. To date the common denominator is the rich fineness of the fruit.
Best year: 1980

Ownership
John and Arda Barry as partners.

Production
About 6000 cases, three-quarters of which is Hermitage.

New Plantings
1.2 hectares of Chardonnay and 2 hectares of Sauvignon Blanc were established in 1981.

Market
Mainly Victoria, with cellar door and mailing list sales becoming of increasing importance.

Winery Visiting Details
10.00 am to 5.00 pm Tuesday to Saturday, 12 noon to 5 pm Sundays (closed Mondays). The address is Moate Lane, Avoca, 3467 Telephone (054) 65 2211.

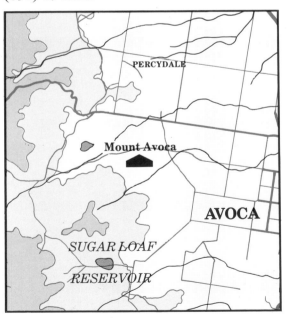

MOUNT MARY

At about the same time as Max Lake and Reg Egan were thrusting cuttings into the sod at Lakes Folly and Wantirna Estate respectively, John Middleton's first hundred or so vines were being similarly introduced at Lilydale in the Yarra Valley.

A perfectionist in a time when severely faulty if not actually diseased wine was the norm, Dr Middleton set about creating his dream vineyard in his beloved valley as a refuge, an achievement and a reward.

Bringing to bear a vineyard and winery hygiene which must have seemed obsessive to many during the development of Mount Mary, he has succeeded in making some of the best red wines Australia has seen, although, it must be said, some of the least Australian in style.

The 5 hectare vineyard is only slightly less spotless than an operating theatre, and the winery equipment is, as the Rolls Royce company were wont to say when asked the horse power of their motor cars, 'adequate'.

Grapes planted and yielding are Cabernet Sauvignon, Cabernet Franc, Merlot and Malbec (the only great Bordeaux variety missing from that line-up being Petit Verdot), Chardonnay, Pinot Noir and Traminer (the plantings of which are intermixed with 10 per cent of Chasselas).

All the wood used is small French oak, some of which are barriques imported made-up, and the white wines are all fermented in barrel.

I have read that there are another 6 hectares of Mount Mary which could be planted should the Middletons decide so, but I would regard any further expansion as unlikely in view of the purist nature of the winemaking.

Winemaker

Dr John Middleton makes all Mount Mary wine. His interest in wine is lifelong and far reaching, embracing very comprehensive experience of European, and, of recent years, Californian wines. Ultimate hygiene is his Holy Grail, and embattled micro-organisms receive very short shrift at Mount Mary. His winemaking approach is such that there is an extreme likelihood that his wines will become even better as vintage follows vintage.

Range of Wines

Mount Mary Cabernets
Mount Mary Chardonnay
Mount Mary Traminer
Mount Mary Pinot Noir

Style

Mount Mary Cabernets

With the 'Bordeaux Mixture' range of varieties to call upon, this wine is never 100% Cabernet Sauvignon, but a blend of this grape with Cabernet Franc, Malbec and Merlot. However, it does exemplify the intrinsic spirit of this noble grape, from the youthful 'cutgrass' austerity to the powerful floral depths of the more mature wines.
Best years: 1978, 1979, 1981

Mount Mary Chardonnay

This is an unusual winestyle with some striking similarities to French Chardonnays. The wine has an emphatic varietal nose, substantial alcohol, comparatively advanced development and frequently a somewhat hurried finish. Although it would be inaccurate not to admit that Mount Mary is close to the top Australian Chardonnays, I do not believe it is one of their number.
Best years: 1978, 1980

Mount Mary Pinot Noir

Pinot Noir is a difficult enough grape even in Burgundy; elsewhere in the world it can be fractious to the point of winemakers' despair. So Mount Mary has experienced its difficult years with the variety. However, it has also produced some glorious Corton-style wines of supreme depth, power, and magnificently intense strawberry overtones.
Best years: 1977, 1980

Ownership

Mount Mary is owned by Dr and Mrs Middleton.

Production

Annual production is about 2000 cases, one-half of which is Cabernet.

New Plantings

(Not yet yielding.) Nil.

Market

All wine is sold by mailing list, except for limited allocations to a handful of specialist retailers.

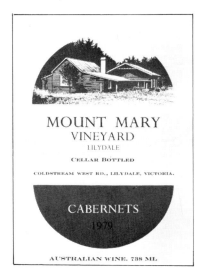

Winery Visiting Details

The winery is not open to the public, but applications to join the mailing list can be lodged by writing to Coldstream West Road, Lilydale, 3140.

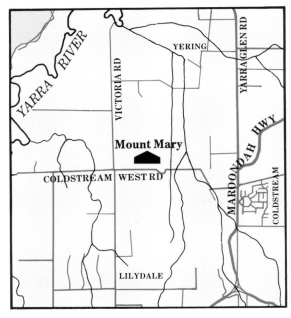

PEEL ESTATE

Perhaps the most quotable quote I have unearthed in researching this book is Will Nairn's answer to a journalist's question about why he turned from farming to viniculture: 'It's more interesting', he responded, 'Lucerne is lucerne year after year, but grapes become wine'. So as a relief from the dismal prospect of watching lucerne remain monotonously unchanged, Will established 13 hectares of Cabernet Sauvignon, Chardonnay, Chenin Blanc, Shiraz, Verdelho and Zinfandel at Baldivis, near Mandurah, on the same freakish strip of Tuart sand which attracted his near winegrowing neighbour Leschenault and the much more distant Conteville.

The first vintage was in 1977, the grapes for which were vinified by Paul Conti at Conteville up at Wanneroo. This arrangement subsisted for the next two years as well, while Will and Helen Nairn were establishing and equipping their own winery. This was completed during 1979, and takes the form of a combined winery, wood-storage and tasting complex, the whole being built into the side of a hill, so that the tasting area is on a mezzanine level directly entered from the higher part of the hill.

1980 arrived and with it the first vintage processed on the Estate. That the consequent wines were of a quality at least equal to the previous three vintages is eloquent testimony to Will Nairn's oenological competence. To date we have seen only the Shiraz, Zinfandel and Chenin Blanc from Peel Estate, as the Cabernet Sauvignon, Chardonnay and Verdelho are not yet yielding, but the former trio of wines have made a very substantial impact on the small vineyard *cognoscenti*.

The Nairns have the land to extend the Peel Estate operation, but have designed the winery for the maximum processing capacity that their present plantings necessitate. Eventually they intend to be crushing 140 to 150 tonnes, which will give them annual sales in excess of 10 000 cases.

Everything Will and Helen are doing is well-conceived and executed, from the varieties they chose to plant, the winery/tasting facility's attractive design, their original and very agreeable labels, to the fine quality of their wines.

Winemaker

Will Nairn has no formal winemaking qualifications but has been advised viticulturally by Bill Jamieson and oenologically by Paul Conti. He is not without his own ideas, however, and was particularly smitten with the white wine wood-aging techniques of the superb small maker Chappellet in the Napa Valley. Hence his own Chenin Blanc wooded style.

Range of Wines

Peel Estate Chenin Blanc
Peel Estate Chenin Blanc (wood-aged)
Peel Estate Shiraz
Peel Estate Zinfandel

Style

Peel Estate Chenin Blanc (wood-aged)

Attractive though the other Chenin Blanc is, it is the wood-aged version which won me hands down at my first smell and taste. It is a big, golden, voluptuous but very stylish wine within whose unstinting generosity of nose and palate I can find no hint of coarseness. Obviously a degree of volatility is an essential component of any wood-aged wine, and those who find such offensive in a white wine can always drink the standard version. For mine, though, this is Chenin Blanc at its very best.
Best year: 1981

Peel Estate Shiraz

Will Nairn has changed the style of this wine slightly from the Conteville made versions of 1977 to 1979, in spite of some dramatic show success generated by the 1979. He is seeking greater finesse and elegance through earlier picking and higher acid. The result has been to add an extra quality dimension to an already admirable winestyle, and to maximize the palate benefit of his beautiful fruit. His use of both French and American oak has also lent greater conviction to the wine. One of the best Shiraz wines in the West.
Best years: 1979, 1980

Ownership

Peel Estate Wines is an equal partnership between the Nairns and 'an English family' who prefer to keep a low profile.

Production

Gradually growing as the vines are reaching maturity, and expected to level out at 10 000 cases.

New Plantings

(Not yet yielding.) Nil, but half the vineyard is only just beginning to yield.

Market

Mostly Western Australia at the moment, but growing interest from Melbourne. At the time of writing, Sydney is yet to discover these wines.

Winery Visiting Details

Seven days a week 10 am to 5 pm (Will doesn't believe in days off). The address is Fletcher Road, Baldivis, near Mandurah. Telephone (095) 24 1221.

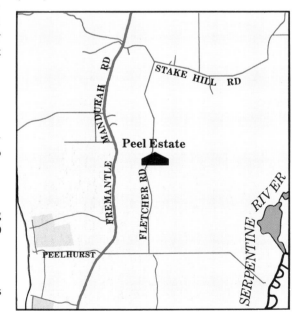

PETALUMA

Oenological guru Brian Croser owns the Petaluma name and the land on which the Petaluma vines are planted. That this fact is a virtual guarantee to the consumer of the future availability of wine of unprecedented quality is a measure of Croser's ability and the respect in which his achievements to date are regarded.

As a label, Petaluma has existed since 1976 — long before a winery was contemplated. In fact it is a fascinating example of Brian Croser's lateral thinking that the whole Petaluma project has developed in precisely the reverse order of every other wine-producing operation in Australia: first the label; then the winery; and finally the vineyard. To date, all fruit processed at the Petaluma winery has been bought-in, but 6 hectares of Chardonnay are planted at the winery and, as I write, are approaching their first modest yield. It is to this fruit that we must look for a definitive statement on Australian cool climate Chardonnay (bearing in mind that, in spite of misleading claims to the contrary, in

the only 'cool climate' site in South Australia is the small area around Mount Lofty wherein Petaluma's Piccadilly vineyard is established). I acknowledge, however, that such statement is yet to be made.

To date the grapes used in Petaluma white wines have come from Cowra (the first three Chardonnays), Coonawarra (the next two), Nagambie (the Rhine Riesling), and Clare (subsequent Rhine Rieslings). The winery is equipped to keep unfermented juice indefinitely by holding it at 1 degree Celsius. This means that Brian could ferment wines all year round if he chose. It also means that the 'small' winery has an effective processing capacity of one many times its size.

Brian Croser is a dedicated perfectionist whose analytically critical view is nowhere brought to bear so strongly as with his own wines. These are of extreme quality and, pedantry aside, should remain so.

Winemaker

Brian Croser was chief white winemaker at Hardy's after returning from studying Oenology at Davis in California. He left that company to initiate the wine courses at the Riverina College, until he found the success of these was forcing him up the administrative ladder to a nonoperational level. He left to set up the Oenotic consultancy with Dr Tony Jordan, and to create his own Petaluma label and winery.

Range of Wines

Petaluma Cabernet Sauvignon
Petaluma Chardonnay
Petaluma Rhine Riesling

Style

Petaluma Chardonnay

It is indicative of the character of the man that the only person I know of who is not satisfied with the quality of the three Petaluma Chardonnays released to date is Brian Croser. Perhaps the 1979 version is not as forthcoming as might be hoped, but the gentle but complex charm and grace of the 1977 and the full-frontal voluptuousness of the 1978 are delightful. But he is much happier with the next two years (yet to be released), because the cooler climate Coonawarra fruit from which they are made enable him more closely to approximate his ideal Chardonnay than did the Cowra fruit of the first three wines. Ultimately (perhaps in both senses of the word) we will be seeing the Piccadilly grown Petaluma Chardonnay.
Best years: 1977, 1978, 1980

Petaluma Rhine Riesling

Here too, there have been different wines. The first of the series, the 1976 from Nagambie fruit, was more a feat of virtuoso winemaking than a great wine (fermented for half a year to produce an almost literally breathtaking intensity of bouquet and flavour). Since then the Clare grown Rhine Riesling has been more sensitively wrought into wine of far greater complexity and subtlety: more like string quartets than the brass band of the 1976.
Best years: 1980, 1982

Ownership

Petaluma's name and the land at Piccadilly are owned by Brian Croser. The winery is jointly owned by Brian, Len Evans and Denis Horgan.

Production

9000 cases of Cabernet Sauvignon, 8000 of Rhine Riesling, and 4000 of Chardonnay.

New Plantings

(Not yet yielding.) The six hectares of Chardonnay at Piccadilly are approaching their first crop.

Market

Specialist retailers and good restaurants, Sydney being particularly well served (a Melburnian, I write with some bitterness).

Winery Visiting Details

None, except by invitation. Telephone (08) 339 4403.

PETALUMA

1981 RHINE RIESLING

750ml

PRODUCE OF AUSTRALIA BOTTLED AT PICCADILLY SA

PETALUMA

1979 CHARDONNAY

735ml

PRODUCE OF AUSTRALIA BOTTLED AT PICCADILLY SA

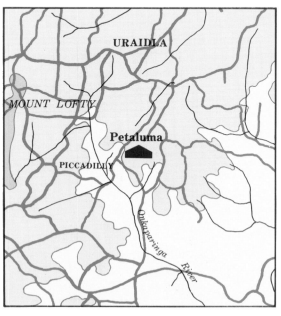

PIPERS BROOK

Andrew Pirie (Master of Agricultural Science, Doctor of Philosophy, Winelover), spent twelve months in France, during which time he decided to establish his own vineyard. A common enough story you might well say, but Andrew did not return to Australia to buy some land in the Barossa Valley or Hunter Valley and plant it out with our traditional 'wine farming' vineyard layout. Rather did he seek out a cool climate site (the other day I heard someone refer to the Goulburn Valley as 'cool climate'; an arbitrary shift of meaning which would make Pipers Brook antarctic by comparison) and plant it with Rhine Riesling, Chardonnay, Traminer, Pinot Noir and Cabernet Sauvignon on the European close-spacing system.

Andrew made an exhaustive study of wine-quality factors and applied these to climatic conditions; not just the obvious ones of temperature and rainfall; not even just the less ob-

vious ones of length of ripening day and mean January temperatures; but down to (and with particular emphasis on) evapotranspiration, the degree to which moisture is lost as vapour through the vines' leaves. This was not, as it may first sound, over-application of theory, but on the contrary an extreme respect for empiricism in trying to identify and recreate the important quality factors affecting the great wines of Europe.

The quality of the wines to date from Pipers Brook would suggest that we should be extremely grateful that Andrew Pirie followed through his research, formulated his convictions and then put them into operation, rather than taking his racehorse to a panel of advisors to have some humps sewn on.

All in all, Tasmania is becoming a depressing prospect for mainland winemakers.

Winemaker

Andrew Pirie's academic qualifications as already mentioned are in Agricultural Science with his Ph.D. being in vine physiology specializing in regulation of pigment formation in red grapes. His year in Europe was spent with Avery's of Bristol, Hugel (Alsace) Remoissenet (Bourgogne) and Siche (Bordeaux). He was also twelve months with the Riverina College as Wine Projects Officer. Since 1980 he has been the full-time manager and winemaker at Pipers Brook.

122

Range of Wines

Pipers Brook Cabernet Sauvignon
Pipers Brook Chardonnay
Pipers Brook Pinot Noir
Pipers Brook Rhine Riesling
Pipers Brook Traminer

Style

Pipers Brook Cabernet Sauvignon

Only one vintage of this has been made at the time of writing, and that is still in wood, so all I can do here is describe the infant in its cradle. It is of extreme beauty and nobility; all the classic young Cabernet hallmarks are present as might be expected, but together with a grace, strength and beauty which no-one could have the right to expect. The infant might one day grow up to be prime minister.
Best year: 1981 (see above)

Pipers Brook Pinot Noir

Another wine with only one vintage under its belt, but for all its eloquently convincing Burgundian fidelity, the 1981 lacks the length of finish to impress as much as the unbelievable Cabernet. For all that, with just one year, Pipers Brook Pinot Noir goes straight to the top rank of this style in Australia.
Best year: 1981 (see above)

Pipers Brook Rhine Riesling

This is a magnificent wine and is at the very forefront of Australian Rhine Rieslings. The unobservant could easily be misled by the wine's great delicacy and gentleness into regarding it as merely straightforward and attractive. By so doing, they would be missing a whole world of subtlety and power hiding in the depths of its glorious nose and palate.
Best year: 1980

Ownership

The project is owned by Pipers Brook Vineyard Pty Ltd, in which Andrew Pirie is the largest of seventeen shareholders.

Production

The maximum will be 800 cases of each of the five varieties.

New Plantings

(Not yet yielding.) A quarter of a hectare of Pinot Noir has yet to come to bear.

Market

Quite unfairly (I write as a Victorian), New South Wales receives 50 per cent of the production, with Victoria and Tasmania having about 25 per cent each, all by mailing list.

PRODUCED BY THE PIRIE FAMILY AT PIPERS BROOK

PIPERS BROOK VINEYARD

1979 RHINE RIESLING

Tasmania

Winery Visiting Details

By appointment only. The address is Pipers Brook, 7254 Telephone (003) 82 7197.

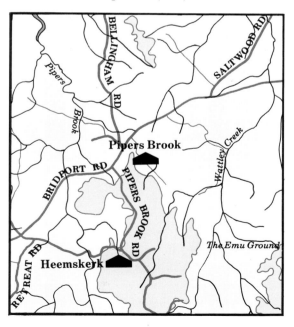

PIRRAMIMMA

Pirramimma is a long established (1900) family-owned winemaking company whose individual profile emerged discernibly only in 1966. Until that year most of their wine (indeed until 1946 all of their wine) was sold to W.A. Gilbey Ltd. of London, and goodness knows what label its bottles ultimately wore.

But in 1966 Pirramimma wines were granted their own livery, and to the consumer it seemed that an instant producer had been spontaneously created. Not so.

Attractive presentation, combined with consistently reliable quality meant the fairly rapid generation of a loyal following both in cellar door visitors and customers of specialist merchants in Melbourne and Sydney. All this happened with what can only be called the barest minimum of advertising and promotion. Indeed if there was any of such, I missed it.

In a way, the changes to Pirramimma being wrought for the last two or three years are even more significant than the dramatic upheaval of 1966, in that they augur a very substantial improvement in quality. Let me quote from som information supplied to me by this company headed General Winemaking Philosophy 'Wine quality is directly related to fruit qualit — where the grapes are grown, how they ar grown and, particularly, when they are picked Therefore fruit flavour is the major picking cri terion, and thereafter modern winemakin, techniques protect that flavour. To this end th company has embarked on a programme of in stalling modern winemaking equipment.' N one could fail to be impressed with the serious ness and sincerity of this statement (the firs part of which reads like a Brian Croser mani festo).

The results of this programme are already be ginning to emerge, but it seems probable tha however impressed we may be with aspects o the last couple of Pirramimma vintages, we'v not seen anything yet. Cambrai, Fern Hill an now Pirramimma — what a splendid an unlooked-for quality development for the area

Winemaker

Geoff Johnston, third generation of the family is the winemaker. Geoff was a student in the inaugural course initiated by Brian Croser a the Riverina College in 1976. After two and half years full-time, he completed the course b correspondence and graduated in 1982.

Range of Wines

Pirramimma Cabernet Sauvignon
Pirramimma Liqueur Port
Pirramimma Maceration Carbonique Shiraz
Pirramimma Mataro
Pirramimma Palomino
Pirramimma Rhine Riesling
Pirramimma Shiraz
Pirramimma Tawny Port
Pirramimma Vintage Port

Style

Note: Because of the changes to the winemaking referred to before, I will describe the style as evinced by the 1980 and 1981 wines only.

Pirramimma Cabernet Sauvignon

It is hard to comprehend that McLaren Vale Cabernet can be like this. Almost the antithesis of the archetypal 'stewed plum' Cabernets of the area, this is now a wine of extraordinary grace and beauty. The 1980 version — light, fine, crisp, sweetly fragrant and tasting of fresh blackberries — needs only a little more stature to give the country's best Cabernets a run for their money.
Best years: 1980, 1981

Pirramimma Rhine Riesling

The nose is stunning — quite the best Riesling nose I have seen from the area. Initial flavour is both fine and dense, particularly with the 1980, and the wine has an attractive long finish. I am troubled by the apparently heavily adjusted acid however, the strong late impact of which I find unpalatable. But this is carping: the fruit is quite admirable, and I look forward with considerable interest to the 1982.
Best years: 1980, 1981

Ownership

Pirramimma is the label for A. C. Johnston & Co. Pty. Ltd., a family-owned company.

Production

Ignoring wines made from vestigial varieties from another era (Palomino, Pedro, Mataro), about 6300 cases.

New Plantings

(Not yet yielding.) To date 5.6 hectares of Riesling have been grafted to Shiraz wines.

Market

Mostly Adelaide and Sydney, with other cities having the occasional bottle in specialist merchant outlets.

PIRRAMIMMA
VINEYARDS

1980
RHINE RIESLING

Vintaged from McLaren Vale fruit, this wine has been processed to protect and enhance the full varietal character.

MADE & BOTTLED BY
A.C. JOHNSTON PTY. LTD.
JOHNSTON ROAD
McLAREN VALE, STH AUSTRALIA
PRODUCE OF AUSTRALIA 750ml

Winery Visiting Details

Monday to Friday 9 am to 5 pm. Saturday 10 am to 5 pm, Sunday noon to 5 pm. The address is Johnston Road, McLaren Vale, 5171 Telephone (08) 383 8205.

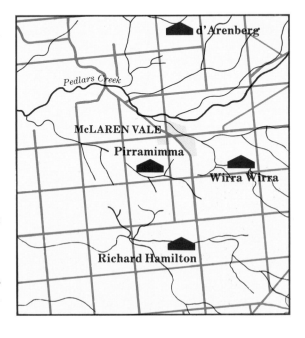

PLANTAGENET WINES Mount Barker, WA

It is intriguing just how many of the last decade's new vineyards were established as diversification from farming interests, particularly in Western Australia. Unlike the other initial reasons for starting a small vineyard which are commonly encountered: hobbyist's whims or enthusiast's dedication, 'diversification' sounds so unromantic. No matter, the wines themselves are all that count, and Plantagenet's contribution to Mount Barker quality has been substantial.

The original intention was merely to grow grapes to sell. Sums hadn't really been done properly, and at less than 5 tonnes per hectare the venture would not have been commercially viable, so a winery was put into operation in 1974, some six years after the establishment of the vineyard. An old apple packing shed was converted for the purpose, and this became the first winery in the Mount Barker district.

The Plantagenet vineyard is of medium size, with some 30 hectares under vine, 5 of which are yet to bear. Varieties yielding at the time of writing are Cabernet Sauvignon, Shiraz and Rhine Riesling: a sound if unimaginative selection. Newer plantings, however, are more interesting: Sauvignon Blanc, a variety which always impresses in the South West; Merlot, to lend complexity and guile to the Cabernet Sauvignon; and of course the current superstar, Chardonnay.

The aim of the partners who own Plantagenet is, unsurprisingly, 'to produce premium table wines using premium varieties'. So is the aim of every other producer in the entire South West, but Plantagenet's additional preoccupation is with Vintage Port — an interesting and potentially significant development for the whole area.

Plantagenet's progression from 'grape farmers' to reluctant winemakers to enthusiastic winemakers to area leaders has been inexorable. They will bear watching in the next few years.

Winemaker

Robert Bowen gained his degree in Wine Science at the Riverina State College in 1978. He has had practical experience with Idyll Vineyard at Geelong as well as working with both Lindemans and Denman Estate. His appointment as winemaker for Plantagenet in time for the 1979 vintage had an immediate influence on the style of the wines, which he is further developing.

Range of Wines

- Plantagenet Cabernet Sauvignon
- Plantagenet Rhine Riesling
- Plantagenet Shiraz
- Plantagenet Vintage Port

Style

Plantagenet Cabernet Sauvignon

Just as Plantagenet has progressed and developed as referred to above, so has their Cabernet Sauvignon. Earlier styles have erred on the side of lack of clarity and finesse, but the latest versions are showing none of such faults. The quality of the fruit flavour is particularly attractive, as is the increasingly distinguished nose. *Best years: 1980, 1981*

Plantagenet Rhine Riesling

The flagship wine of the Plantagenet vineyard, at least in terms of quantity, and perhaps even in quality. Sweet, pretty fruit whose shyness belies an innate understated power and depth. The wine lives well and develops slowly. *Best years: 1979, 1980*

Plantagenet Shiraz

Perhaps even more than the Cabernet Sauvignon, this is a swiftly evolving style, the last three years having lightened and fined down considerably, to the wine's greater benefit. This is quite a complex Shiraz, and reasonably elegant — improbably so considering the slightly jammy versions of a few years ago. *Best years: 1980, 1981*

Ownership

Plantagenet is a partnership between three families: those of A. F. Smith and R. W. Devenish (both local), and of M. Meredith-Hardy of England.

Production

Currently about 4300 cases, being Rhine Riesling 2000, and the balance equally Cabernet Sauvignon, Shiraz and Port.

New Plantings

(Not yet yielding.) 2.5 hectares of Chardonnay, 1.2 of Sauvignon Blanc and a small amount of Merlot are yet to bear.

Market

Intriguingly, 40 per cent goes to Sydney, with 15 per cent each to Melbourne and Perth, the balance being cellar door.

Winery Visiting Details

Monday to Satuday 9 am to 5 pm. The address is Mount Barker, 6324 Telephone (098) 57 1150.

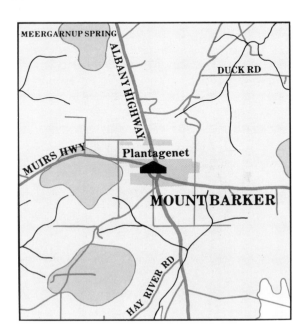

PRINCE ALBERT

Bruce Hyett planted his vines in 1975 on a site which had previously been planted one hundred and twenty years earlier. At 2 hectares it is just a little bigger than Romanee Conti, a fact which must be heartening for Bruce, who doubtless wishes the smaller French venture well.

Determined to plant only one variety, he read, talked and pondered for a year before deciding to establish Pinot Noir, as 'the soil type looked just like the colour photographs of Burgundy with rich red clay with marl showing on the surface'. At first thought this may seem a delightfully inconsequential reason for such a decision, but climatically and microclimatically there was no good reason why the variety should not do well, and Bruce obviously was wary of making the mistake of 'throwing out the baby with the bathwater' (a common enough error in these days of the new technological pedantry). The vineyard is directly between the two Geelong cement works, which fact may be significant if one is to make a virtue of necessity.

I cannot resist quoting some of the background information which Bruce supplied: 'Careful planning of initial and maximum requirements plotted the way for the winery and storage, which always looked to be some distant goal, but which arrived at lightning speed to the total dismay of the erstwhile benign bank manager. Fortunately the excellent Government publication on the cost of establishing a vineyard had not yet been published.

'The next fifty years are likely to be the worst while we investigate a few of the possible combinations of vineyard and winery practices in search of the ultimate Pinot Noir.'

An honest, good-humoured, but deadly serious quest would seem to be afoot. May resounding success attend these efforts.

Winemaker

Bruce Hyett describes himself as an enthusiastic amateur. He reads every viticultural and oenological tome he can get his hands on, and absorbs much from conversation with other winemakers. He was fortunate in being the recipient of unstinting help from Stuart Anderson, under whom he worked for two vintages at Balgownie. With candour which can only be described as unprecedented, he claims to be 'urgently in need of further training and experience in France'.

PRINCE ALBERT

PINOT NOIR

1978

PRINCE ALBERT VINEYARD
1857—1885   RE-ESTABLISHED 1975

2 HECTARES OF PINOT NOIR PLANTED IN
RED SOIL ON A NORTH FACING LIMESTONE
SLOPE OVERLOOKING THE WAURN PONDS
VALLEY NEAR GEELONG VICTORIA

PRODUCE OF AUSTRALIA
750 ML

Range of Wines

Prince Albert Pinot Noir

Style

Prince Albert Pinot Noir

This wine is in the process of developing a style. Bruce Hyett would be the last person in the world to suggest that the wines to date are anything but naive and experimental. He would also be too modest to point out that the quality of the fruit is unexcelled in this country. So far they have been pretty but very straightforward wines, particularly on the palate, where the abruptness of the finish is almost startling. The bouquet has more components; with hints of coffee, burnt toast and earth among the more expected strawberry overtones. It seems inexorable that in the fullness of time Prince Albert will produce some of our greatest Burgundies. In the meantime these Pinot Noirs make charming and attractive drinking.

Best years: 1978, 1981

Ownership

Entirely owned by Bruce and Sue Hyett and Neil Everist.

Production

A mere 800 odd cases is all that can be made.

New Plantings

Nil.

Market

Almost all by mailing list, Victoria receiving the lion's share, and New South Wales about 30 per cent.

Winery Visiting Details

By appointment only. The address is Lemins Road, Waurn Ponds, 3221 Telephone (052) 43 5091.

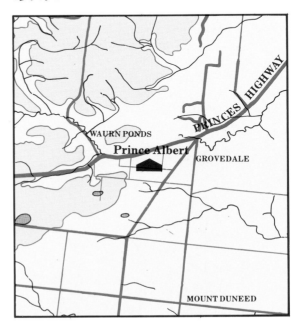

Some people love red wine. Neill and Sally Robb are two such, so they did something about it. And in a most unusual way: the seventies decade saw a lot of small plantings of premium grape varieties in very good areas as many wine lovers decided to become closely involved with winemaking and grape growing. Some of these are now household names to lovers of boutique wines. Others developed and cherished their small vineyards, but did not progress to the stage of building wineries and acquiring the necessary oenological expertise to turn their grapes into wine.

Were it not for the Redbank operation, these grapes would be lost as anonymous ingredients in big company blends: unwept, unhonoured and unsung. Redbank buy their grapes and make individual small parcels of wine from them, giving adequate attribution to each grower (exactly as is the case with Ed Joualt's 'Allandale' in the Hunter Valley). The only stipulation Neill makes is that the viticultural practices are to his perfectionist satisfaction. He has a horror of irrigation with which many would disagree — mostly those, coincidentally, who irrigate.

On their own vineyard, identified on labels as 'Sally's Paddock', the vines were not even irrigated when first planted, thus maximizing root development and consequent fruit complexity, but at the expense of yield. The vineyard is planted to Cabernet Sauvignon, Merlot and Pinot Noir.

The winery was specifically designed to be able to cope with small quantity batch processing using techniques which neatly combine Californian technology with European tradition. Cap plunging is carried out by hand; pressing is in hand-operated cage presses; fermentation is open; and there is no temperature control necessary, the ambient temperatures during vintage — usually April — being so low that it is occasionally difficult to initiate fermentation, and small batches generate little heat.

Winemaker

Incredibly, Neill Robb has no formal qualifications in oenology. On the other hand, his practical experience is formidable: a year with Berri co-operative, another with Hardy's, and four years with Chateau Remy. All this came about through an active disinclination to remain a Clerk of Courts or a cog in the Ampol wheel: two of his past areas of endeavour wherein he felt unfulfilled. For this latter fact, let us all give thanks.

Range of Wines

Redbank Carisbrook Cabernet Sauvignon
Redbank Carisbrook Shiraz
Redbank Marong Shiraz
Redbank Marong Vintage Port
Redbank Maryborough Balzac
Redbank Mountain Creek Cabernet Sauvignon
Redbank Mountain Creek Shiraz
Redbank Mugana
Redbank Myers Flat Cabernet Sauvignon
Redbank Sally's Paddock
Redbank Sulky Cabernet Sauvignon
Redbank Sulky Pinot Meunier

Style

Redbank Sally's Paddock

I have selected this wine to describe rather than any of Neill Robb's other labels because I feel that it is both most typical of the Redbank paradigm, and also one of the best series of wines produced by him to date. Neill's feeling for wine is remarkable, and he is achieving spectacular results, albeit idiosyncratic, with the Redbank releases. Redbank reds, I should here observe, have that rare ability (shared by Bordeaux first-growths) to look young, lusty and purple even after some five years in the bottle, and while the Sally's Paddock wines are not of such an age, they too have the tight vinosity to achieve such promise of slow aging. The bouquet is both intense and austere, and so is the fruit quality as perceived in the mouth: dense, tannic (with grape tannin) and brightly acid. To look at the young wine is to peer through a keyhole, as the wine's promise is without limit, and a cursory inspection is misleadingly unyielding. Potentially a great wine.
Best years: 1980, 1981, 1982

Ownership

Entirely owned by Neill and Sally Robb.

Production

Currently the winery is producing about 1000 cases per year, operating at half capacity due to the limited availability of high enough quality grapes for Neill's purist standards.

New Plantings

(Not yet yielding.) 'Sally's Paddock' is being increased by one hectare of Cabernet Sauvignon.

Market

Most sales are by mailing list, and most are, surprisingly, to Sydney. Good specialist retailers have limited allocation.

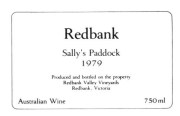

Winery Visiting Details

The winery is open 9 am to 6 pm Monday to Saturday, noon to 5 pm Sundays. The address is Redbank, near Avoca, 3467 Telephone (054) 67 7255.

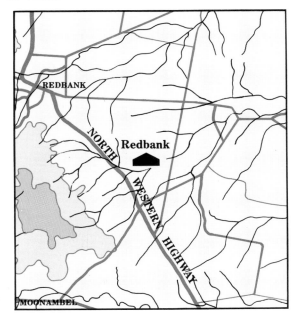

REDMAN

As we know it, Redmans came into being in 1965, when Owen and Edna Redman sold their Rouge Homme vineyard and winery to Lindemans, and promptly purchased another vineyard, previously owned by Arthur Hoffman. The new vineyard was well tended, and planted entirely to Shiraz, so there was no impediment to the creation of the new 'Redman' label and release of the 1966 vintage.

Coonawarra was supreme in the mid-1960s of Australian viticulture, and the new wine was of a quality not merely to support, but to justify this Terra Rossa adulation. Redmans flourished. Appointing a distribution house with access to national outlets, the Redman reputation quickly outgrew their production capacity, and the resultant dearth of their wine completed the job of creating an instant reputation and desirability. All this with just one wine.

In 1970, the Redman list of products doubled to two. Cabernet Sauvignon, planted by virtue of Owen Redman's quietly faultless foresight, had come on stream. It was Owen who decided to bottle the Cabernet in magnums only, a decision which puzzled many, but added greatly to what was fast becoming the Redman mystique. The release some years later of the same wine in Imperials was, I think, a false step, as the wine was too important a jewel in Australia's vinous crown to be wasted on such an arrantly publicist impracticality (how many dinner parties do you give for 50 people?).

Redmans, in a mere fifteen years, has become an essential aspect of Australia's wine. It is a comforting thought for self-interested consumers like me that a trio of wine-interested, oenologically competent sons, Bruce, Owen and Malcolm, appear to assure us of the continued existence of Coonawarra's leading vineyard, and its produce.

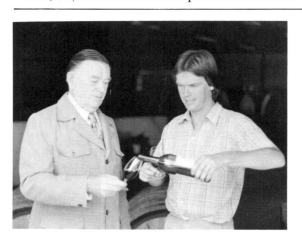

Winemaker

Owen Redman has made all of the wines to date, but son Bruce has a rapidly increasing influence on vinicultural decisions, albeit with his father's guidance. Bruce is a graduate in Oenology from Roseworthy, and worked for two vintages with Reynella (1976 and 1978) as well as spending the 1977 vintage at Swan Hill. 1979 saw him at Krondorf, and 1980 at Chateau Beau Site in Saint Estephe. He has also travelled widely through the winegrowing districts of France and Germany before returning to take over as winemaker for the family concern.

Range of Wines

Redman Cabernet Sauvignon
Redman Claret

Style

Redman Cabernet Sauvignon

This is a very fine wine. Dark, tight and intense, the wine has a delightful soft power in the bouquet and considerable depth of flavour components. Like a Victorian bordello, it is rich, lusty, velvety and expensive, and caters to an exclusive and appreciative clientele.
Best years: 1972, 1976, 1979, 1981

Redman Claret

One of this country's famous labels, and one we are all proud to serve to bibulous overseas visitors. Only in Coonawarra can Shiraz make a Bordelaise style wine, and nowhere better than Redmans who annually are able to produce a soft but tightly balanced wine, with sweet fruit and a long finish, and which ages with grace in the medium to long term.
Best years: 1966, 1970, 1976, 1981

Ownership

A family-owned company, the principles being Owen and Edna Redman.

Production

Average is 25 000 cases, being 17 500 cases of 'Claret' (Shiraz) and 7500 cases of Cabernet Sauvignon. (A 'case' of magnums contains six double size bottles.)

New Plantings

Nil.

Market

This information has been withheld, goodness knows why.

Winery Visiting Details

The winery is open from 9.00 am to 5.00 pm from Monday to Saturday. Sundays are by appointment only. The address is just Coonawarra, South Australia, 5263 Telephone (087) 36 3331.

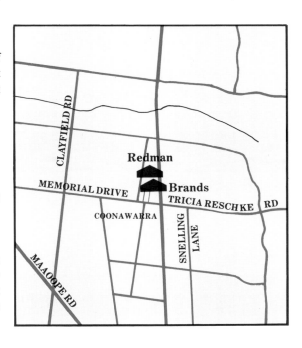

133

RICHARD HAMILTON

To be a member of the Hamilton family is to be conscious of a vinicultural heritage stretching back nearly one and a half centuries. And, as we have all seen so often, to be a doctor of medicine drastically increases the probability of becoming infected with the winemaking urge. To be both a Hamilton and a doctor renders the outcome inevitable. Undoubtedly, Richard succumbed to this urge much earlier in his life than is the case with most vinous medicos, and 1972 saw him commencing his plantings at, or rather near, Willunga, just down the road from McLaren Vale.

The land he chose is slate and gravel over a deep drained limestone base. Climatically quite mild and maritime, the vines enjoying much the same sort of untroubled circumstances as those of Pirramimma and Wirra Wirra at little distance north, Richard Hamilton's vineyard presents very few unlooked-for viticultural problems. Plantings now comprise 17 hectares Rhine Riesling 6.5, Cabernet Sauvignon 3.7 Chardonnay 3.2 and 1.2 hectares each of Traminer, Chenin Blanc and Muscat of Alexandria.

Richard has always been particularly interested in white wines, and both his vineyard plantings and his winemaking reflect this. His especial predilection is wood-aging of whites, and one can readily imagine that this must have generated some bewilderment amongst the McLaren Vale winemaking fraternity a decade ago.

It would be unjust if any summary of the Richard Hamilton winery story — however brief — did not pay due attention to the immensely important role played by Richard's father Burt. Burton Hamilton has been Richard's mentor, exemplar, consultant, manager and amanuensis, but would describe himself as being merely an assistant. His career in wine has been notably distinguished, but he is publicity shy in an industry remarkable for its tumid egos. Now aged 78, he still fulfils all of the functions mentioned above, and in the words of his son: 'his background experience judgment and attention to detail have been indispensable to the quality and reputation of Richard Hamilton wine'. (I'm sorry, Burt, but no one can avoid publicity forever.)

Winemaker

Dr Richard Hamilton is now the winemaker for both his Willunga vineyard and the newly acquired Leconfield. His interest is wine and his training is medicine — a marriage which is apparently not just made in Heaven, but massproduced there. He is one of many who have found the disciplines of medical science of immense benefit in winemaking endeavours.

Range of Wines

Richard Hamilton Auslese Riesling
Richard Hamilton Cabernet Sauvignon
Richard Hamilton Chardonnay
Richard Hamilton Chenin Blanc
Richard Hamilton Egremont Muscat of
   Alexandria
Richard Hamilton Rhine Riesling
Richard Hamilton Egremont Vintage Port
Richard Hamilton White Burgundy

Style

Richard Hamilton Auslese Riesling

I am sure that Richard enjoys making this wine, offering as it does the opportunity to exercise his 'white wine in oak' preference to the full. The fruit is very late-picked Rhine Riesling with a little equally late Semillon. Fermentation itself is in hogsheads, and the wine is then given 12 months oak maturation before bottling. Obviously the style is deep, honeyed and softly full, but less expectable is the finesse which offsets the lusciousness. A wine for substantial aging, and incidentally a style which is, very sensibly, available in half bottles.
Best years: 1977, 1979

Richard Hamilton Chenin Blanc

This is a variety which in Australia has been treated as a White Burgundy workhorse particularly in the Swan Valley, where most of the plantings are. Richard Hamilton is much more interested in the recreating for it the role it plays in the Loire Valley, where it stands very little less tall than Sauvignon Blanc. Again it generously repays wood-aging, as Peel Estate in the West and Chappellet in the Napa Valley have discovered so successfully. Rich and fine, with intense varietal undertones, this is a unique wine for the area.
Best year: 1981

Ownership

Owned by Dr Richard Hamilton and his wife Jette.

Production

About 5600 cases a year: Rhine Riesling 1600, Chardonnay 1500, Chenin Blanc 1000, Cabernet Sauvignon and Sauternes 500 each, and Port and Muscat 250 cases each.

New Plantings

(Not yet yielding.) Nil.

Market

Cellar door, mailing list and retail outlets, but for wines like the Chenin Blanc or the Auslese Riesling it is wisest to write to the winery.

Winery Visiting Details

Monday to Saturday 10 am to 5.30 pm. Sunday noon to 5 pm. The postal address is PO Box 117, Willunga, 5172 Telephone (085) 56 2288.

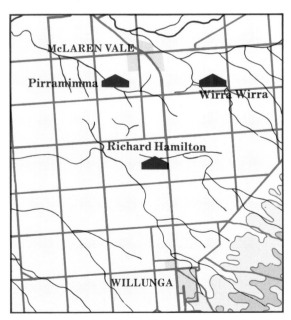

ROBINSONS FAMILY VINEYARDS   Ballandean, Qld

The idea of growing grapes and making wine was kindled for John Robinson by his marriage to Heather Salter, whose grandfather was the proprietor of Saltrams at Angaston in the Barossa Valley.

John, who lived for a time at Lyon in France — close to the vineyards of Burgundy and Beaujolais — looked around Toowoomba and Southern Queensland for suitable land on which to plant vines and settled on Lyra, Ballandean, which is just off the New England highway and only 10 km north of the Queensland/New South Wales border.

As his wife and family helped initially with the planting of the vines he decided to incorporate the word 'Family' into the label and name.

The granite soil and comparatively temperate ripening conditions at Lyra have proved ideal for the growing of Chardonnay and Cabernet Sauvignon. Amateur climatologists may be surprised to learn that Ballandean is classifiable as only 'warm', being some 3 degrees cooler in Mean January temperature than Cessnock.

In the modern winery complex (completed in 1979) John refrigerates his grapes before crushing as he regards this as an essential requisite in the making of quality wines. For the 1982 vintage he has a small but efficient filtration and bottling plant.

There are 10.5 hectares in production, 5 of which are Cabernet Sauvignon, 3.5 being Chardonnay, with the balance made up of Pinot Noir, Traminer, Shiraz and Rhine Riesling. Very little Shiraz was planted as he worked on the principle that local growers would plant the variety. This proved to be the case.

Winemaker
John Robinson is a solicitor by profession. He studied under Brian Croser at Riverina College of Advanced Education doing the Wine Science course. Prior to this he spent one of the vintages with Dr Max Lake in the Hunter. In 1975 he visited the Wine Research Institutes at Beaune and Bordeaux in France.

Range of Wines

Robinsons The Family Cabernet Sauvignon
Robinsons The Family Chardonnay
Robinsons The Family Pinot Noir
Robinsons The Family Shiraz Cabernet
Robinsons The Family Shiraz

Style

Robinsons The Family Cabernet Sauvignon

This wine has been a remarkable achievement for a state which had failed markedly to distinguish itself for quality wine production. Fruit, as might be expected, is generous — indeed, almost overwhelmingly so — but without the jammy coarseness which has too often characterized Queensland wines. Sensitive use of oak adds further tightness, and the wines to date promise to live well in the medium term. *Best years: 1979, 1980*

Robinsons The Family Shiraz

Another very big wine with attractive sweet fruit and mitigating oak treatment. Making good dry red wine (particularly Shiraz) in this climate is really an exercise in trying to make an overweight girl look beautiful. It would appear that John Robinson is unusually talented at this, the wine being notably attractive and intense of flavour, but balanced and clean finishing. *Best years: 1979, 1980*

Ownership

Robinsons Family Vineyards is family-owned.

Production

In a normal year production is Cabernet 1500 cases, Chardonnay 1500 cases, Pinot Noir, Traminer and Shiraz between them making up a further 600 cases.

New Plantings

(Not yet yielding.) Chardonnay 2 hectares, Malbec 0.5 hectares, Pinot Noir 1 hectare, Cabernet 0.5 hectare. Additional plantings of Chardonnay may be made from year to year.

Market

Cellar door sales. A mailing list has accounted for the bulk of sales to date, although some orders have been placed by wine merchants and licensed restaurants in Queensland.

Winery Visiting Details

The winery may be visited from 9 am to 5 pm daily including Saturdays and Sunday, excluding Christmas Day and Good Friday. The address is Lyra Church Road, Lyra, Ballandean, 4382 Telephone (076) 84 1216.

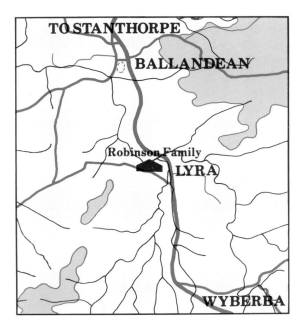

THE ROBSON VINEYARD

Murray Robson, apart from having perhaps the most appalling handwriting in Australia, has one of the most beautiful (and, proportionately one of the most heavily capitalized) vineyards and wineries. His 4 hectares of vines were planted on the 8 hectare property commencing in 1971, and the 'vineyard in miniature' now comprises 1.4 hectares of Chardonnay, 1.2 of Cabernet Sauvignon, .4 each of Traminer and Merlot, and .2 each of Malbec, Pinot Noir and Sauvignon Blanc.

Clearly, the winery has been designed and constructed to deal with the specialized requirements of very small parcels of individual wines. Murray feels very strongly about not seeing himself as a hobbyist, and quite reasonably points out that he, as proprietor, works full-time. In fact the business somehow supports a full-time staff of five, not including the dog Vertsy, who joined the company in 1979 in the capacity of Director of Security.

The wines are what Murray describes as 'ex-pensive' (at an average of $6.50 per bottle I do not believe this is the case) and he says they will become more so. Anyone who cares to investigate the economics of small-parcel quality winemaking could hardly object to either the prices or the likelihood of an imminent increase in same.

A delightful feature of the Robson vineyard from a winery visiting or tourist standpoint is 'Squire Cottage' — a charming double-storey cottage standing in a copse of trees in the middle of the vines overlooking the tiny valley of Mount View. Those with the forethought to book the cottage at least three months ahead (or the good fortune to fluke a cancellation) can stay in this attractive base while they raid the area's wineries.

Murray, whose bank manager I should like to meet, is building a refrigerated cool room to store customers' wines, and to establish a base of longer cellared Robson wines with a view to releasing them at optimum age.

Winemaker

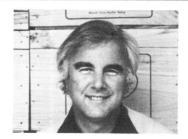

Murray Robson is the winemaker, and describes his qualifications far more trenchantly than could I: 'Trial, error, persistence, hope, luck, reading, Riverina College seminars and, above all, help and advice from others in the wine industry'. He adds 'and our own experimentation'. Fair enough.

Range of Wines

The Robson Vineyard Cabernet/Merlot
The Robson Vineyard Cabernet Sauvignon
The Robson Vineyard Chardonnay
The Robson Vineyard Hermitage
The Robson Vineyard Late Harvest Semillon
The Robson Vineyard Malbec
The Robson Vineyard Pinot Noir
The Robson Vineyard Semillon
The Robson Vineyard Traminer
The Robson Vineyard Vintage Muscat

Style

The Robson Vineyard Cabernet Merlot

Murray Robson is making some of the most immaculately clean wines in the country, and his Cabernet Merlot is illustrative of this. The young wines are like purple rubies in their brilliant translucency, and the nose is as faithful to the varieties as one could want. Unfortunately the quantities available are ridiculously small, so not many have the opportunity to taste one of Australia's best reds.
Best years: 1979, 1980

The Robson Vineyard Chardonnay

This is a beautiful Chardonnay, very much in the Australian style, but aristocratic withal. Gentle, delicate and indeed, almost fragile in its lissom elegance, its oak character can over-whelm the unemphatic fruit when young, but age brings integration, and integration brings depth.
Best years: 1979, 1980

The Robson Vineyard Hermitage

Perhaps Murray's best wine: a veritable *tour de force* of virtuoso Pokolbin Shiraz treatment. Clean, limpid, emphatic and elegant, the wine has superb balance, great grace and a notably long finish. An adornment to the Hunter Valley.
Best years: 1979, 1980

Ownership

Entirely owned by Murray Robson.

Production

Maximum for a good year is 5000 cases, being Chardonnay 500, Traminer 200, Cabernet Sauvignon 500, Pinot Noir 100, Malbec 50, Cabernet/Merlot 200, Cabernet Port 100, Semillon 1500, Late Harvest Semillon 150, Hermitage 1500, Vintage Muscat 200.

New Plantings

(Not yet yielding.) None envisaged.

Market

About 95 per cent cellar door and mailing list, the remaining 5 per cent reserved for a handful of specialist retailers and a few restaurants, mostly in Sydney.

Winery Visiting Details

Monday to Saturday 9 am to 5 pm, Sunday noon to 5 pm. The address is Mount View Road, Mount View, 2325 Telephone (049) 90 3670.

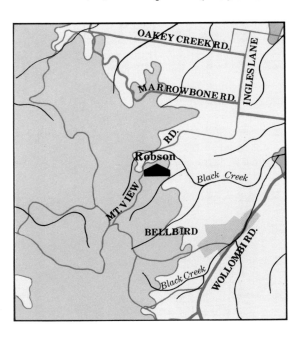

ST. HUBERTS

It is not easy for us to comprehend that the very specific surge of interest in fine, cool climate, expensive wine which is now bringing the Yarra Valley into a position of prominence, and even pre-eminence, had its antithesis at about the turn of the century, to the extent that the area withered as a vignoble. Even St. Huberts (Mark One), covered in glory in the latter part of last century, ceded to economic pressures as the Barossa and Rutherglen areas became paramount, the latter wines' richness, softness and inexpensiveness being more to the public taste.

St. Huberts (Mark Two) shows how far the wheel has turned. That a young operation like this can charge $17 per bottle for their Cabernet Sauvignon, whether or not they incur as a result a raised eyebrow or two from the other makers, is an indication of the consumer's changed attitude.

The vineyard was established, or re-established if you like, in 1968, and now comprises 16 hectares: Cabernet 4, Shiraz 3, Rhine Riesling 3, Pinot Noir 2.5, Chardonnay 2.5, and

for no good reason one hectare of Trebbiano

The winery is spacious, very well-equipped and unattractive, being of the 'Chateau Lysaght' genus, a circumstance imposed by economic necessity. Maturation is in small wood, both American and French oak being used. Not everything in the St. Huberts garden is rosy but they have always been exemplary in their winery hygiene, and one is most unlikely to encounter an unsound St. Huberts wine. Similarly the quality of the fruit in all their wines has been convincing and expressive of emphatic varietal style.

St. Huberts have shown considerable courage and individualism in establishing their image and their marketing strategies. One must return again to that $17 Cabernet for example both courage and individualism are amply demonstrated here. And it can be asked: is this wine too expensive, or are other cool climate Cabernets too cheap? Certainly I feel that the latter is true, and if $17 were too expensive the public wouldn't buy the wine. They do.

Winemaker

Peter Connolly is the chief winemaker for St Huberts, assisted by Alex White (who also has his own small vineyard not far away). Peter's particular interest is in the creation and establishment of styles which are both robust and elegant, and his winemaking reflects this admirable preoccupation.

Range of Wines

St. Huberts Cabernet Sauvignon
St. Huberts Chardonnay (not yet released)
St. Huberts Rhine Riesling
St. Huberts Shiraz
St. Huberts Trebbiano

Style

St. Huberts Cabernet Sauvignon

All right then, what does one get for $17? The Cabernet is opulently coloured and moderately clear to the eye; its nose is both deep and subtle with slight but attractive cedar undertones; and the palate is poised and elegant and hints at mint, crushed grass and spice. The wine is admirably long-finishing. So much for the general profile, but vintage variations are substantial, not so much in terms of quality but of style. My personal favourite is still the 1976, but the last couple of vintages may well rival the former. Certainly one of Australia's top wines.
Best years: 1976, 1979, 1980

St. Huberts Rhine Riesling

Rather embarrassingly, St. Huberts are in acute danger of surpassing their notorious, if excellent, Cabernet with the quality of their Rhine Riesling. Still a comparatively experimental wine, the style is consequently variable, but at best it is overwhelming, particularly in the late harvest version: an intense but beautifully proportioned and tightly knit wine whose citrus and passionfruit nuances are deepened by a touch of botrytis. A remarkable wine, but still to be developed as a style.
Best years: 1980, 1981.

St. Huberts Shiraz

A lovely Yarra Valley 'Claret Shiraz', as are so many of the district's wines from this variety. The much lower price than that of the Cabernet is certainly not reflected in the wine's quality, elegance, longevity or style. Entirely to be recommended.
Best years: 1976, 1979, 1980

Ownership

The principals are coy about the company structure, and as I am a wine writer and not an investigative journalist, I left it at that.

Production

About 6000 cases, roughly two-thirds of which is made up of equal quantities of the two reds.

New Plantings

(Not yet yielding.) Nil, the Chardonnay and Pinot Noir are only now beginning to yield.

Market

The lion's share is cellar door and mailing list, with most Melbourne and only two Sydney specialist merchants carrying stock. Currently 10 per cent is exported.

Winery Visiting Details

Weekends only: Saturday 10 am to 5 pm, Sunday noon to 5 pm. The address is Maroondah Highway, Coldstream, 3770 Telephone (03) 739 1421.

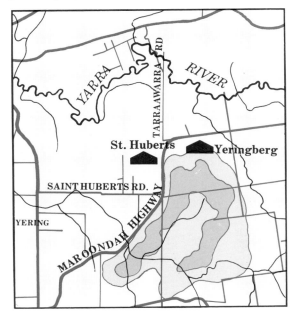

141

SEVILLE ESTATE Seville, Vic.

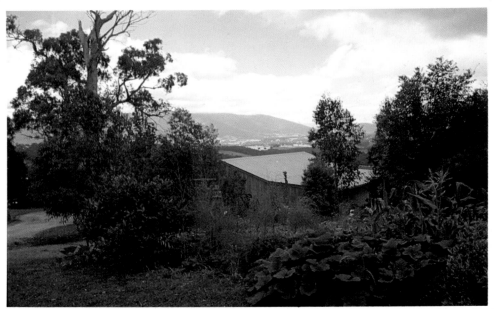

Let me quote in its entirety Peter McMahon's fascinating response to my request for background information about his vineyard:

'The son of a Lilydale medical practitioner I have spent my whole life in the Yarra Valley and grew up with its history and beauty around me.

'About 1962 I discovered a small vineyard on red soil, at Wandin North. It was owned by a Swiss Italian migrant with a wonderful sense of humour. He influenced me to plant a few vines at our home in Lilydale advising me to leave three buds per rootling when planting, two for cane and one for the Rechabite Rabbit. My first efforts at wine making were in 1964.

'By 1970 after twenty years in general practice Margaret and I decided that our future was in viticulture. Our purchase of land at Seville was dictated more by the beauty of the position than by its suitability as a vineyard. However, the necessary north eastern aspect was there, as was soil of great fertility, not necessarily a good thing!'

What Peter is too modest to emphasize in the above is that his love affair with Rhine Riesling has now reached epic, Wagnerian proportions, and has devolved in a winestyle which is unique in the southern hemisphere (his Trockenbeerenauslese and its attendant Beerenauslese). But more of this later.

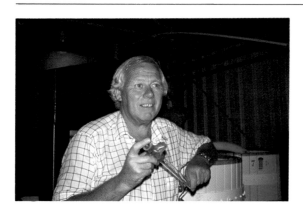

Winemaker

With Seville Estate, yet again (for perhaps the fortieth time in the history of Australian wine) we have a doctor as owner/winemaker. Peter McMahon, in common with many of his kith, has found his medical training to be of immense advantage in making wine, because, as he says, a basic knowledge of chemistry, biochemistry and microbiology is common to both disciplines. He also regards as of immense value his pilgrimages to France, Germany and California during the time of their vintage.

Range of Wines

Seville Estate Cabernet Sauvignon
Seville Estate Chardonnay
Seville Estate Pinot Noir
Seville Estate Rieslings (Dry)
Seville Estate Rieslings (Botrytis affected)

Style

Seville Estate Cabernet Sauvignon

Richly powerful and slightly chocolatey dry reds with a curious but attractive sweet vinosity in the bouquet. The fruit quality is quite exemplary although the wines lack that ultimate finesse and elegance which would take them to the very pinnacle of Australian Cabernet quality. For all that these are certainly among our best dry reds.
Best years: 1977, 1979

Seville Estate Chardonnay

A patchy wine, sometimes very good and occasionally less so, but never either superb or poor. In good years the fruit is of great beauty, but without any flinty depths of complexity. A lesser year can produce an almost cheesy palate and straw smell which I find unpalatable.
Best year: 1980

Seville Estate Pinot Noir

One of the prettiest Pinot Noirs one could find in a day's march, even if that march were from Dijon to Chagny. Beautifully coloured, strawberry-smelling and tasting wines of grace and balance, and in my experience of a degree of soundness and health which is sadly rare for this variety in Australia. When one considers the quality of this and also Mount Mary Pinot Noir, the Yarra Valley suggests itself as an ideal area for this grape.
Best years: 1977, 1980

Seville Estate Riesling Trockenbeerenauslese

I select this to review rather than one of the other Rieslings, although it has been made only once, because it most represents the maker's ambitions with this variety and will be made again (conditions permitting). It is both magnificent and unique. Gloriously powerful, deeply golden and slumberously viscous, the wine has a strongly botrytis nose with complex volatile components (not a fault for this style of wine) and a luscious, long finishing palate with substantial residual sugar. To be drunk a long time hence.
Best year: 1980

Ownership

Family-owned Proprietary Limited Company.

Production

About 1000 cases, 75% of which is red.

New Plantings

(Not yet yielding) 0.5 hectares each of Merlot and Chardonnay.

Market

Mailing list takes care of most, with a little reserved for selected merchants and restaurants.

Winery Visiting Details

By appointment only. The address is Linwood Road, Seville, 3139 Telephone (059) 64 4556.

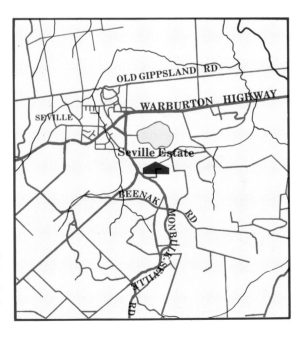

SEYMOUR VINEYARDS

Back in those heady days of 1968, winegrowing beckoned like a siren to many afloat on the sea of business (what a tedious metaphor!) and both takeovers and new vineyard ventures were rife. By the mid seventies those who had smashed themselves on the vinicultural rocks included the Fitzpatrick brothers with their Seymour Vineyards project. Enter Maurice Bourne, whom many at first thought to be merely a company vulture, but whose dedication to the vineyard's salvage has been wholehearted, painstaking and long-lasting.

There are in fact two vineyards: 'Chinaman's Garden' on the Hume Highway at Seymour, and 'Northwood' about 5 kilometres further north on the Goulburn River. Each is of twelve hectares, varieties planted being Rhine Riesling, Traminer, Sylvaner, Semillon and Sauvignon Blanc in Chinaman's Garden, and Cabernet Sauvignon, Shiraz, Grenache, Malbec and Merlot in Northwood.

The years since Maurice acquired the business in 1976 have not been easy for him. Much viticultural tidying up had to be underaken; his talented young winemaker Ian Deacon left in 1979; Maurice found himself struggling a little at first making the wines himself; and now a Californian winemaker arrives annually to lend some much appreciated advice and instruction. Persistence pays, and it is very much to Maurice's credit that dividends in terms of wine quality are beginning to emerge.

It is fashionable nowadays to sneer a little at tourist-trade cellar door sales, but such has probably been largely responsible for the continuing existence of the Seymour Vineyards operation, whose particular advantage it is to have its eye-catching octagonal tasting and sales area right on the Hume Highway and only 100 kilometres north of Mebourne. Also the company's comparative lack of market penetration in terms of distribution outlets to date may well appear with hindsight to be a boom when one considers the past variability of quality. Now that higher standards are being achieved, doubtless greater distribution will be sought.

Winemaker

Maurice Bourne is the winemaker, and is quietly determined to acquire the expertise to meet his very high standards. Not formally trained, he gained considerable experience from Ian Deacon, until he assumed the vinicultural responsibility himself in 1979. He is now assisted by Jim Clendenen who comes across from California each vintage.

Range of Wines

Seymour Vineyards Cabernet/Merlot/Malbec
Seymour Vineyards Cabernet Sauvignon
Seymour Vineyards Gewurztraminer
Seymour Vineyards Grenache
Seymour Vineyards Rhine Riesling
Seymour Vineyards Sauvignon Blanc
Seymour Vineyards Shiraz

Style

Seymour Vineyards Cabernet/Merlot/Malbec

These three varieties always opt for a *menage a trois* with unseemly alacrity. The Seymour version has a delightful composite nose of considerable quality. The colour lacks vitality, but the palate fulfills the bouquet's promise, being surprisingly generous for a wine of only medium body. Balance and finish are good.
Best year: 1980

Seymour Vineyards Gewurztraminer

Gewurztraminer has always been one of the more impressive styles from Seymour Vineyards, and recent vintages have entrenched my respect for the wine. Intensely spicy in the nose, the palate is soft, crisp and extraordinarily pretty without, it must be said, any great complexity. Most attractive drinking.
Best years: 1980, 1981

Seymour Vineyards Sauvignon Blanc

The impact of Sauvignon Blanc always reminds me of sitting on freshly cut grass and eating peaches, the nose of the former and the flavour of the latter being notable components of this variety. This is particularly the case with the recent Seymour Vineyards versions, the wine being entirely beguiling and very true to style.
Best years: 1980, 1981

Ownership

Seymour Vineyards is a private company owned by Maurice Bourne.

Production

Total average production is around 8000 cases.

New Plantings

(Not yet yielding.) None envisaged, although some grafting may be carried out.

Market

Predominantly cellar-door, with small lots placed in specialist retailers.

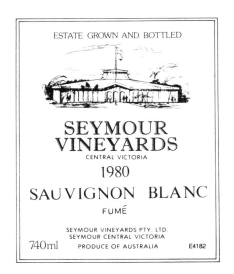

Winery Visiting Details

9 am to 6 pm Monday to Saturday, noon to 6 pm Sunday. The address is Hume Highway, Seymour, 3660 Telephone (057) 92 1372.

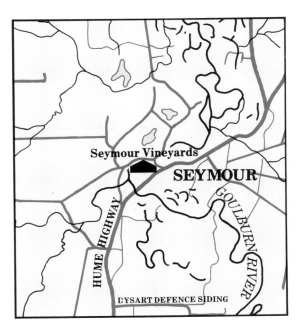

STANTON & KILLEEN

Stanton & Killeen's Gracerray Winery was established in 1925 by John Charles Stanton as an offshoot from his father's 'Park View' winery. He was a fourth generation winemaker (his great grandfather having started making wine in the early 1870s). One decade was much like any other in Australian wine from the twenties through to the early sixties, and the business flowed at an orderly and comfortable pace.

The permanent disruption of this vinous tranquillity started, as we all know, in the mid-sixties, and for Stanton & Killeen the new era coincided with Norm Killeen's taking over as winemaker after fifteen years of being involved with the agricultural rather than viticultural side of the partnership's interests.

It was a baptism of fire for him as the sluggish mainstream of Australian wine tastes and consumption grew to an unpredictable torrent. Norm had urgently to learn not merely the techniques of winemaking but the intricacies of table wine (in which he had never been particularly interested) while the market went berserk. As he puts it, he had to re-establish a place for Stanton & Killeen in an industry which it had almost deserted.

He planted the Moodemere vineyard as soon as he took charge, and began to develop the table wine range of Stanton & Killeen, while still maintaining the traditional range of the area's famous sweet fortified wines. Since 1972 his son Chris has taken an increasing part in the annual vintage, and his formal training at Wagga introduced a new elegance into a range of table wines which were already lighter and finer than those for which the area was known.

1981 saw the first vintage from a new vineyard established by Stanton & Killeen and called 'Quandong' after the name of an old winery on the property in the 1890s.

Winemaker

Chris Killeen has been being groomed as Stanton & Killeen winemaker since he left school in 1972. As vintage followed vintage he gained more practical experience, and he gained further theoretical knowledge by completing the Wine Science Course at the Riverina College. Chris became a member of the partnership in 1979, and in 1981 he took over as winemaker from his father Norm.

Range of Wines

Stanton & Killeen Moodemere Cabernet
   Sauvignon
Stanton & Killeen Moodemere Cabernet/Shiraz
Stanton & Killeen Moodemere Shiraz
Stanton & Killeen Moodemere Vintage Port
Stanton & Killeen Moodemere Muscat

Style

Stanton & Killeen Moodemere Cabernet Sauvignon

This is a wine remarkable for its depth and
elegance when you consider the area in which
it is grown. Deep brick-red in colour without
the inkier depths of a cooler climate Cabernet,
it has neither the fierceness of the Baileys nor
the flaccidness of its Rutherglen counterparts,
but is a nicely fruited, softly tannic dry red of
some grace.
Best years: 1979, 1980

Stanton & Killeen Moodemere Shiraz

Probably the best of the winery's dry reds, this
maker having demonstrated over the years an
increasing sensitivity with Shiraz, which is after
all a classic grape for the area. Soft but powerful, the wine has an unexpected lightness of
flavour and approachability which makes for
most agreeable drinking.
Best years: 1975, 1978, 1980

Stanton & Killeen Vintage Port

This is a massive but graceful vintage port style
in the traditional mould of Rutherglen fortifieds
so far as strength of flavour is concerned, but
with a fine tight austerity in the back of the
palate to offset the sheer weight of the wine. It
must be said however that North Victoria is a
long way from Portugal, in more ways than
one.
Best years: 1972, 1977

Ownership

Stanton & Killeen is a long-standing family
partnership.

Production

Current production is about 6000 cases per
year, 60 per cent of which is fortified and the
balance dry red.

New Plantings

About 5 hectares are not yet in full bear.

Market

As with all Rutherglen wineries, cellar door
sales account for a substantial proportion of the
production. This and retail outlets in Victoria
take about 80 per cent, New South Wales is 15
per cent, with 5 per cent to other states and
export.

Winery Visiting Details

Monday to Saturday 9 am to 5 pm. The address
is Graham Road, Rutherglen, 3685 Telephone
(060) 32 9457.

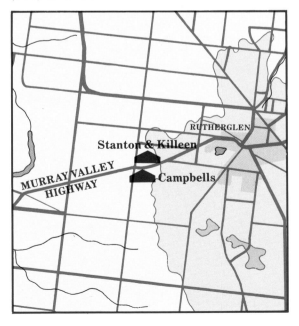

TALTARNI Moonambel, Vic.

A remarkable venture, the story behind the establishment of Taltarni reads like the scenario of a sprawling three act play. Act One: a Ballarat based group of investors acquire 100 hectares of land at Moonambel near Stawell in Victoria and plant about half with vines in 1969. By 1972 it was apparently all too much for them (in spite of no wine yet having been made), so it was time for Act Two. Which begins with the entry of a *deus ex machina* in the form of Bernard Portet, who was seeking quality vineyard sites 'around the world'. Bernard had already selected the Clos du Val site in the Napa Valley, and bought Taltarni for his American backers. Brilliant young winemaker David Hohnen, who was Davis (California) trained, was installed to manage Taltarni, and made some wine which was, I think, sold to Seppelts, where it disappeared.

Act Three begins with Bernard Portet making the 1977 vintage and bottling it under the Taltarni label for the first time; David Hohnen going back to his native West Australia to make the superb Cape Mentelle wines in Margaret River; and Bernard's younger brother Dominique arriving from France to take over as vineyard and winery manager and winemaker. Vintage follows vintage, and Taltarni is off and running. Curtain.

Despite the happenings above, Dominique Portet *is* Taltarni so far as you and I are concerned. And I am sure he will not object to my observing that he has not yet settled on a definitive style for the label, with the possible exception of the Cabernet Sauvignon. His particular interest in Champagne augurs well for the future if Dominique's skill even nearly matches his admirably purist good intentions.

All the above irreverence apart, Taltarni is one of the most promising vineyard projects in Australia, and I think we can look forward with some excitement to Act Four.

Winemaker

Dominique Portet is the son of Andre Portet who for twenty years was Technical Director of Chateau Lafite. He graduated from Montpellier with degrees in Oenology and Viticulture and has worked in several wineries in the south of France before assuming control of Taltarni. He is assisted by Greg Gallagher, who is an Oenology graduate from Roseworthy College and has worked with Seppelts.

Range of Wines

Taltarni Blanc de Blancs (100% Chardonnay)
Taltarni Brut (White Hermitage/Chenin Blanc)
  (Both the above are Champagne styles)
Taltarni Cabernet Sauvignon
Taltarni Chenin Blanc
Taltarni Malbec
Taltarni Rhine Riesling
Taltarni Sauvignon Blanc
Taltarni Shiraz

Style

Taltarni Cabernet Sauvignon

Already respected as one of the great wines of Australia, this is not a straight Cabernet Sauvignon, but, like most of the noble Bordeaux reds, a blend of Cabernet Sauvignon, Cabernet Franc, Merlot and Malbec. Rich, big but fine, it contains within its immense depths stylistic undertones of the Medoc and the Napa Valley, overlaid with solid Australian muscle.
Best years: 1977, 1978

Taltarni Chenin Blanc

In a surprisingly short time, this beguiling wine has become one of Melbourne's restaurant favourites. Anywhere outside Western Australia Chenin Blanc could well be termed an unexpected variety, but the Taltarni version demonstrates the grape is perfectly happy at Moonambel. Crisp, attractive and clean finishing, the wine has integrity without assertive varietal character.
Best years: 1979, 1981

Taltarni Brut (Champagne)

A somewhat negative wine of non-committal style, but well-made, well-balanced and undeniably popular. Aficionadoes of the bubble might be better advised to await the appearance of the straight Chardonnay champagne from this maker, particularly the 1980.

Taltarni Shiraz

This is a wine which has varied considerably in style during its short career to date, probably because of lack of knowledge (by its French winemakers) of the unique characteristics of Australian Shiraz. For all that, each vintage has produced a good wine; sometimes charming, sometimes belligerent.
Best years: 1977, 1978, 1980

Ownership

Taltarni is owned by 'Red Earth Nominees Pty Ltd' The management is tight-lipped about who in fact are comprised by such, and I couldn't be bothered to do a 'company search'.

Production

Increasing annually, but currently about 25 000 cases.

New Plantings

(Not yet yielding.) A few hectares of Merlot and Chardonnay are about to start bearing. No further plantings are envisaged.

Market

Victoria 40 per cent, United States of America 35 per cent (!), New South Wales 15 per cent, the balance to Queensland, South Australia, Europe, South East Asia and New Zealand.

Winery Visiting Details

Monday to Friday 9 am to 4.15 pm, and Saturdays 10 am to 5 pm. The address is simply Moonambel, 3478 Telephone (054) 67 2218.

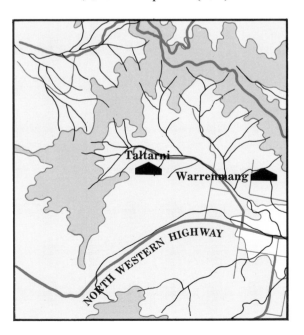

TAMBURLAINE

Tamburlaine was the third new vineyard to be established in the Hunter Valley this century, after Lakes Folly and Belbourie. It grew out of Dr Lance Allen's lifelong wine interest which culminated in his acquiring in 1966 a 34 hectare paddock at Pokolbin, densely planted to dead trees and mouldering stumps. Much dynamiting and bulldozing later, the cleared sections were sown with legumes to be ploughed into the heavy clay soil. This was to be the pattern for future development.

Actual planting began in 1967 using cuttings from Tyrrells and Draytons, and the first crop appeared in 1971. This and the next two years' vintages were fermented elsewhere, but in 1974 partly, and 1975 onwards wholly, Tamburlaine grapes have been vinified at the Tamburlaine winery.

In the early 1970s more land was purchased nearby at Rothbury Ridge, as Dr Allen named it, and further plantings followed. The current area under vine is about 15 hectares: 12 on the Tamburlaine property and 3 at Rothbury Ridge. Varieties established are Shiraz (6.4 hectares), Cabernet Sauvignon (2.2 hectares), Semillon (2.8 hectares at Tamburlaine and 2 at Rothbury Ridge), Chardonnay (0.8 hectares) and Sauvignon Blanc (0.2 hectares), the latter two being at Rothbury Ridge.

Lance Allen's aim is to produce small quantities of good quality wines, using low yielding, non-irrigated vines. His wine-making methods are traditional, and he uses small wood maturation. Red grapes are fermented on the skins for three days in the open concrete vats, with regular plunging of the cap. Wood-aging is from 18 to 24 months.

The white wines are fermented in stainless steel with temperature control. Some of the whites are given a period of maturation in new German oak casks.

Winemaker

Dr Lance Allen likes a change. After 15 years as a pharmacist, he decided to become a doctor of medicine, so he did. Another 15 years saw his decision to become a winemaker, so perhaps the syndrome is cyclic. Although he has had no formal training in oenology, he finds his pharmaceutical and medical experiences a considerable asset in winemaking.

Range of Wines

Tamburlaine Cabernet Sauvignon
Tamburlaine Chardonnay
Tamburlaine Hermitage Vat 9
Tamburlaine Hermitage Vat 10
Tamburlaine Pokolbin Semillon
Tamburlaine Rothbury Ridge Semillon
Tamburlaine Shiraz/Cabernet

Style

Tamburlaine Cabernet/Shiraz

Generally this wine, although lighter and finer than the 'Hermitage' styles, is somehow less convincing. Elegance, rather than weight, is their hallmark, but depth is lacking. For all that, an agreeable winestyle for fairly early drinking.
Best years: 1979, 1980

Tamburlaine Hermitage

Tamburlaine make some of the district's best Shiraz styles, which is saying quite a lot. Emphatic but complex and sensitively balanced, they are tight, long-finishing reds with exemplary varietal character. Vat 9 has more wood, being matured in French hogsheads; Vat 10 being aged in 500 gallon American oak.
Best years: 1978, 1979, 1980

Tamburlaine Semillon

A beautiful wine, showing the stylistic advantages of cold fermentation with early-picked grapes in creating gentle but assured varietal character. The wood-aged versions have been created with care so that the fruit character is not overwhelmed by the oak.
Best years: 1979, 1980

Ownership

Tamburlaine is family-owned.

Production

The Hunter Valley is ungenerous with yields: only 2500 cases are annually produced from the 15 hectares, 1500 red and 1000 white.

New Plantings

(Not yet yielding.) None yet to bear, but it is to be hoped that vine maturity will increase the tonnage.

Market

Entirely by mailing list and cellar door.

Winery Visiting Details

Monday to Saturday 10 am to 4.30 pm. The address is McDonalds Road, Pokolbin, 2321 Telephone (049) 987 570.

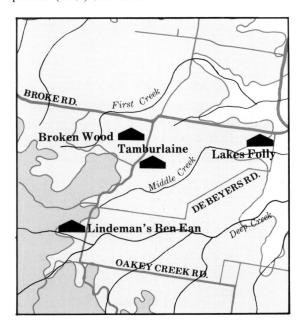

TERRACE VALE

To say that Terrace Vale happened by mistake would be neither accurate nor complimentary, but its creation was certainly unusual. Rather like a science fiction writer's idea of a group of Martians reproducing, the concept popped out quite naturally from the conjoint enthusiasm of about twenty wine-loving families back in 1971, who decided to do more than just talk about wine.

Ignoring the rest of this formidable *dramatis personae*, we can concentrate on the two prime movers of the group, Dick Tiley and Michael Wood who, catalyzed by Murray Tyrrell's enthusiasm for the district, devised the project with such efficiency that 1972 saw the beginning of plantings of what is now a 38 hectare vineyard on loamy creek flats not far from the Hermitage Estate. Varieties planted included the compulsory Hunter staples of Shiraz and Semillon, together with Chardonnay, Traminer, Sauvignon Blanc, Cabernet Sauvignon and Pinot Noir. It is interesting to note that more whites than reds were planted,

amazing market prescience in an industry noted for its 20-20 hindsight but blunderingly myopic foresight.

The winery was more of a problem, and indeed won't really be completely finished until 1986, when it will be capable of handling the full potential Terrace Vale crush of 250 tonnes. I must be critical of the company's brochure, amongst whose expectable hyperbole we find the ill-considered words: 'We're certain that the age-old methods are by far the most rewarding when it comes to making fine wine. By all means, add a little twentieth century technology, but keep it to a minimum.' I don't really believe they mean that quite literally, and the quality of the wines so far produced would suggest that a much more responsible attitude is in fact the case.

Terrace Vale is utterly Hunter, and a welcome addition to this drought-beleaguered and fluoride-threatened vignoble. Wine-lovers anywhere should wish them well.

Winemaker

Alain Leprince was working on research projects involving chemicals in grape production in liaison with Loire Valley winemakers, when he decided he would like to join their ranks. This proving impossible, he came to Australia and worked at the Rothbury Estate. In 1973 he joined Terrace Vale, and was appointed their chief winemaker in 1977.

Range of Wines

Terrace Vale Cabernet/Hermitage
Terrace Vale Cabernet Sauvignon
Terrace Vale Chardonnay
Terrace Vale Hermitage
Terrace Vale Pinot/Hermitage
Terrace Vale Sauvignon Blanc
Terrace Vale Semillon
Terrace Vale Semillon/Chardonnay
Terrace Vale Traminer
Terrace Vale Vintage Port

Style

Terrace Vale Chardonnay

Probably the vineyard's most successful wine to date, both because of its enviable record in three successive Hunter Valley Wine Shows, and the general desirability of a well-made Chardonnay. Not wines of great subtlety or power, they are nevertheless most attractive examples of this superb variety, whose flavour and charm they ably demonstrate.
Best years: 1978, 1979, 1980

Terrace Vale Hermitage

A wine in the Tyrrells mould, although not lavishly so, and sweet-fruited rather than muscular. However this is no lightweight, and the integrity and depth of the Hunter Shiraz character is admirable, as is its balance.
Best years: 1977, 1979, 1980

Terrace Vale Sauvignon Blanc

This is a beautiful Sauternes style wine made only when botrytis affects the grapes. An intriguing 'smoky straw' smell underlies the pretty varietal nose with its hint of noble rot character, and the palate is quite beguiling. I admire this style very much, and will keep my fingers crossed for the frequent occurrence of the conditions essential to its production.
Best year: 1980

Terrace Vale Semillon

There are in fact two: the Bin 1 and the Bin 1A, described by the makers as Chablis and White Burgundy styles respectively. Without wishing to seem intransigently uncooperative, this is nonsense — the Bin 1 is lighter, that's all. Terrace Vale Semillon is wonderfully typical of the area's unique white wine, and ages with grace to suggest hints of the fabled old Lindeman Semillons whose finesse, however, they lack.
Best years: 1978, 1979, 1980

Ownership

A private company with some nineteen shareholders who are all, I am told, publicity shy.

Production

Currently a little over 4000 cases, being Hermitage 1000, Semillon Bin 1 and Bin 1A 800 each, Chardonnay, Traminer and Cabernet 500 each, Vintage Port 200 and Sauvignon Blanc 50 cases.

New Plantings

(Not yet yielding.) 2 hectares of Chardonnay.

Market

90 per cent is placed within New South Wales, with Victoria and Queensland sharing the remainder.

Winery Visiting Details

Monday to Saturday 10 am to 4 pm, Sunday noon to 4 pm. The address is Deasy Lane, Pokolbin, 2321 Telephone (049) 98 7517.

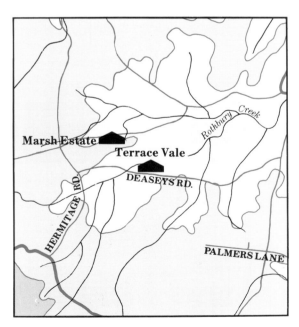

TISDALL MOUNT HELEN Strathbogie Ranges, Vic

Perhaps the best orchestrated launch of a project in Australia's wine history has been Tisdall's. Dr Peter Tisdall could never be accused of hobbyism in his spectacularly whole-hearted foray into wine, starting in 1972 with 80 hectares of plantings at Rosbercon in the Echuca district. This massive beginning was barely under way when it became obvious that the future of the quality market would depend upon higher, cooler climate areas.

No whit disturbed, he purchased suitable land (after a considerable search for what every producer is pleased to call 'the ideal site') in the Strathbogie Ranges. This was planted with Cabernet Sauvignon, Merlot, Pinot Noir, Chardonnay, Rhine Riesling, Sauvignon Blanc and Traminer, and was named Mount Helen.

The combination of retaining one of the best winemakers in the country, the designing of a tasteful, dignified and attractive label, and extremely intelligent advertising engendered almost instant respect for the Tisdall image And a great deal of good luck to the Rosbercor wines, which have no further place in thi book.

Mount Helen, on the other hand, has been revivifying influence on the entire Victoria wine scene, and the credit for this must be laid at the feet of winemaker John Ellis. His and vineyard manager Greg Elford's manipulation of the viticultural aspects of Mount Helen ha been both painstaking in effort and rewardin in quality, and has been paid that ultimate com pliment accorded only to tall poppies: bitchy remarks from other winemakers (except thos big-hearted enough — like Max Lake — to giv credit wherever it is found due).

Barring natural and unnatural disasters, you and I can look forward hopefully to a decade o three of rewarding Mount Helen wines unti times as Ellis retires, opts out, or is cloned.

Winemaker

John Ellis graduated dux of Roseworthy Col lege in 1971, and has since worked with Le Buring, Krondorf, Yalumba and Rosemount be fore joining Tisdall in 1978. He had the goo fortune to marry Anne Tyrrell in 1980 and thu formed a nexus which, knowing John, coul one day lead to a takeover of the Hunter Valle by Victoria. Together with a few other en lightened winemakers he believes strongly ii the overriding importance of creative viti culture as distinct from 'vine farming'.

154

Range of Wines

Mount Helen Cabernet Sauvignon
Mount Helen Cabernet Merlot
Mount Helen Chardonnay
Mount Helen Chardonnay/Riesling
Mount Helen Fume Blanc
Mount Helen Gewurztraminer
Mount Helen Pinot Noir
Mount Helen Rhine Riesling

Style

Mount Helen Cabernet Sauvignon

A wine of the most remarkable equipoise; fine, limpid, gently powerful, and languidly unhurried on the finish; redolent of the more noble aspects of Cabernet character, and of a balance to suggest quite lengthy maturation without noisome taint. Near the top rank of Australian Cabernets, and destined, once the vines are a little older, to take an honoured place within that rank.
Best years: 1979, 1981

Mount Helen Chardonnay

Seemingly fragile in its delicacy and yet so well-knit as to deny such fragility, this is a wine in the mould of Oregonian rather than Californian or French Chardonnays. Again, the vines are young, and it is to be hoped that successive vintages will see the emergence of greater power to accompany the exemplary elegance.
Best years: 1979, 1981

Mount Helen Pinot Noir

Pinot Noir is an odd grape, and one which appears determined to remain intractable in most of its Australian plantings. Mount Helen is an exception; density of colour which has most rival winemakers insisting that Shiraz pressings have been used (they are wrong), and sweet Pinot fruit yet with an almost Cabernet tightness so unlike the all too common 'pretty Pinot Roses' which result from this variety in the antipodes.
Best years: 1979, 1981

Ownership

Solely owned by Dr Peter and Mrs Diana Tisdall.

Production

Mount Helen produces 14 450 cases a year, being: Cabernet Sauvignon 500 cases, Cabernet Merlot 500 cases, Pinot Noir 1700 cases, Chardonnay 4000 cases, Rhine Riesling 1500 cases, Fume Blanc 750 cases, Chardonnay/Riesling 5000 cases and Gewurztraminer 500 cases.

New Plantings

(Not yet yielding.) Nil.

Market

Victoria 53 per cent, New South Wales 30 per cent, Queensland 10 per cent, South Australia, Tasmania and Western Australia 7 per cent.

Winery Visiting Details

The Tisdall winery is at Echuca (no winery at Mount Helen). The hours are: Monday to Saturday 9.00 am to 5.00 pm, Sunday noon to 6.00 pm. The address is Cornelia Creek Road, Echuca, 3625 Telephone (054) 82 1514.

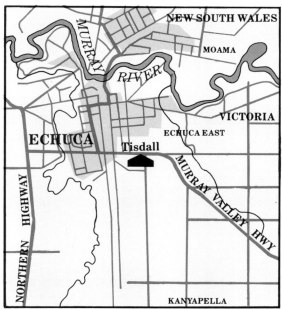

TRENNERT

Imagine a couple, wearying of the mundanities of an albeit successful business life, deciding to seek a haven in the hills south of Adelaide, acquiring same, indecisively wondering which particular bucolic endeavour to pursue ('cows, goats, horses, silkworms, donkeys?'), and finally opting for wine.

It sounds like an enjoyable recipe for vinous disaster, but the results speak differently.

Don and Barbara Paul, for all their amiable hedonism, are both purist and perfectionist in their approach to wine. Their almost apologetic explanation for this fact is typically Trennert: 'We realized that if we were unable to dispose of our wines, we would have to retire to the cellars and set about drinking them. It would be really traumatic to have to force ourselves to drink vast quantities of something we actively disliked . . .' As convincing a reason for making good wine as any I've heard.

Trennert wines are hand-made, even to cap plunging, an operation as unrelievedly time consuming as feeding a litter of puppies with a baby's bottle, or painting the Sydney Harbour bridge. The winemaking style could be described as traditional but painstaking, and the results are exemplary for the area, which can incline towards overly soft, big-breasted wines. I have never tasted a flaccid Trennert.

The annual crush is kept to only 50 tonnes, so that Don and Barbara are happy about maintaining the closely controlled quality which is traditionally associable with Trennert wines, a quality which has made these wines perhaps the most sought-after in South Australia.

Winemaker

Don and Barbara Paul are plangent exceptions to the normally very reliable dictum that good intentions alone don't make good wine. That is precisely what they did even when they were fumbling in the oenological dark. Since those days in addition to experiencing a dozen vintages, they have done the laboratory course for small winemakers at Riverina College, and have attended every possible seminar, technical conference and so on.

Range of Wines

Trennert Bin 3 Shiraz
Trennert Bin 7 Shiraz
Trennert Cabernet Sauvignon
Trennert Rhine Riesling
Trennert Shiraz/Cabernet

Style

Trennert Bin 3 Shiraz

Made from grapes which include, as well as some quality bought-in fruit, the Shiraz grown on the Trennert vineyard, Bin 3 is tight, fine and deep 'claret' style which lives quite well in the medium term.
Best years: 1973, 1975, 1976, 1978, 1979

Trennert Bin 7 Shiraz

A softer, more Burgundian style, perhaps the most typically Southern Vales of the Trennert range; and as such, without quite the stylish elegance which characterizes this maker. For all that, an attractive and agreeable dry red.
Best years: 1975, 1978, 1979

Trennert Cabernet Sauvignon

As might be expected, the flagship of the Trennert fleet; authoritative and emphatically Cabernet in character, with good deep fruit (grown at Langhorne Creek) and a desirable level of austerity in the finish. A nicely balanced, high quality wine which lives well.
Best years: 1978, 1979, 1980

Trennert Rhine Riesling

The only wine of the range made entirely from fruit grown on the Trennert vineyard, this is a crisp but generously endowed Riesling style with hints of honey in the back palate.
Best years: 1979, 1980

Ownership

Trennert is entirely family-owned (Don and Barbara Paul and two daughters).

Production

Average is about 350 cases of each wine. (Total 1750 cases).

New Plantings

(Not yet yielding.) Nil.

Market

Victoria 35 per cent, South Australia 20 per cent, New South Wales 20 per cent, Queensland 15 per cent, Western Australia and Tasmania 10 per cent. Effectively all of this is by mailing list.

Winery Visiting Details

9 am to 5 pm Monday to Saturday, as long as there is no sign on the gate reading 'Go Away', 'No Wine', 'Gone Fishing', 'Back in 5 years' etc. The address is Piggott Range Road, Happy Valley, 5159 Telephone (08) 383 6052.

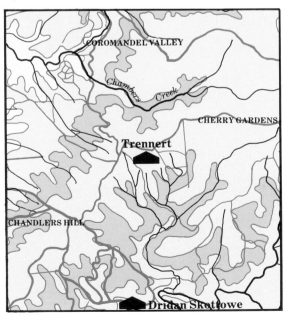

VASSE FELIX

Vasse Felix was the first of the new wave of Margaret River plantings, being established in 1967, just two years after Dr John Gladstone's conclusion of his investigations into the suitability of the South West for premium wine grape production. (I say 'new wave' because the area from Yallingup to Bunbury had included some winegrowing from as far back as 1830.)

Let's clear up the background to the unusual name first: in the district's very early days a quixotic figure was a Monsieur Vasse who played a significant part in opening up the area before going bush and living with the aborigines (version one) or drowning in a long-boat (version two). Whatever his fate, he left his name in quite a few places around the area, notably the township of Vasse some 45 kilometres north of Margaret River. Scholars and those of classical bent will not need to be told that 'Felix' is Latin for happy or 'in a state of contentment'. There you go.

Eight hectares were developed, the plantings being of Rhine Riesling, Cabernet Sauvignon, Traminer and Shiraz, and the owner and developer being Dr T. B. Cullity, a Perth cardiologist. Like many others, his aim was to produce as high a quality of wine as possible, with no commercial compromise. Unlike many others, he achieved just that.

Eastern States readers will probably never have heard of Silvereyes, rampaging birds who

welcomed vineyard establishment in the South West with far greater enthusiasm than the veriest connoisseur, and who can effectively destroy an entire vintage. The Vasse Felix method of coping with their voracity is intriguing: after trying to dissuade their attentions with falconry (hence the feathered predator symbol), winemaker David Gregg heard of the birds' preference for figs, so fig trees were planted around the vineyard to give them a more desirable option to their grape diet. This system, used in conjunction with sonar blocking devices in the vineyard itself, worked so well that it is now possible to vintage the grapes in undamaged condition at optimum ripeness. And the Silvereyes are most grateful for the figs, which keep them regular.

Winemaker

David Gregg is an expatriate Englishman whose formal qualifications are in the field of Dairy Technology. However his enthusiasms are for wine, and he came to Vasse Felix in 1973 for the second 'commercial' vintage, after spending some time in the region observing the burgeoning of viticulture. His lack of oenological training is neatly counterbalanced by his annually making some of the area's best wine.

Range of Wines

Vasse Felix Cabernet Sauvignon
Vasse Felix Hermitage
Vasse Felix Riesling (dry and late-picked styles)
Vasse Felix Traminer

Vasse Felix Cabernet Sauvignon

From one point of view it is perhaps unfortunate that Vasse Felix Cabernet is always going to be compared with the same district's Moss Wood. From another, it could be said to be an enviable stroke of luck to have such a pace-maker. Certainly, there are many common denominators, particularly within the depth and quality of the fruit. These serve also, though, to point up the disparities, which are: colour — Vasse Felix is deeper and darker; nose — Vasse Felix is less forthcoming and with a touch more vinosity; palate — Vasse Felix is more emphatically uncompromising in its Cabernet character. A comparative tasting of ten year old wines would be interesting.

Best years: 1973, 1977, 1979, 1980

Vasse Felix Riesling

One of the most beautiful white wines in Australia, this is a softly beguiling, deeply floral Riesling of crispness and length of finish. Small quantities of Traminer sometimes find their way in the Rhine Riesling, and this if anything adds a greater depth to the wine. Of further charm is the light golden hue of this wine, even when quite young. It ages very well.

Best years: 1977, 1979, 1981

Ownership

The vineyard and winery are owned by Dr Cullity with David and Anne Gregg as partners in the enterprise.

Production

About 4600 cases, being Cabernet Sauvignon 3000 cases, Riesling 1200 cases, Traminer and Hermitage each 200 cases.

New Plantings

(Not yet yielding.) Nil.

Market

Western Australia 50 per cent, Victoria and New South Wales each 20 per cent, others 10 per cent.

Winery Visiting Details

Monday to Saturday 10 am to 4 pm but first ring to make sure there is wine available. The address is Harmans Road South, Cowaramup, 6284 Telephone (097) 55 5242.

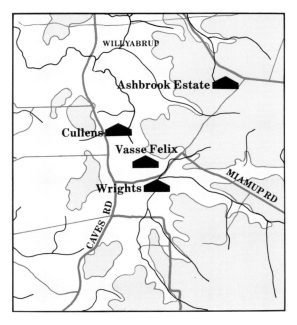

VIRGIN HILLS Kyneton, Vic

The unkind could describe this as a dream which went wrong. Before I am taken to task for being one of such, let me make it clear that I refer only to the extrinsic limitations which circumstance has imposed on Tom Lazar's quality aspirations.

Tom, variously described as restaurateur, entrepreneur and maverick, wanted to crown his undoubted achievements by masterminding a vineyard and winery producing an ultimate quality dry red. By the expenditure of some of his illimitable resources of sheer energy, he created the 18 hectares of Cabernet Sauvignon, Shiraz, Malbec and Pinot Noir together with a winery not far from Kyneton. Yield was low — appallingly low — but quality was very high indeed.

Vicissitudes ensued, together with some consequent variation in ownership details. Nevertheless, a Virgin Hills wine has appeared every year, and has for the most part been met by an enthusiastic and loyal following. Tom's idea of making just one wine (a dry red) and giving no varietal attribution on the label is, after all, the very stuff and essence of the practice of any of the great red wines of Europe. His reticence about conveying such information verbally, or for publication, is not relatable to the European practice, however.

Tom Lazar makes wine almost by intuition, but having said that, he brings to bear an intelligence, a vitality and an ability which can produce some formidable results. We will discuss the style of the wine later, but the style of the winemaker is breathtaking. Lack of confidence has never been Tom's weak point, and he combines technological expertise with an abiding respect for traditionalism to an extent unequalled outside Bordeaux. Nevertheless, I doubt that I am alone amongst Australian consumers in feeling that the promise of the Kyneton project has never been fulfilled, and we wait in vain for some definitive vinous statement on the wine's style.

Winemaker

Tom Lazar is a creative and extremely able person with an international palate and boundless singlemindedness. His winemaking experience includes having worked with Owen Redman at Coonawarra at a time when Tom decided he wanted to work towards the establishment of his own vineyard. His friendship with Brian Croser has certainly not impeded the development of his oenological competence.

VIRGIN HILLS

1975

Produced in Australia, Kyneton, Victoria. 738 ml.

Tom Lazar

Range of Wines
There is but one: 'Virgin Hills' (a dry red).

Style
Virgin Hills
Continuity of style has been difficult, if not impossible to observe in the handful of vintages so far released. The 1975 wine was a cracker: deep and tight, with fine fruit, softly austere tannin and overtones of Coonawarra in the wine's suppleness. The following year saw a much bigger but more flaccid wine which promised much but delivered less. Subsequent years have been rather disappointing, with some apparent volatility discernible in the 1977, and good fruit and suspect balance in the 1978. However the unalterable basic promise of the vineyard, together with the restlessly resilient ability of the winemaker render probable some superb Virgin Hills reds in the near future, particularly if a little more purism is allowed to hold sway.
Best year: 1975

Ownership
I understand that the Virgin Hills complex is now owned by Melbourne businessman Marcel Gilbert.

Production
No figures are available.

New Plantings
(Not yet yielding.) No vines are yet to bear fully, but there are plantings of Chardonnay, Traminer and Rhine Riesling which, although yielding, have not yet produced wine presented to the public.

Market
Mailing list and specialist outlets only.

Winery Visiting Details
Almost uniquely among the 90 wineries covered within this book, there is no cellar door facility. The address is PO Box 54, Kyneton Telephone (054) 22 2151.

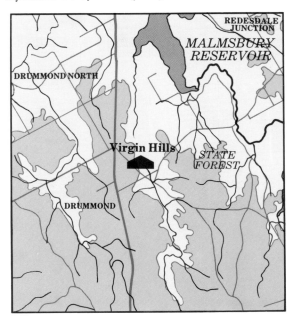

WAKEFIELD RIVER ESTATES Balaklava, SA

Arguably, I am assured, this is the smallest commercial vineyard in Australia. This does not mean that I wish to have an argument about it — this kind of statement usually brings out of the woodwork all manner of previously unheard-of contenders. Before any such take me to task, be advised that Wakefield is the proud possessor of 2135 vines, two-thirds Shiraz and one-third Cabernet Sauvignon.

Technically, I suppose that this operation is of dubious relevance to a book on small wineries, as they have no winery. However the Wakefield grapes are fermented and bottled separately from any other fruit, and the same winemaker — Jim Irvine, who is a partner in the venture — does all of the vinification regardless of which winery's facilities are used. As a matter of interest, the Krondorf winery was used for 1975 to 1977, Saltram from 1978 to 1981, and future vintages will be processed at Hamiltons Eden Valley winery. But, to labour the point, all made by Jim Irvine.

So much for all that: the concept grew from a property at Balaklava (about 100 kilometres north-west of Adelaide) owned by George Heritage, a retired master mariner who became infected by the vineyard establishment epidemic of the 1970s. Vines were planted, a label was created, and some quality bought-in wine was marketed (all white). This is still part of the Wakefield practice — always with adequate attribution on the label — but I do not feel such wines have a place in this book.

The reds, on the other hand, are all their own work, and of a quality to warrant inclusion. To date, the two varieties are made as a blend, but it is intended that they will be kept separate from 1984 onwards.

Winemaker

Jim Irvine has had formidable experience as a winemaker, being the man who established the Hardy's Siegersdorf label and who created the superb Krondorf Bin 4 Shiraz in the early seventies, as well as having risen to senior executive status in the Saltram empire. Jim now operates his own wine consultancy.

Vineyard Diary

SEPTEMBER 1972 –
1420 Shiraz vines planted.
OCTOBER 1972 –
715 Cabernet Sauvignon vines planted;
32 rows in total.
DECEMBER 1972 –
Trellising to single wire completed.
FEBRUARY 1973 –
All trellising including two wire T-arms
finished. 80% of Shiraz hand trained to
single wire, balance trained to T-trellis,
four arms.
OCTOBER 1973 –
First crop indications, replanting of
missing vines. Vine training continues
throughout season.
MARCH 5th 1974 –
First crop picked. 1.45 tonnes of Shiraz.
Wine made at Krondorf, excellent full
bodied style.
NOVEMBER 1974 –
Training of all vines completed.
MARCH 14th 1975 –
Picking – Shiraz 7.1 tonnes, Cabernet
1.0 tonne, 86% Shiraz – 14% Cabernet.
MARCH 20th 1976 –
Picking – Shiraz 8.8 tonnes, Cabernet
1.9 tonnes, 82% Shiraz – 18% Cabernet.
MARCH 26th 1977 –
Picking – Shiraz 11.7 tonnes, Cabernet
3.7 tonnes, 76% Shiraz – 24% Cabernet.

· WAKEFIELD RIVER ESTATES ·

1977 · PREMIER VINTAGE
· SHIRAZ & CABERNET SAUVIGNON ·
· APPELLATION QUALITY ·

Winemaker's Notes

The vineyard of 1.8 hectares is situated
on the alluvial soil banks of the River
Wakefield at Balaklava, some 100
kilometres north-west of Adelaide. This
soil consists of rich, sandy loam over red
clay.

The two grape varieties are picked
separately but fermented together to
obtain the individual vineyard style. This
style will vary slightly, from year to year,
until the vineyard is in full bearing. The
increasing amount of Cabernet, having a
"firming" effect on the total wine.

Vintaged at Krondorf Winery and
matured in oak puncheons, this wine
carries a wealth of fruit and richness of
taste. The warm dry summers in a very
dry (14" rainfall) area seem to add
"generosity" to the palate and bouquet,
soft, rounded, voluminous, somewhat
full-bodied, and with finesse.

Range of Wines

Wakefield River Estates Shiraz/Cabernet

Style

Wakefield River Estates Shiraz/Cabernet
Give a man like Jim Irvine some good fruit to work with and you can be certain of good wine. Here we have the results of young vines grown in an area of low rainfall (340 mm) with extremely limited supplementary water resources. Flavour and complexity are thus greatly enhanced, and yield — already far from princely from only 1.8 hectares — is of course the loser. Obviously there is very little of their wine: more's the pity, because it is a fine, deep, intense red with powerful Cabernet character, sweet fruit and clean, astringent finish. A very good winestyle, totally disparate from Barossa or McLaren Vale dry reds.
Best years: 1976, 1977

Ownership

A private company owned by Dr Doug Hewitson and Messrs George Heritage, Jim Irvine and Ron Westwood.

Production

Varies between 600 and 1000 cases.

New Plantings

(Not yet yielding.) Half a hectare of Cabernet Sauvignon is expected to produce its first grapes in 1984.

Market

Ninety per cent is in Victoria, with a little to New South Wales and tiny parcels to other states. Remarkably for a South Australian vineyard, only 1 per cent is placed within that state.

Winery Visiting Details

As there is no winery, I suppose this is the wrong heading. However 'cellar door' sales facilities have now been arranged at Balaklava, but quantities sold this way are expected to be insignificant. Hours have not been fixed, so one should ring first. The address is just Balaklava, SA Telephone (088) 62 1201.

WANTIRNA ESTATE Wantirna South, Vic.

If not exactly unknown, it is at least rarely acknowledged that Reg and Tina Egan's Wantirna Estate was established almost simultaneously with Lakes Folly. Consider what this means: in 1963 there was no 'wine boom'; there had been no small vineyards established for donkeys' years; and, no doubt, no dearth of advice from well-meaning friends and bank managers not to touch the project with a barge pole.

Wantirna Estate wines represent a nexus with 19th century Melbourne, when the 'Yarra Valley' vignoble extended patchily from South Yarra to past Lilydale, and fine, light clarets washed down our great-grandfathers' roast beef. It is effectively a Metropolitan vineyard — a common enough phenomenon in Adelaide, Perth or Bordeaux, but unlike such, it was established *within* the Metropolitan area as distinct from being engulfed by the suburban sprawl.

The original plantings included varieties which the hindsight of the 1980s would lend one to deprecate — Grenache, Pedro Ximenez and Clare Riesling (as it was then known) were planted as well as Shiraz and Cabernet Sauvignon — but predicting vinous fashions was not quite so easy in 1963.

Four hectares were established, much of which had been replanted since with more Cabernet, Chardonnay, Pinot Noir, Merlot and Rhine Riesling.

The vineyard is situated in an 800 hectare tract of proposed parkland which is to be administered by the Melbourne and Metropolitan Board of Works (!) but I am assured by Reg Egan that co-existence is probable. A thin topsoil overlays heavy yellow clay on the vineyard's eastern slopes, and the only water available is that which is precipitated with the compliments of the Bureau of Meteorology.

Winemaker

Until 1979 Reg Egan made all Wantirna Estate wines. He still makes the major winemaking decisions, but his own perfectionism is now potentiated through the retention of Ian Deacon as winemaker. Ian's background includes some years of practical experience at Seymour Vineyards after gaining qualifications studying under Brian Croser at the Riverina College at Wagga.

Range of Wines

Wantirna Estate Cabernet/Merlot
Wantirna Estate Chardonnay
Wantirna Estate Clare Riesling/Pedro
Wantirna Estate Pinot Noir
Wantirna Estate Riesling
Wantirna Estate Shiraz

Style

Wantirna Estate Cabernet/Merlot
To discuss this vineyard's Cabernet Merlot is an exercise in avoiding overuse of superlatives. The nose carries overtones of St Emilion and undertones of coffee, both partially obscured by dense but graceful Cabernet fruit. Merlot makes its presence felt more in the palate, which, for all its generosity and power, has an elegance and almost fragility which I find both intriguing and attractive.
Best years: 1977, 1978

Wantirna Estate Pinot Noir
This is very close to being the Southern Hemisphere's best Pinot Noir. The colour gives no hint of an Australian provenance, being both deeper and darker as well as limpid. The nose too has depths which are unfortunately not normally associable with Australian Pinot, and the palate is convincing, subtle, firm and notably long-finishing. If this is to be taken as an indication of the quality achievable from Wantirna (a Melbourne suburb) then we should start pulling down houses.
Best year: 1978

Ownership

Wantirna Estate is entirely owned by Reg and Tina Egan.

Production

Annual production is about 1000 cases of red and 500 of white. When replanting is completed and all vines are yielding, total production will approximate 2000 cases.

New Plantings

(Not yet yielding.) About 2 hectares of the replanting programme are still to come on stream, being Cabernet Sauvignon, Merlot, Chardonnay and Pinot Noir.

Market

Entirely by mailing list, most of which are Melbourne based. A small quantity is sent to Adelaide, but virtually none to other states.

Winery Visiting Details

The winery is not open to the public, but applications to join the mailing list can be lodged by writing to PO Box 231, Glen Waverley, 3150 Telephone (03) 221 2367.

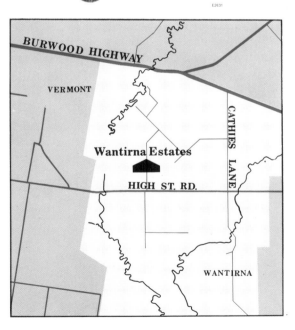

Jack Church is a quiet, friendly, rather private man who is modest about his achievements and equally modest about his vineyard. The modern cant expression 'low profile' would seem to be particularly appropriate.

Jack has had a lifelong interest in wine which eventually devolved in his purchase of nine hectares of land on the lower slopes of the Yarra Valley's Warramate Hills in 1969. During the next two years he planted out two hectares with Rhine Riesling, Shiraz and Cabernet Sauvignon. To create the winery he dug into the hill fairly extensively, and used log cabin structures for extensions.

The winery equipment is adequate, although far from optimum. It is being progressively added to, the next stage being refrigeration facilities which will make the whites particularly more in the current fashion.

Those of pedantic bent find it behoves them to sneer at hobbyism in winemaking: the technological revolution having generated a breed of extremely vocal, professionalist purists. Jack must indeed be a target for their curled lips, as he overtly states that his winemaking endeavours are a hobby. But what a hobby — tending and vintaging five acres of vines, and making and nurturing the wines could hardly be compared to pottering with stamp collections or tying trout-flies when the mood may strike. The world of wine is both rich and varied, and covers a wider gamut, thank goodness, than the purists would consider ideal.

May good fortune attend Jack Church's efforts.

Winemaker

Jack Church is a Bachelor of Science in Chemistry, whose profession is in some highly specialized, recondite corner of the printing industry. He has attended numerous courses of oenological subjects at the Riverina College of Advanced Education, and reads whatever viticultural and winemaking books he can lay his hands on.

Range of Wines

Warramate Cabernet Sauvignon
Waramate Rhine Riesling
Warramate Shiraz

Style

Warramate Cabernet Sauvignon

This is a beautiful wine of mammoth proportions: not coarse, but immensely generous in both American oak flavours and the typical 'mashed grass' characteristics of fine young Cabernet. At the moment all these formidable attributes tower from a somewhat slender base but a few years aging should engender more integration and lengthen the finish.
Best years: 1977, 1979

Warramate Rhine Riesling

This is a wine which evokes some measure of nostalgia for me: for the 'bad old days' before modern white wine making equipment became ubiquitous in Australian wineries. Although heavy, and perhaps a little flat, the wine has profound reaches within its full palate, and the nose is both emphatic and direct. In neither aspect, it must be admitted, is there much detectable Rhine Riesling character, but I like the style and find it a little sad that the new equipment soon to be installed will make yet another Bo Derek out of Sophia Loren.
Best years: 1977, 1979

Ownership

Entirely owned by J. R. and J. M. Church.

Production

Average is 150 cases of Shiraz, 250 of Cabernet Sauvignon and 300 of Rhine Riesling.

New Plantings

(Not yet yielding.) None at the moment, but Jack Church plans to establish some of the other red Bordeaux varieties to deepen the complexity of his Cabernet Sauvignon.

Market

Virtually all Victoria, and virtually all by cellar door and mailing list.

WARRAMATE
Riesling
1979

This wine is made from Rhine Riesling grapes grown on the lower slopes of the Warramate Hills overlooking the Yarra Valley of Victoria.

Bottled by the Makers:
J. R. & J. M. CHURCH,
GRUYERE, VICTORIA.

Produce of Australia.   738 mls.

Winery Visiting Details

Saturdays 9 am to 6 pm, Sunday noon to 6 pm, or by appointment. The address is simply Gruyere, Victoria Telephone (03) 328 2017.

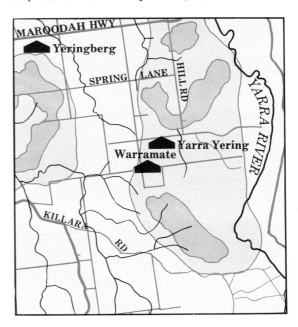

WARRENMANG Moonambel, Vic

Harking back to the story on the establishment of Taltarni, readers with eidetic memories may recall that the Ballarat based group of businessmen mentioned felt that they could not cope with the large scale of the Moonambel plantings, and so sold the vineyard to Bernard Portet. In fact they retained ownership of a little corner of the plantings and built a winery to deal with the tiny but high quality production. Warrenmang was born. Now read on.

An important factor in the Warrenmang development has been Leo Hurley, a man whose wine career at Seppelts Great Western spanned from 1923 to 1973, most of which time was as right-hand man to the great Colin Preece. Hurley made the first few Warrenmang wines, up to and including the remarkably successful 1980 Cabernet Sauvignon — a wine which represents a culmination of all of the preceding vintages. Importantly, Leo Hurley's influence does not stop there: during this time he himself had a right-hand man, Russell Branton (one of the owners), and Russell has taken over the winemaking responsibility having 'drunk at the fount' for half a decade.

Warrenmang now fills an important role in Victoria's Western District winemaking. The vignoble is of increasing significance viticulturally, with other newcomers Taltarni, Redbank, Chateau Remy, Mount Avoca, Boroka and Montara all joining the 'old men' of the area: Seppelts and Bests. And Warrenmang's very small, very good production helps to keep consumer expectation of area quality at a high level.

The winery is small, but efficiently designed specifically for the production of high quality red wine in small parcels. Oak storage (about 50 per cent new wood each year) is underground. The vineyard is about 10 hectares, of which 7 are fully yielding. Varieties bearing are Shiraz 4 hectares, Cabernet Sauvignon 2 hectares, and Chardonnay 1.3 hectares. To date no white wine has been made at the Warrenmang winery as the current equipment is not suited to its production.

Winemaker

Russell Branton now makes the Warrenmang wines, in collaboration with consultant Neill Robb. (For Neill's background and experience see 'Redbank'.) Russell was infected with winemaking ambitions back in the days when his work in the hotel business with Menzies, the Oriental and the Federal group started to develop for him an international palate. He was singleminded enough to achieve this ambition, and is also idealistic enough to have the potential to make great wine.

Range of Wines

Warrenmang Cabernet Sauvignon
Warrenmang Shiraz

Style

Warrenmang Cabernet Sauvignon

While maintaining a distinct continuity of common denominators, the style of this wine has fluctuated somewhat, the two extremes being the 1978: a big, slumbrous, tannic wine rather like a Colin Preece which had been given new wood; and the 1980: an elegant, fine but deep version of impeccably Bordelaise breeding. However, all the Cabernet Sauvignons to date have also had marked sibling resemblances, particularly in the minty, almost eucalyptus undertones of the impressively powerful bouquet. It seems most likely that Russell Branton will seek to maintain and develop this elegance of the 1980 in his future vintages.
Best years: 1977, 1980

Warrenmang Shiraz

A wine with the potential to rival Neill Robb's Redbank versions, but so far such potential is unrealized. Colour and depth of flavour are not problems, but stylishness and charm have been. It seems probable that the combination of Russell Branton's seeking after grace and harmony with consultant Neill Robb's unquestionable sensitivity with the variety will generate some vintages of greater felicity.
Best years: 1978, 1980, 1982

Ownership

Warrenmang is jointly owned by winemaker Russell Branton and Ballarat restaurateur Luigi Bazzani.

Production

Current production is 1200 cases of Shiraz and 800 cases of Cabernet Sauvignon.

New Plantings

(Not yet yielding.) Still to bear are an additional 0.8 hectares of Cabernet Sauvignon, and 0.6 of Merlot, Rhine Riesling and Traminer.

Market

Specialist merchants and, increasingly, mailing list accounts for all the production.

Winery Visiting Details

By appointment only. The address is simply Moonambel, 3478 Telephone (054) 67 2233.

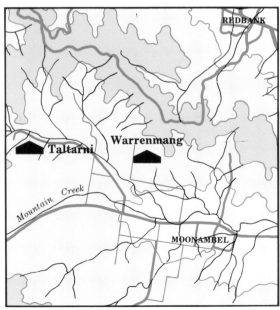

WATER WHEEL VINEYARDS Bridgewater-on-Loddon, Vic

As with many of the Victorian areas planted with vines during the 1970s, the Bridgewater planting was a re-establishment rather than the creation of a new vignoble, wine having been made in the district in the last century. The project was begun by Water Wheel Flour Mills Pty Ltd in 1972, an era when diversification into wine was rife.

The varieties planted are interesting: as well as the expectable Cabernet Sauvignon and Shiraz, the vineyard includes Cabernet Franc, Ruby Cabernet, Mondeuse and Pinot Noir. More interesting still are the Portuguese Port varieties — Mourisco Preto, Bastardo, Touriga and Souzao. Chardonnay and Rhine Riesling were added in 1977.

In 1980 a new winery was completed, housing an underground cellar whose temperature variation from summer to winter is less than 4° Celsius. Excavated soil from the cellars was bulldozed into mounds pushed against three walls of the winery to insulate this too against temperature fluctuations. All of the oak storage is underground, and the stainless steel handling tanks are located on the ground floor of the winery.

Water Wheel wines have a small but loyal following within Victoria. The wines are intense in varietal character, and generously endowed with both fruit and flavour. Area under vine totals 10 hectares, most of which is Cabernet Sauvignon and Shiraz.

The Water Wheel Vineyards venture has been an unusual one, in that everything has been done without involving any of the high-powered viticultural or oenological consultants whose influence has been so marked over the last ten years. A a result an intriguing and idiosyncratic style has emerged for their wines, a style which often means individuality at the expense of elegance. In these days of 'me too' boutique wines, one can only admire this individualism.

Winemaker

David von Saldern was born and educated in Germany, where he graduated with honours in 1953 from the wine college Weinsberg Wurttenburg. He joined Water Wheel Vineyards in 1976, and has been solely responsible for the winemaking from 1977 onwards.

Range of Wines

Water Wheel Cabernet Franc
Water Wheel Cabernet Sauvignon
Water Wheel Hermitage
Water Wheel Pinot Chardonnay
Water Wheel Rhine Riesling
Water Wheel Vintage Port

Style

Water Wheel Cabernet Sauvignon

There are in fact two versions of this: the 'Private Bin' and the 'Standard'. Surprisingly the 'Standard' is the bigger and firmer of the two, and consequently the longer lived. For all that, the common denominators are marked — substantial fruit character, rich colour, very grapey aroma and high vinosity.
Best years: 1975, 1977, 1978, 1980

Water Wheel Hermitage

The same double label system applies for the Hermitage as the Cabernet Sauvignon. The style is lighter than might be expected, with good soft tannin and beguilingly pleasant fruit. Again the 'Private Bin' wine is the more drinkable when young of the two.
Best years: 1977, 1980

Water Wheel Pinot Chardonnay

An intriguing and most unusual winestyle with, in latter years, 20% of Rhine Riesling added to lend crispness and lightness, and to mitigate the almost cheesy strength of the Chardonnay. The wine has stylistic roots in the traditional Australian 'White Burgundy' genus rather than Californian or French versions. However, Chardonnay being Chardonnay, it is much more complex than such White Burgundies.
Best years: 1980, 1981

Ownership

The vineyard and winery are owned by Water Wheel Flour Mills Pty Ltd, which is in turn owned by Water Wheel Holdings Ltd, a listed public company.

Production

Annual production is 5000 to 6000 cases, most of which is Cabernet Sauvignon and Shiraz.

New Plantings

(Not yet yielding.) Nil.

Market

Cellar door, mailing list and a few specialist outlets in Melbourne and Sydney.

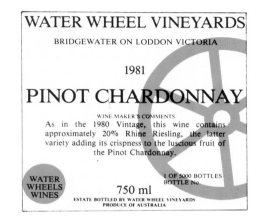

Winery Visiting Details

Monday to Friday 10 am to 5 pm, Saturdays by appointment. The address is Mill Road, Bridgewater-on-Loddon, 3516 Telephone (054) 37 3000.

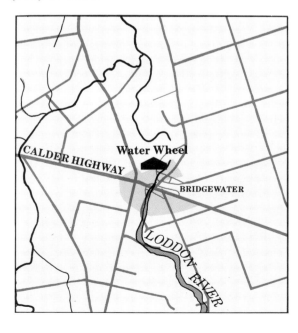

WIRRA WIRRA

Spearheading the McLaren Vale quality revolution is the small, or fairly small, winery of Wirra Wirra. The place has quite a history, which is amusingly and eloquently recounted in a Wirra Wirra press handout — not a branch of literature normally known for either humour or stylistic excellence — but which space availability precludes from repeating here. Anyway, from it we glean that the original vineyard was established in 1894 by Robert Wigley, who had been banished to McLaren Vale by his family when he was 29, apparently after having found time (apart from his Law and Architecture studies, and playing cricket for South Australia) to outrage the Adelaide establishment by riding horses in the Adelaide Town Hall, etc.

Apparently he was a drinking man, so he decided to ameliorate his rusticated lot by becoming a winegrower. The first wine was made in 1897. Within a few years he was one of the bigger winegrowers of the area, and there en-

sued a couple of decades of supplying the London market through Burgoynes before he died in 1924. Within a few years, there was just a disused winery and a handful of untended vines as his family sold off the property.

Enter Greg and Roger Trott, cousins who acquired the derelict winery and 3 hectares of the original property in 1969. Restoring the building (rather magnificently) and purchasing some of the surrounding land, they planted Cabernet Sauvignon, Shiraz, Grenache, Rhine Riesling, and more recently Merlot, Pinot Noir, Chardonnay, Chenin Blanc and Sauvignon Blanc.

The Trotts' respect for the romantic and historical aspects of re-establishing the Wirra Wirra winery did not extend to a slavish desire to emulate the traditional style of the area. On the contrary their quest for finesse and elegance in their winestyles is unremitting, and their score on the board is mounting.

Winemaker

Greg Trott is the Wirra Wirra winemaker. He is also the Wirra Wirra stonemason, bricklayer, carpenter, glazier, cooper, manager and factotum. He is without formal oenological training, but spent some five years with the

Southern Vales Cooperative, during which time, as he puts it, he 'became familiar with the rudiments of winemaking'. From the style of the wine, I would suspect that the services of the Oenotec consultancy are now used.

Range of Wines

Wirra Wirra Cabernet Sauvignon
Wirra Wirra Church Block (Shiraz/Grenache)
Wirra Wirra Rhine Riesling
Wirra Wirra Shiraz
Wirra Wirra Tawny Port
Wirra Wirra Vintage Port

Style

Wirra Wirra Church Block

I think that this is one of the more attractive wines in the district. It scales no pinnacles of excellence, and indeed has no pretensions to nobility, but in its own way possesses both beauty and charm. Made from grapes grown in a small paddock which also encompasses a ruined church, the vinosity of the Shiraz is lightened by the lowly Grenache to produce a fine, pretty dry red of faintly Burgundian aspect.
Best years: 1976, 1977

Wirra Wirra Rhine Riesling

All of Greg Trott's Rhine Rieslings have been impressive, and the most recent vintages are nothing short of remarkable. Pondering the wine's aristocratic power, intensity of flavour and length of finish, it is difficult to believe that it is not a cool climate wine, but the fruit is all McLaren Vale. A splendid achievement for the Southern Vales.
Best years: 1979, 1980

Ownership

Wirra Wirra is a partnership between Greg and Roger Trott.

Production

Not counting wine made for bulk sales, production is currently about 6000 cases per year.

New Plantings

The plantings of Merlot, Pinot Noir, Chardonnay, Chenin Blanc and Sauvignon Blanc already referred to have yet to bear.

Market

Mostly cellar door and mailing list, with modest representation in licensed outlets.

Winery Visiting Details

Monday to Saturday 10 am to 5 pm, Sunday 11.30 am to 5 pm. The address is McMurtrie Road, McLaren Vale, 5171 Telephone (08) 383 8414.

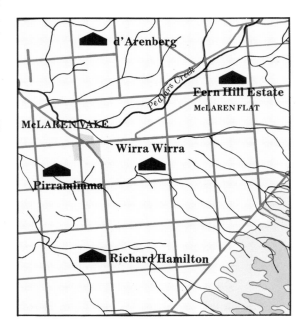

WOLLUNDRY

Fascination with an old Victorian dessert wine led Ron Hansen and his wife Kay to make forays into the north eastern Victorian wine growing areas in the late sixties. Eventually, the quest for drier styles (and a little closer to home) led them to the Hunter where they travelled throughout the area sampling and buying the wines. The unique Hunter styles were to leave their mark.

Becoming increasingly disenchanted with city life, the rural alternatives of the Hunter Valley offered more appeal and the decision to change lifestyles came with a gift of an old Hunter style white burgundy made at the now defunct (1960) 'Glanders' winery. This wine made such an impression on them that they were determined to make a similar style.

A chance meeting with Andy Phillips, Max Lake's then vineyard manager, saw them settling for a delightful property on the northern side of the Pokolbin vineyard area. Grapes had not previously be grown at Wollundry, but ample heavy volcanic clay type soils would obviously provide a fine complement to the historical Hunter varieties of Hermitage and Semillon.

By 1971, most of the major new expansion plantings had taken place and Ron Hansen was quick to notice the imbalance in the ratio of red varieties to whites in the expanded plantings as well as the consumer swing to white wines. The result was that when planting commenced in the winter of 1971, it was his aim to plant equal areas of red and white varieties. As well

as the two traditionals Hermitage and Semillon, Blanquette, Traminer and Cabernet Sauvignon were planted in 1974. In 1979, Chardonnay was included which brought the total area under vine to 24 hectares.

Wollundry reds are made in the traditional Hunter fashion, open concrete fermenters with hand plunging of the cap of skins to extract colour and tannin in a method that has been used throughout the valley from its beginning. Maturation is in mostly American oak with a specially selected vat being matured in Yugoslavian oak hogsheads. The whites are cold fermented in stainless steel and to this stage have not had any wood aging. Maturation without wood has produced soft fragrant wines that show all the fruit characteristics while maintaining a light honeyed character unique to the Hunter. 1982 Vintage sees the first wood matured whites from Wollundry with Semillon and the recently planted Chardonnay being matured in new French Nevers oak puncheons.

Winemaker

Ron Hansen spent some of his early years learning basic winemaking technique at Lakes Folly together with a quality control course at Roseworthy College. His wines are basically made as he feels they should be made, on analysis of the fruit from each paddock. He believes that the basis for quality wines begins in the vineyard and his meticulously maintained vineyard bears testimony of this belief.

Range of Wines

Wollundry Blanquette
Wollundry Cabernet Sauvignon
Wollundry Gewurztraminer
Wollundry Hermitage (American Oak)
Wollundry Hermitage Bin 80 (Yugoslavian Oak)
Wollundry Semillon

Style

Wollundry Hermitage

Although Ron Hansen is one of the 'come lately' makers, he has a profound respect for the traditional Hunter styles: Hermitage and Semillon. As a result most of his plantings are of these two varieties. The Hermitage is a big, firm, tight but sweet-fruited wine with a minimum of the humid armpit smell of traditional Pokolbin Shiraz. I am never quite certain what winemakers mean by Australian 'Claret' or 'Burgundy', but Wollundry is clearly Burgundian in both intent and achievement. The wine ages softly and well.
Best years: 1975, 1976, 1979, 1980

Wollundry Hermitage Bin 80

Bin 80 Hermitage is matured in Yugoslavian oak hogsheads which imparts a full astringent finish; somewhat different from the softer American oak. It is suggested that an additional bottle maturation of at least two years is recommended to allow the wine to soften and develop its full complexity.
Best years: 1976, 1979, 1980, 1981

Ownership

Wollundry is a family partnership between Ron and Kay Hansen.

Production

Average annual production is about 5000 cases which is predominantly the two traditional Hunter varieties of Hermitage and Semillon.

New Plantings

(Not yet yielding.) Nil.

Market

The majority of sales are cellar door and mailing list. Distributors have been appointed for Sydney and Melbourne where selected retail outlets have a limited range of some wines.

Winery Visiting Details

Monday to Saturday 10 am to 5 pm, Sunday 10 am to 2 pm. The address is Palmers Lane, Pokolbin, 2321 Telephone (049) 98 7654.

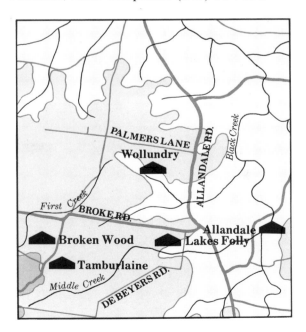

175

WRIGHTS WINES Cowaramup, WA

Henry Wright lived for many years in South Africa and Kenya before moving to Western Australia in 1964. He purchased a property at Cowaramup in the Margaret River district and established not vines, but beef cattle and pigs. An unlikely enough beginning to a winemaking venture, and it was ten years later before the idea of planting wine grapes arose.

'We were looking for an interesting way of making a living, and as we were both interested in wine, we felt that establishing our own winery and vineyard could be the answer.' Thus spake Henry Wright in a recent newspaper interview. Sounds nice and laid-back.

There are 9 hectares planted to date, roughly three each of Rhine Riesling, Cabernet Sauvignon and Shiraz, with plantings not yet bearing of Semillon and Chardonnay. Soil type is gravelly loam over clay, so there are no problems either with root development or yield.

The winery is a basic but attractive building just barely visible between two huge peppermint gums, set back some 30 metres from the Miamup road, and girdled by Willyabrup Creek. Idyllic.

Henry and Maureen Wright are, in fact, quite as easy-going as all this sounds. Although deadly serious about their winemaking venture, they are not of the technologically obsessed mould of current small makers, where those makers are either brilliant young graduates from XYZ college or single-minded enthusiasts with medico/scientific backgrounds.

For all that the wines are sound, clean, definite reds and whites which could well serve as benchmarks in defining the characteristics of the area, as distinct from some of the superstar neighbours' product, superb though they are, which more represent individual feats of virtuoso winemaking.

Winemaker

Henry Wright has had no formal training in oenology. However he is fortunate to be in a district which abounds in winemakers of brilliance, and Henry avails himself of their unstinting advice and support. The quality of his wine attests eloquently to the success of his methods, admittedly without actually rivalling any of the area's superstars.

Range of Wines

Wrights Cabernet Sauvignon
Wrights Hermitage
Wrights Hermitage/Cabernet Sauvignon
Wrights Rhine Riesling
Wrights Rose
Wrights Vintage Port

Style

Wrights Cabernet Sauvignon

A curious but successful blend of the old and the new: the style is more 'traditional' than is found elsewhere in the area, yet the fine quality of the Cowaramup fruit is associable with recent developments. Both earthy and spicy, this is a wine of considerable substance which should live very well.
Best years: 1979, 1980

Wrights Hermitage

A good, fine tight Shiraz with some muscle but no lack of beauty. Again the fruit quality impresses although the warmth and complexity of the palate is somewhat mitigated by a frequently rather hard finish. It should age well in the medium term.
Best years: 1978, 1980

Wrights Rhine Riesling

A somewhat unusual wine, of considerable attractiveness, this style shows some evidence of skin contact which has a coarsening effect on the palate. However, the perfumed power of the nose and the lusty beauty of the palate — more peach than passionfruit — make for an intriguing and quite enjoyable Rhine Riesling of almost White Burgundian proportions.
Best years: 1979, 1981

Ownership

Owned and operated by Henry and Maureen Wright.

Production

Cabernet Sauvignon 1500 cases, Hermitage 1750 cases, Rhine Riesling 1250 cases, plus Semillon 1750 cases and Chardonnay 250 cases when in full production.

New Plantings

(Not yet yielding.) 2.5 hectares of Semillon and 0.4 of Chardonnay are beginning to bear.

Market

Cellar door 30 per cent, mailing list 30 per cent, Western Australia 30 per cent, New South Wales and Victoria 10 per cent.

Winery Visiting Details

Monday to Saturday 10 am to 4.30 pm. In the off-season, appointments are preferred for weekdays. The address is Miamup Road, Cowaramup. 6284 Telephone (097) 55 5314.

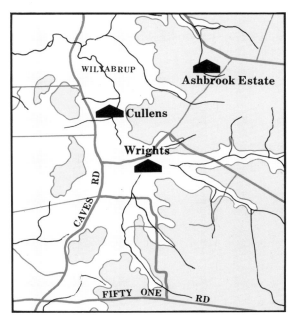

177

YARRA YERING

Part of the questionnaire form sent out to all the wineries covered in this book contained a request for information regarding 'the background, as distinct from the history, behind the establishment of the vineyard and winery'. By a very long chalk the briefest response came from Yarra Yering: 'I don't really understand the question. I wanted to make really good wine'. I suppose one cannot argue with that, however difficult it makes my task in filling out this page.

Dr Bailey Carrodus is by training a botanist whose specialty is plant physiology. A decade of wanderings in Europe entrenched for him a dedication to a dream of establishing his own vineyard and making wine. To this end, while working with the CSIRO, he purchased some gently sloping land at Coldstream in the Yarra Valley and planted some 12 hectares with vines.

Very much a devotee of European (French) viticultural winemaking techniques, Dr Carrodus rejected most of the traditional Australian practices (except, for some reason, low density planting) and established some varieties which even the most radical of other Australian growers were only thinking about at the time.

1973 saw the first Yarra Yering wines. They were complex and elegant, although, like the next few vintages, they possessed an unpalatable level of volatility which was quite wrongly seen by most wine buffs as auguring a swift demise in the bottle. Bailey trenchantly opposed that view with the undeniable Yarra Yering apophthegm that you can't have oak without volatility. Nevertheless recent vintages have been much healthier and represent some of the area's finest wines.

Plantings at the vineyard include experimental patches of the rare Viognier variety, and (also experimentally) the entire gamut of Chateauneuf du Pape varieties.

Winemaker

Dr Bailey Carrodus has a Ph.D. in plant physiology, which one would imagine must be of substantial advantage viticulturally. He also studied Oenology at Roseworthy College, emerging with his diploma. Somewhat of a winemaking maverick, he can perhaps be credited with having pioneered the now burgeoning preoccupation with viticulture, as well as effectively being the pioneer of the Yarra Valley re-establishment.

Range of Wines

Yarra Yering Dry Red No. 1
Yarra Yering Dry Red No. 2
Yarra Yering Dry White
Yarra Yering Pinot Noir

Style

Yarra Yering Dry Red No. 1

This is the Bordeaux version of the dry reds, being constructed from Cabernet Sauvignon, Malbec and Merlot. Willowy rather than plump, the wine is deep and fine with a superb balance imparting an aging potential improbable for its apparent delicacy.
Best years: 1976, 1978

Yarra Yering Dry Red No. 2

Basically Shiraz, with sometimes substantial Pinot Noir and, one assumes, minute admixtures of the Rhone Valley fruit salad, this is remarkably different from those thunderously Australian Hermitages which grip the drinker by the throat. A light but profound red which, were it not for the possibility of a misprint, one might almost term ascetic.
Best years: 1976, 1978

Yarra Yering Dry White

One of the unsung beauties amongst the bustier chorus girl line-up of Australian whites, this is a wine which I have always found very much in the Graves style, chalkily dry, but with gently sweet fruit. A lovely wine.
Best years: 1978, 1980

Yarra Yering Pinot Noir

Much as I would like to, I have not tasted this wine so my comments on its style, while impartial, would be uninformed. However I understand that the 1980 version particularly is a wine of great beauty.

Ownership

Dr Carrodus is the sole owner.

Production

Average total production is 2500 cases of which about 1600 cases is the 'Dry Red No. 1'.

New Plantings

(Not yet yielding.) Nil.

Market

No information given, but cellar door/mailing list would probably account for nearly all of the wine.

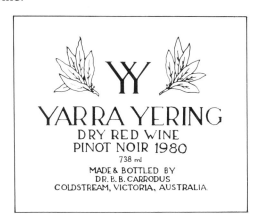

Winery Visiting Details

Saturdays and public holidays 9 am to 5 pm; Sundays noon to 5 pm (no week days). The address is Yarra Yering Vineyard, via Coldstream 3770 Telephone (059) 64 9267.

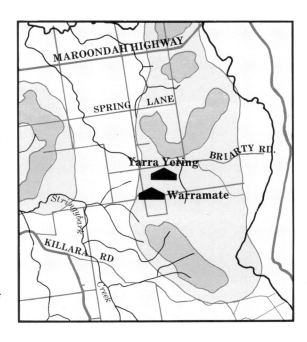

YERINGBERG

A slight hiatus of half a century broke the continuity of production of Yeringberg wines (1921 to 1969). For all that, continuity is very nearly the right word as the re-establishment was not merely in the same area, or even the same property, but actually on part of the same land which had produced Yeringberg wines for 60 years from 1862. Moreover, the original winery has been re-equipped, and, to cap it all, the new vines were planted by the grandson of the original vigneron, ownership of the property having stayed with the de Pury family. A most romantic dynastic nexus!

Guillaume de Pury accomplished the Yeringberg re-establishment in a small way, with only 1.6 hectares. Several varieties have been tried, and some of these (Shiraz and Rhine Riesling) have been taken out having failed to meet Guill's high standards. Currently the winery produces four wines only: Cabernet (Cabernet Sauvignon, Merlot and Malbec), Pinot Noir, Chardonnay and Marsanne.

Obviously, from such a small vineyard only small parcels of wine are produced: 200 cases of each of the four wines. Equally obvious is that expensive large-scale equipment is unnecessary, so each Yeringberg wine is almost literally hand-made. Guill's aim was, and remains, to make small quantities of high quality wine, using only grapes grown on the property. The red wines are given up to two years in French oak hogsheads, and the whites also have a few months of French oak.

To a degree, it could be said that Yeringberg wines are 'collector's items' even now. This is likely to be much more the case as it becomes more and more apparent to the consumer that the Yarra Valley is one of the Southern Hemisphere's best quality wine producing areas. At 200 cases of each wine per year, there is not much to go around.

Winemaker

Guillaume de Pury has a degree in Agricultural Science and of Doctorate of Philosophy in biochemistry from Melbourne University. He has combined the management of his grazing property with university research in biochemistry, but is no longer active in the latter, having given over all of his time to grazing and winemaking.

Range of Wines

Yeringberg Cabernet
Yeringberg Chardonnay
Yeringberg Marsanne
Yeringberg Pinot Noir

Style

Yeringberg Cabernet

The Yarra Valley is a cool area, and Yeringberg can be particularly so, resulting in occasional difficulties with ripening. As a result the Cabernet, for all its tightness and austerity, has a gentleness and almost fragility which prompts comparisons with some Tasmanian reds. Wine of considerable beauty.
Best years: 1976, 1977, 1979

Yeringberg Chardonnay

A 'Chardonnay-in-miniature' under whose initially light impact lies a surprising density of fruit. Wood treatment adds further complexity, and the crispness of the finish rounds off a most beguiling wine.
Best years: 1979, 1980

Yeringberg Pinot Noir

One of a very small handful of convincing Australian wines from this variety, this is no strawberry-cordial Pinot Noir but a fine, firm, tight and balanced dry red of emphatically Burgundian associations. Well worth the very considerable trouble you will have to take to acquire some.
Best years: 1977, 1979, 1980

Ownership

Yeringberg is owned as a partnership between G. & K. de Pury.

Production

As mentioned, a mere 800 cases, equally divided between the four wines of the range.

New Plantings

(Not yet yielding.) 0.5 hectares have been planted to Chardonay, Merlot and Malbec.

Market

A little Yeringberg wine finds its way to specialist merchants and restaurants, but it is safer to be placed on the mailing list.

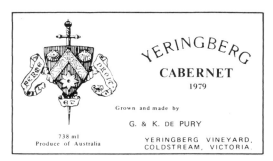

Winery Visiting Details

By appointment only. The address is Yeringberg, Coldstream, 3770 Telephone (03) 739 1453.

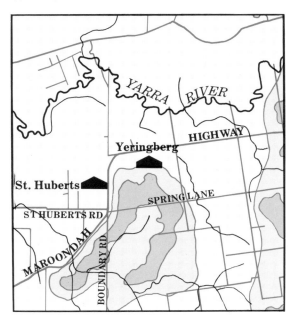

Area Maps

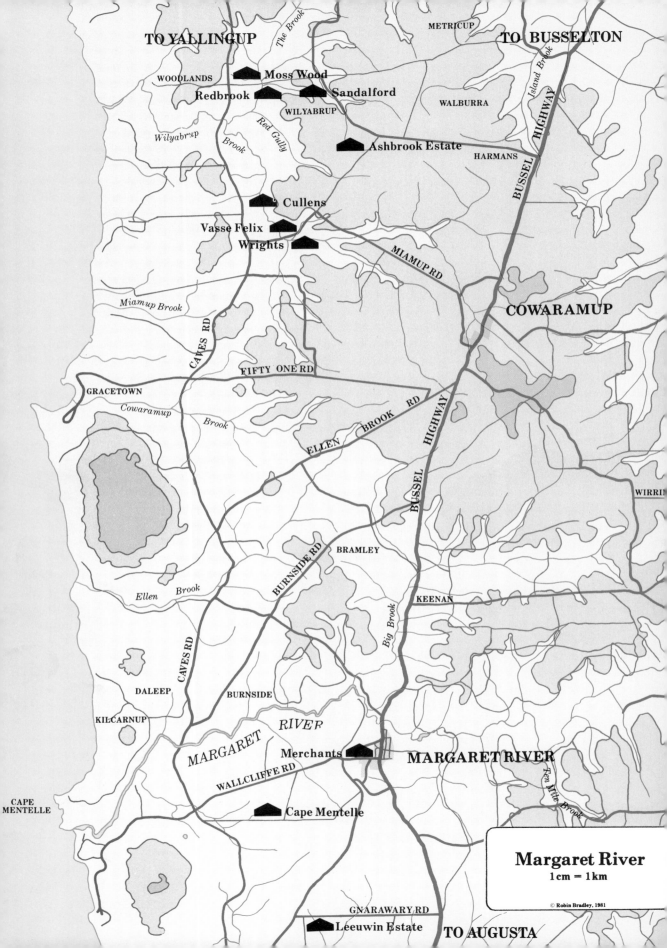

Margaret River

1 cm = 1 km

© Robin Bradley, 1981

LAKE JOONDALUP

LAKE GOOLELAL

Conteville

WANNEROO

WANNEROO RD

GREENWOOD

TUART HILL

BALGA

GNANGARA LAKE

BEACH RD

KINGSWAY

GNANGARA RD

GNANGARA
PINE PLANTATION

BENARA RD

MARSHALL RD

Bennet Brook

ORD RD

Riverside

SWAN RIVER

Banara

Farm

Valencia

EAST
GUILDFORD

WEST SWAN

WEST
MIDLAND

Sandalford

GREAT EASTERN HIGHWAY

CAVERSHAM

MIDDLE SWAN RD

HENLEY BROOK

Evans & Tate

WEST SWAN RD

SWAN

RIVER

Houghton

Westfield

Ellen Brook

Helena River

GREAT NORTHERN

HIGHWAY

UPPER SWAN

TOODYAY RD

MIDDLE SWAN

HERNE HILL

Swanville

OAKOVER RD

Vignacourt

Jane Brook

Swan Valley

1cm = 1km

© Robin Bradley, 1981

Susannah Brook

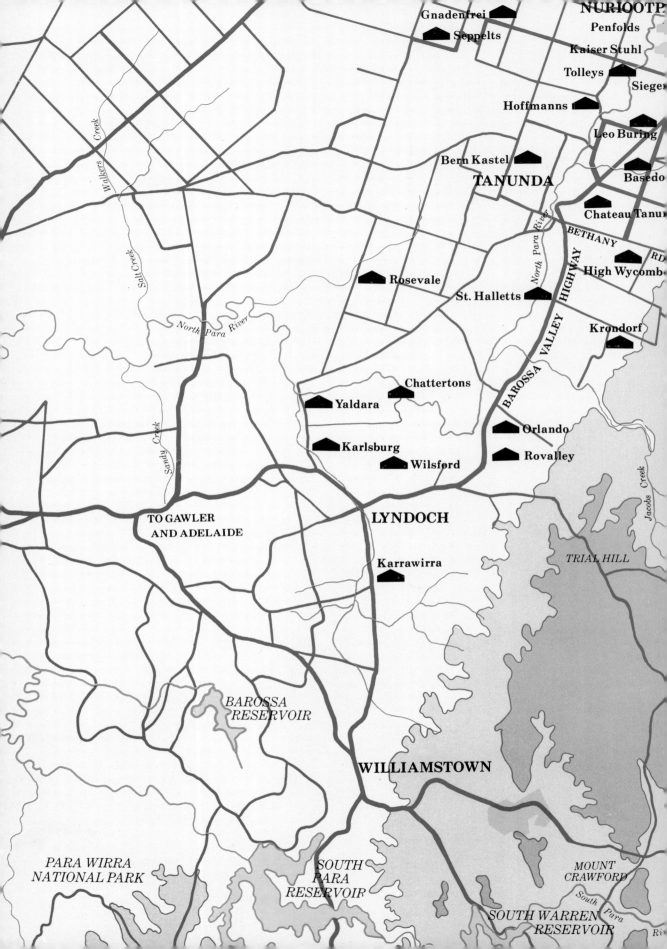

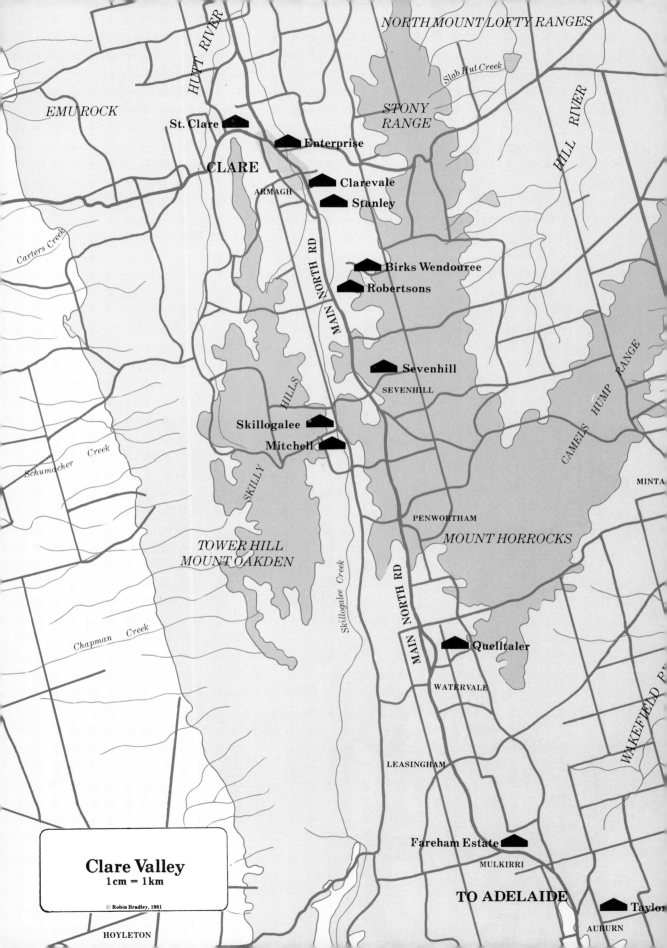

NORTH MOUNT LOFTY RANGES

Slab Hut Creek

EMU ROCK

HUTT RIVER

St. Clare

Enterprise

CLARE

ARMAGH

Clarevale

Stanley

STONY
RANGE

HILL RIVER

Carters Creek

Birks Wendouree

Robertsons

MAIN NORTH RD

Sevenhill

SEVENHILL

Schumacher Creek

Creek

HILLS

SKILLY

Skillogalee

Mitchell

Skillogalee Creek

TOWER HILL
MOUNT OAKDEN

PENWORTHAM

MOUNT HORROCKS

CAMELS HUMP RANGE

MINTA

Chapman Creek

MAIN NORTH RD

Quelltaler

WATERVALE

WAKEFIELD R

LEASINGHAM

Fareham Estate

MULKIRRI

Clare Valley

1cm = 1km

© Robin Bradley, 1981

TO ADELAIDE

Taylor

HOYLETON

AUBURN

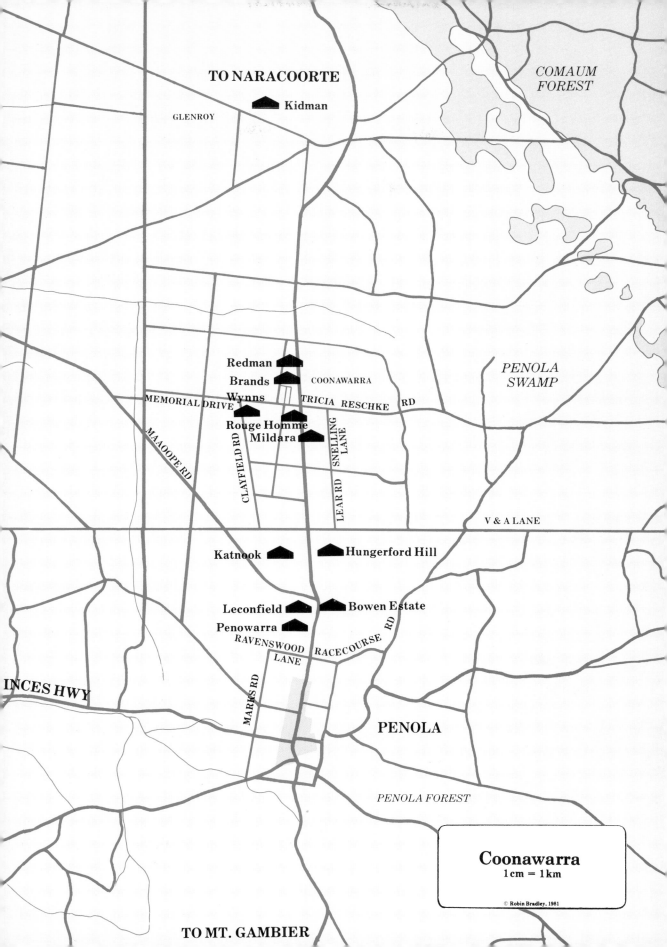

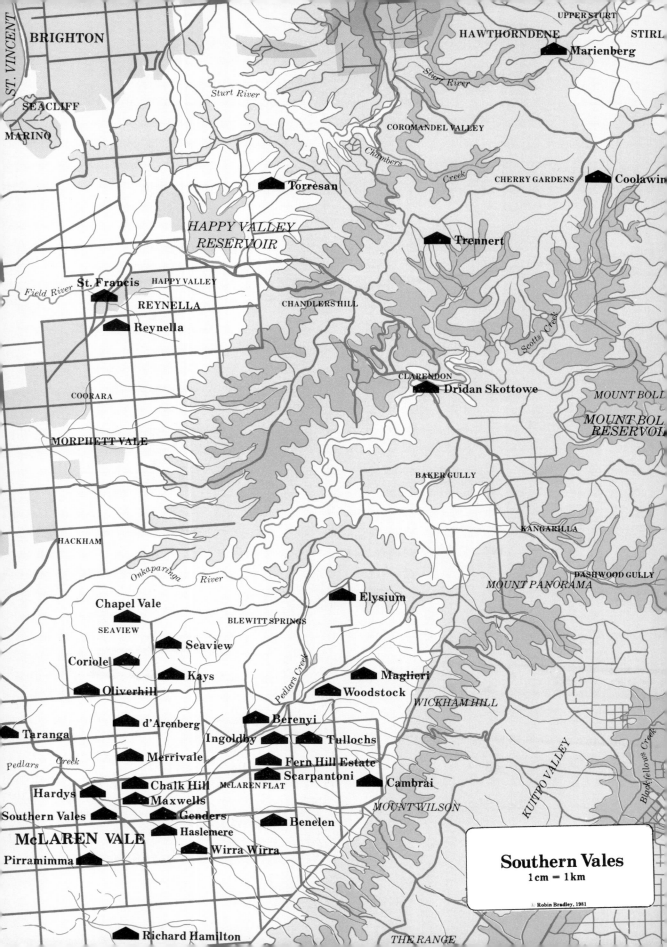

Myers Creek

Ridgwood River Channel

MYERS FLAT

EAGLEHAWK

Myers Flat Channel

BENDIGO

Balgownie

LONG GULLY

MAIDEN GULLY

HIGHWAY

RD

WEST BENDIGO

Bendigo Creek

MARONG

CALDER

EDWARDS

OLYMPIC

Spencers Hill Channel

PDE

Marong & Lockwood Channel

KANGAROO FLAT

HIGHWAY

CRUSOE RESERVOIR

LOCKWOOD

Chateau Le Amon

CALDER

BIG HILL

SHELLBOURNE EAST

LOCKWOOD SOUTH

Central Victoria

1 cm = 1 km

© Robin Bradley, 1981

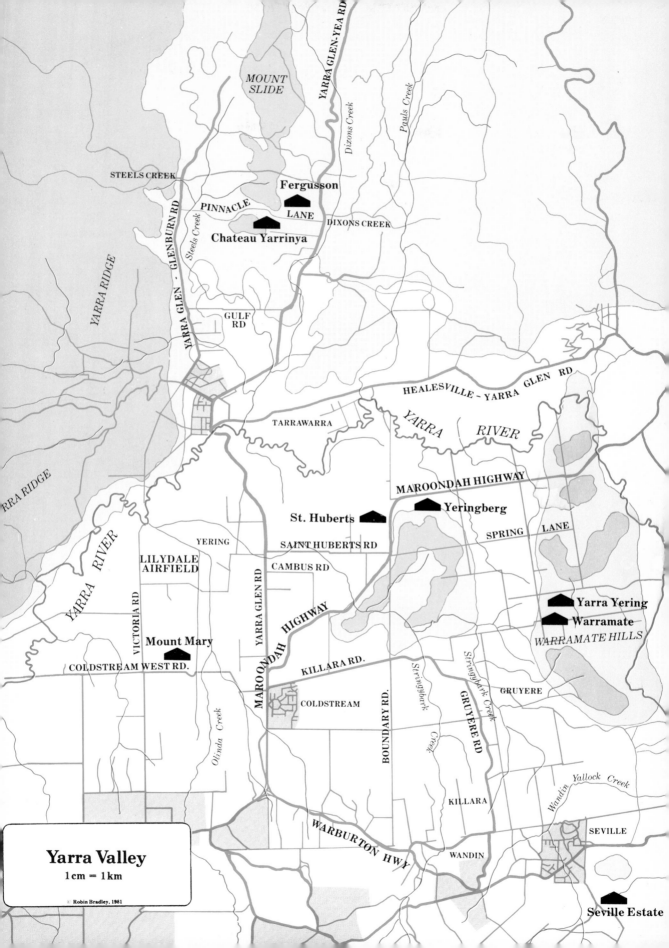

MOUNT
SLIDE

STEELS CREEK

Fergusson

PINNACLE

LANE

DIXONS CREEK

Chateau Yarrinya

YARRA RIDGE

GLENBURN RD

YARRA GLEN – GLENBURN RD

Steels Creek

Dixons Creek

Pauls Creek

GULF
RD

HEALESVILLE – YARRA GLEN RD

TARRAWARRA

YARRA   RIVER

RRA RIDGE

YARRA   RIVER

MAROONDAH HIGHWAY

St. Huberts

Yeringberg

SPRING   LANE

YERING

SAINT HUBERTS RD

LILYDALE
AIRFIELD

CAMBUS RD

VICTORIA RD

YARRA GLEN RD

Yarra Yering

Warramate

WARRAMATE HILLS

Mount Mary

COLDSTREAM WEST RD.

MAROONDAH   HIGHWAY

KILLARA RD.

COLDSTREAM

BOUNDARY RD.

Stringybark Creek

Stringybark Creek

GRUYERE RD

GRUYERE

Olinda Creek

KILLARA

Wandin Yallock Creek

SEVILLE

WARBURTON HWY

WANDIN

Seville Estate

Yarra Valley

1 cm = 1 km

© Robin Bradley, 1981

WINTON NORTH

LAKE   MOKOAN

TAMINICK

Booths

Baileys

WARBY RANGE

TAMINICK GAP

MOUNT WARBY

*MOUNT
GLENROWAN*

GLENROWAN

WARBY
SPRINGS

Fifteen Mile Creek

HUME HIGHWAY

LACEBY

One Mile Creek

WANGARATTA

Croppers Creek

KING   RIVER

HIGHWAY

BOWSER

OVENS

Reedy Creek

RIVER

Yellow   Creek

Tea Garden Creek

Brown Bros

MILAWA

N. E. Victoria
1 cm = 1 km

© Robin Bradley, 1981

to Markwood

GREAT WESTERN

Bests

Sep

Hyde Park

WESTERN HIGHWAY

STAWELL

Pleasant Creek

BELLELLEN RD

Creek

BLACK RANGE

McCall

ILLAWARRA

BUNJILS
CAVE

Sugarloaf Creek

BELLELLEN

Basin Creek

Pentland Creek

MOKEPILLY

BELLELLEN

Creek

RD

Mile

to Monta

Nine

Mount William Creek

JALLUKAR

LAKE FYANS

Salt

POMONAL

Boroka

BORONIA PEAK

MOUNT CASSEL

Western Districts
1 cm = 1 km

© Robin Bradley, 1981

HALLS GAP

LAKE
BELLFIELD

BELLFIELD SETTLEMENT

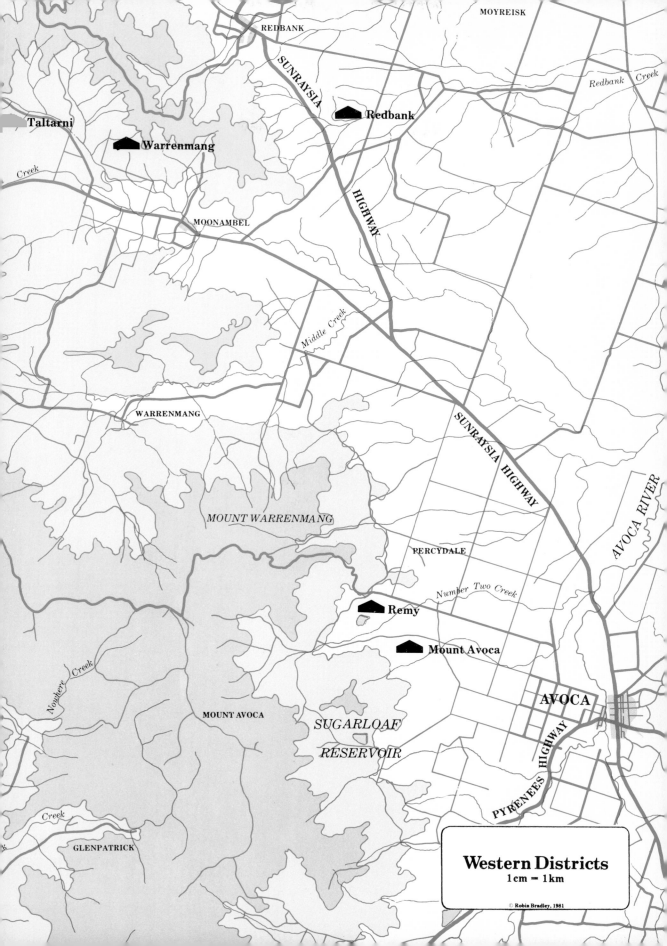

MOYREISK

REDBANK

SUNRAYSIA

Redbank Creek

Taltarni

Warrenmang

Redbank

HIGHWAY

Creek

MOONAMBEL

Middle Creek

WARRENMANG

SUNRAYSIA HIGHWAY

MOUNT WARRENMANG

AVOCA RIVER

PERCYDALE

Number Two Creek

Remy

Nowhere Creek

Mount Avoca

AVOCA

MOUNT AVOCA

SUGARLOAF

RESERVOIR

PYRENEES HIGHWAY

Creek

GLENPATRICK

Western Districts

1 cm = 1km

© Robin Bradley, 1981

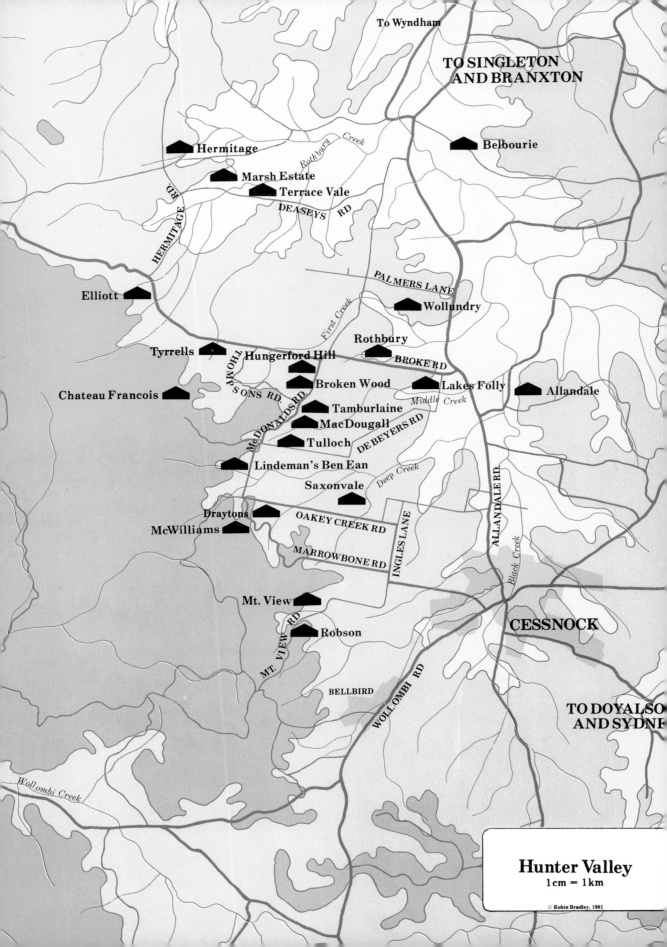

Hunter Valley

1 cm = 1 km

© Robin Bradley, 1981

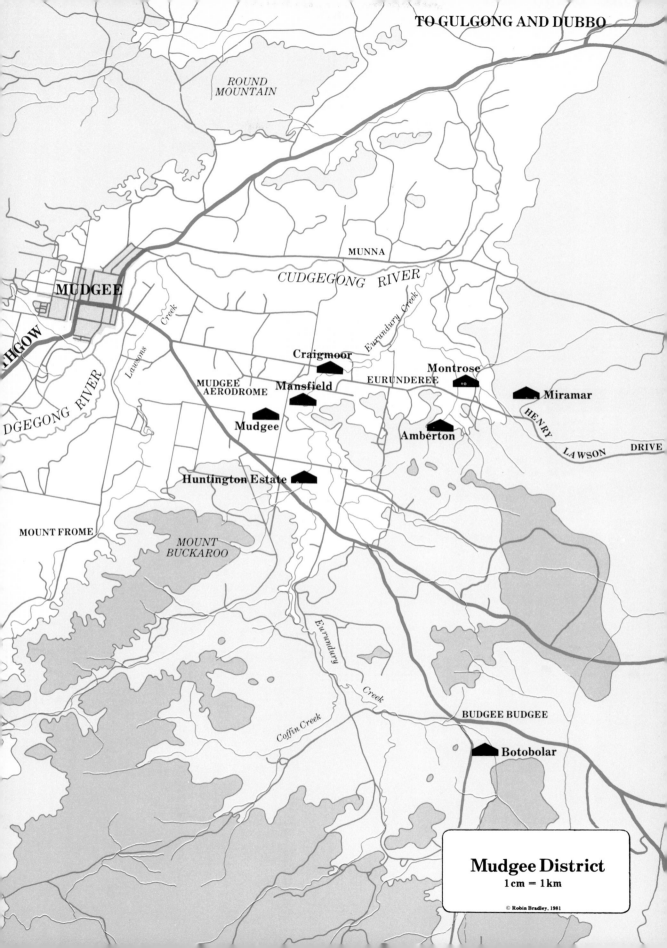

TO GULGONG AND DUBBO

ROUND MOUNTAIN

MUNNA

CUDGEGONG RIVER

MUDGEE

Eurunbury Creek

Lawsons Creek

Craigmoor

Montrose

**MUDGEE
AERODROME**

Mansfield

EURUNDEREE

Miramar

GOW

DGEGONG RIVER

Mudgee

Amberton

HENRY LAWSON DRIVE

Huntington Estate

MOUNT FROME

*MOUNT
BUCKAROO*

Eurunbury

Creek

BUDGEE BUDGEE

Coffin Creek

Botobolar

Mudgee District

1 cm = 1 km

© Robin Bradley, 1981

Index

Alba Institute of Oenology, 108
Albert, Tony, 30–1
Alcorso, Claudio, 110
Alcorso, Julian, 110
Amerine, Professor Maynard, 90
Anderson, Stuart, 8, 14, 40, 112, 128
Atallah, W., 5

Barry, Arda, 115
Barry, Brian, 66
Barry, John, 114–5
Batley, Brian, 10
Bazzani, Luigi, 169
Becker, Dr Helmut, 54, 76
Beeston, John, 30–1
Belgiorno-Nettis, Franco, 108–9
Best, Charles, 18
Best, Henry, 18
Birks, Andrew, 6
Bourne, Maurice, 144–5
Bowen, Doug, 26–7
Bowen, Joy, 26–7
Bowen, Robert, 126
Brand, Bill, 28
Brand, Eric, 28
Brand, Jim, 28
Branton, Russell, 168–9
Breen, Bernie, 22–3
Breen, Cordelia, 22–3
Brill, Beverley, 7
Bulleid, Nick, 30–1

Campbell, Colin, 34
Campbell, John, 34
Cartwright, Bob, 94
Carrodus, Dr Bailey, 178–9
Chatterton, Brian, 46
Chatterton, Roland, 46
Church, Jack, 166
Clendenen, Jim, 144
Connolly, Peter, 140
Conti, Paul, 48, 96, 118
Corino, Carlo, 108
Crappsley, Bill, 64
Croser, Brian, 6, 28, 40, 84, 120–1, 124, 160, 164
Cullen, Diana, 56–7
Cullen, Kevin, 56–7
Cullity, Dr T. B., 158–9

d'Arenberg, Frances Helena, 58
Deacon, Ian, 144, 164
de Pury, Guillaume, 180–1
Devenish, R. W., 127
Devitt, Brian, 10
Devitt, Tony, 10
Digby, Ken, 104
Dridan, David, 60
Dunstan, David, 26

Egan, Reg, 116, 164–5
Egan, Tina, 164–5
Elford, Greg, 154
Elliott, Stephen, 66–7
Ellis, John, 154
Evans, Len, 121
Evans, John, 65

Farr, Gary, 16
Fergusson, Michael, 69
Fergusson, Peter, 68–9
Fesq, Bill, 74
Forsell, Andrew, 68
Franklin, Dr Colin, 7

Gallagher, Greg, 148
Garnham, Ian, 20
Geisenheim Institute, 18, 54, 76
Gilbert, Marcel, 161
Gladstones, Dr John, 56, 158
Gregg, Anne, 159
Gregg, David, 158–9
Guy, Robert, 72–3

Hall, Don, 45
Hall, Jan, 45
Halliday, James, 17, 30–1
Hamilton, Burton, 134
Hamilton, Jette, 135
Hamilton, Dr Richard, 92–3, 134–5
Hamilton, Syd, 92
Hansen, Kay, 174–5
Hansen, Ron, 174–5
Haselgrove, Colin, 74
Heitz 'Martha's Vineyard', 4
Henschke, Cyril, 76
Henschke, Johann Christian, 76
Henschke, Stephen, 76

Heritage, George, 162–3
Hewitson, Dr Doug, 163
Hickinbotham, Ian, 8
Hickinbotham, Stephen, 8
Hoffman, Arthur, 132
Hohnen, David, 38–9, 148
Hohnen, John, 38
Holmes, Leon, 78–9
Holmes, Leonie, 78–9
Hooper, Stuart, 16–7

Horgan, Denis, 94–5
Horne, R. H., 'Orion' 42
Hurley, Leo, 168
Hyett, Bruce, 128–9
Hyett, Sue, 129

Irvine, Jim, 162–3
Irwin, Ian, 31

Jackson, Cynthia, 7
Jackson, Dr Ted, 7
James, Walter, 72, 114
Jamieson, Bill, 48, 118
Johnson, Hugh, 12
Johnston, Geoff, 124
Jordan, Dr Tony, 28, 40, 84, 120
Joualt, Ed, 4–5, 130
Just, Jacob, 82
Just, Rosina, 82

Kay, Colin, 86
Kay, Cuthbert, (Cud) 86
Kidd, Ray, 98
Kidman, Ken, 88
Kidman, Sid, 88
Killeen, Chris, 146
Killeen, Norm, 146
Killerby, Dr Barry, 96–7
Killerby, Betty, 97
Kitchener, Dr Peter, 7
Knappstein, Olive, 62
Knappstein, Tim, 62–3, 66, 106

Lake, Dr Max, 14, 30, 90, 112, 116, 136, 154, 174
Lake, Stephen, 90
Lange, Judy, 2–3
Lange, Merv, 2–3
Lazar, Tom, 160
Leamon, Alma, 40–1
Leamon, Philip, 40–1
Leprince, Alain, 152
Le Soeuf, Leslie, 38
Light, Brian, 50
Lloyd, Dr Hugh, 32, 52
Lloyd, Mark, 52

MacRae, Ian, 104–5
Maltby, Tom, 8–9
Mann, Dorham, 48

Marsh, Peter, 102–3
Marsh, Robyn, 103
Mast, Trevor, 18
McCracken, David, 22
McMahon, Margaret, 142
McMahon, Dr Peter, 142
Meredith-Hardy, M., 127
Middleton, Dr John, 116–7
Miller, Graeme, 44–5
Mitchell, Andrew, 106–7
Mitchell, Jane, 106–7
Mondavi, Robert, 94–5
Murphy, Dan, 88

Nairn, Helen, 118
Nairn, Will, 118

O'Callaghan, Robert, 46
Oenological Research Institute, Surrey, 80
Oenotec, 84, 120
Osborn, Francis d'Arenberg (d'Arry), 32, 58–9
Osborn, Francis Ernest, 58
O'Shea, Maurice, 112

Packham, Dr Gordon, 105
Pannell, Dr Bill, 112–3
Pannell, Sandra, 112–3
Paul, Barbara, 156–7
Paul, Don, 156–7
Pearse, Betty, 48–9
Pearse, Tony, 48–9
Phillips, Andy, 174
Pirie, Dr Andrew, 122–3
Platt, Barry, 54
Portet, Andre, 148
Portet, Bernard, 38, 148
Portet, Dominique, 148
Potts, Frank, 20
Potts, John, 20
Pratten, Elizabeth, 37
Pratten, Dr Peter, 36–7
Preece, Colin, 168
Pridham, Geoffrey, 100
Pridham, Ursula, 100
Purbrick, Alister, 42
Purbrick, Eric, 42
Purbrick, John, 42

Redman, Bruce, 132
Redman, Edna, 132–3
Redman, Malcolm, 132
Redman, Owen, 132–3, 160
Redman, Owen Jr, 132
Rees, Tony, 31
Riverina State College, 4, 6, 20, 22, 24, 28, 40, 46,
    68, 80, 82, 84, 106, 114, 120, 122, 124, 126, 136,
    146, 156, 164, 166
Robb, Neill, 130–1, 168
Robb, Sally, 130–1

Roberts, Bob, 80–1
Roberts, Wendy, 80–1
Roberts-Thomson, D., 5
Robinson, John, 136
Robson, Murray, 138–9
Rocca, S., 5
Roseworthy Agricultural College, 10, 16, 26, 34, 42,
    50, 62, 66, 70, 72, 82, 86, 94, 104, 106, 132, 154,
    174, 178
Rossetto, Frank, 31
Rozentals, John, 6–7
Rumball, Peter, 66–7

Salmon, Alan, 38
Salter, Heather, 136
Salteri, Carlo, 108–9
Sefton, Dr Daryl, 82–3
Sefton, Nini, 82–3
Seville, Peter, 31
Smith, A. F., 127
Soper, Ray, 31
Stanford, Guy, 114
Stanton, John Charles, 146
Station de Recherches Viticoles et Oenologiques,
    Alsace, 8
Stehbins, Ray, 84
Stehbins, Wayne, 84
Stevens, Graham, 32–3, 52, 70
Stockhausen, Karl, 98

Taperell, Dr Quentin, 102
Tate, John, 64–5
Thomas, Patricia, 71

Thomas, Wayne, 70–1
Thomson, Viv, 18
Thomson, Frederick, 18
Tiley, Dick, 152
Tinson, Harry, 12
Tisdall, Diana, 155
Tisdall, Dr Peter, 154–5
Trott, Greg, 70, 172–3
Trott, Roger, 172–3
Tschelitscheff, Andre, 90
Tyrrell, Anne, 154
Tyrrell, Murray, 152

Van Heyst, Cyrille, 54–5
Van Heyst, Jocelyn, 54–5
Vautin, Dr Bill, 7
Velzeboer, Maartin, 105
Vialard, Louis, 14
Vickery, John, 26
Von Saldern, David, 170

Wahlquist, Gil, 24–5
Wahlquist, Roland, 24
Wahlquist, Vincie, 25
Ward, Ken, 88
Weinsberg Wurttenburg Wine College, 170
Westwood, Ron, 163
White, Alex, 140
Wigley, Robert, 172
Wiltshire, Graham, 74
Wood, Michael, 152
Wright, Henry, 176–7
Wright, Maureen, 176–7